American Monarchy

A SOCIAL GUIDE
TO THE PRESIDENCY

Also by Jerrold M. Packard

THE QUEEN & HER COURT
A GUIDE TO THE BRITISH MONARCHY TODAY

American Monarchy

A SOCIAL GUIDE TO THE PRESIDENCY

Jerrold M. Packard

DELACORTE PRESS/NEW YORK

Published by
Delacorte Press
1 Dag Hammarskjold Plaza
New York, New York 10017

PRINTED IN THE UNITED STATES OF AMERICA

FIRST PRINTING

Library of Congress Cataloging in Publication Data

Packard, Jerrold M.
American monarchy.

Bibliography: p.
Includes index.
1. Presidents—United States—Homes and haunts.
2. Presidents—United States—Staff.   I. Title.
E176.1.P33   1983   353.03′1′09   83–7168
ISBN 0-385-29278-3

FOR MERL, TOO

Contents

CONTENTS

Introduction

IF GEORGE WASHINGTON had been a man of somewhat different views on the general fitness of affairs, the newly united states might indeed have become a monarchy. Simply because the colonists had recently fought a war to detach themselves from one kingdom was not at the time considered compelling logic that they should not themselves become yet another kingdom. At the end of the eighteenth century monarchy—that is, the system of government headed by a sovereign king, usually hereditary—was absolutely *de rigueur* over nearly all the "civilized" world, with revolutionary France the major exception.

Had Washington accepted the throne considered by the young federation, Americans would today very possibly be subjects under the sovereign House of Washington-Custis or perhaps some related descendant branch. Unquestionably *our* monarchy would have devolved in an entirely constitutional manner, Americans being a naturally constitutional folk, and the monarch's few real powers would be held in close check by the House and Senate—the bodies wisely laid down by the framers of our system.

Of course, the Constitutional Congress correctly read the antimonarchial sentiments of the newly independent colonists and didn't offer a crown; instead, Washington became a temporary "president" of the freely associated states. We Americans thus avoided a royal house and family, with its inevitable indiscreet princesses, philandering grand dukes, and mad monarchs. In place of a European-style court we got our own unique kind of American monarchy.

From its becomingly modest beginnings, the office of the presidency grew slowly at first, only in recent years taking off in the giant leaps that have made it stronger than any constitutional jurisdiction in world history. Through the greater part of the nineteenth century the President got along with one or two "clerks," mostly just to help out with the mail; there certainly wasn't any "executive office" in the modern sense of that term. For many years a new President made his own way to Washington unaided, then unceremoniously found the White House and as a matter of necessity made do with the very few perquisites and resources attendant upon the office. The young Republic very consciously decreed that its chief lawmaker shouldn't be allowed to forget the temporary nature of his elevation, and rather pointed pains were taken to ensure this. For example, no President until Theodore Roosevelt at the beginning of this century had the cushion of an expense allowance—the salary was considered perfectly adequate to cover all of the chief executive's needs. The amount? Through most of the nineteenth century it hadn't exceeded $25,000 a year—and this had to provide for the President's social expenses as well.

At the end of the first third of this century change started to come in substantial increments when Franklin Roosevelt's brand of populism inevitably put a close to the era of the bucolic presidency. By the end of the century's second third the office had settled very comfortably and permanently into a role of unparalleled magnificence, the chief executive heir to every imaginable luxury, his official establishment bloated to a point where it resembled an only slightly scaled-down version of the court at Versailles, and his political powers far in excess of what George Washington and his compatriots would have ever been able to envision as appropriate or necessary for the head of a republic.

This book is meant as a guide to the social aspects surrounding the executive branch of government—the home in which our

Presidents live, the offices they and their staffs work in, the presidential environment beyond the White House—the Executive Office Building, Blair House, Camp David, the private presidential homes which become "Summer" or "Western" or "Texas" White Houses—the Vice Presidential Residence; the protocol and diplomatic life which form a courtly backdrop for the presidency; and the many diverse elements which together make up the way of life of the American Chief Executive. Its purpose is to let light in on a world and life-style visible around its edges but still in the main a realm unknown to the people it is meant to serve.

American Monarchy

A SOCIAL GUIDE
TO THE PRESIDENCY

I

Presidential Abode

THE WHITE HOUSE

The President's mansion is a chaste and republican building.
Etiquette at Washington . . . , 1857

THE KENNEDYS probably did it best. During their thousand days in the White House it became a royal palace for a republican America. No family before had quite the same attributes: youth, physical beauty, wealth, golden oratory, a stated commitment to provide an equality of opportunity for all of the country's people. No family since has presided over an America nearly so idealistic, trusting, and financially secure. When Jacqueline Kennedy filled the White House with antiques, she was almost universally acclaimed for doing so; when Nancy Reagan parallels the Kennedy elegance, she is castigated for it nearly as universally. Though different standards apply to its occupants today, the White House nonetheless continues to serve as the nucleus of this country's national life, both political and social. The style of its occupants historically has tended to set a tone for the country, with Americans coming to emulate in both overt and subtle ways the signals sent from the President's home. The residents of the White House have become everyone's neighbors through the constant media attention focused on them, and their graces and foibles immediate grist for the praisemaker and faultfinder alike.

It wasn't this way in the beginning, of course. During the first half century of the American presidency Washington was not much more than a backwater southern town made slightly extraordinary by the presence of the federal government, in those decades a small and wieldy bunch of legislators and clerks housed in a very few official buildings. Washington City itself was only the central portion of the District of Columbia, the federal capital territory; two other towns within the District—Georgetown, on the Maryland side of the Potomac, and Alexandria, on the Virginia bank—rivaled it in size. The Virginia part of the District—about a third of the total—would be retroceded to that state in 1846 by request of the Virginia legislature; Washington City and the remainder of the District of Columbia would wait until 1888 before becoming a coterminous entity.

When it was decided in the last decade of the eighteenth century to locate the new nation's capital in a mosquito-infested swamp on the Potomac—a location chosen in large part to mollify the contentious southern states—the city's planners wanted to make the President's home and the legislative building the two most important elements of Pierre L'Enfant's grand design. These key buildings were to be connected by a great boulevard—today's Pennsylvania Avenue—one visible to the other, a symbolism connoting the keeping of each other in political check. Andrew Jackson's placement of the Treasury Building a quarter century later blocking the view put an end to the symbology.

To design the President's House (after an aborted attempt by L'Enfant), a contest was held with the prize of $500 to go to the winner. L'Enfant wrote that it should have "the sumptuousness of a palace and the agreeableness of a country seat." One of the entrants signed his architectural drawing "AZ"; not until 1915 was it discovered that "AZ" was really Thomas Jefferson, who evidently felt that it would be unethical for a man in his high position to enter the competition publicly. Fortunately Jefferson's top-heavy design was rejected.

In 1792 the competition commissioners chose as the winner James Hoban of Charleston, South Carolina. Born in Ireland, where he studied and practiced architecture, Hoban had emigrated to the United States at the end of the Revolutionary War and was working at his profession in Charleston when he learned of the competition. President Washington himself approved the young architect's design, specifying only that the size of the original three-story plan be increased by one-fifth, which, because of the geometric effect, increased the cubic space by nearly 73 percent. But when it appeared that the project might be scrapped altogether because of a shortage of funds, the commission decreed that the house should be limited to two floors and a basement, and Hoban's three-story plan was accordingly altered. The planned porticoes for the two main fronts were also eliminated because of the lack of money. Penny-pinching wasn't given as the public justification, but rather that the mansion "should not sink the neighboring buildings so much."

Hoban's design was Palladian in inspiration, as was Jefferson's, but of a more graceful, neoclassical form. Three manor houses from his native Ireland probably served as the architect's inspiration, but the plan for the American presidential mansion was in no way a copy of any of them. It was true that Leinster House, Castletown, and Lucan all had elements that would be repeated or suggested in the White House: elliptical rooms, room placements, window pediments, and swags, even the classical Palladian room proportions as ratios of width to length. But Hoban's results produced an altogether new building.

Work on preparing the site had started a year earlier in 1791, nine years before Washington City would officially become the seat of government of the new Republic. Slaves were rented from nearby plantations to dig the excavations for the cellar; these workmen were barracked in the President's Square—now Lafayette Park—across Pennsylvania Avenue. It was hoped that the sale of lots would help finance the project, but little interest was shown by private builders anywhere near the swampy site. It's useful to keep in mind that L'Enfant's grand design for the capital was just that at first—a design showing a fully conceived city, but one not to be a reality for many decades. The prospect of leaving the modern comforts of New York or Philadelphia or Charleston for a sleepy Potomac village held little appeal in the 1790s.

Nevertheless, the cornerstone was laid on October 13, 1792, the ritual being carried out according to the Masonic rite. It was exactly 300 years and one day after Columbus's discovery of America. An engraved brass plate noting the occasion was used to cover the cornerstone. Unfortunately the President wasn't able to attend the ceremony; records show that Washington was in Philadelphia on the historic day.

Work on the mansion proceeded hardly at all for the first years, the very contemporary problem of a shortage of funds being the chief villain. Not until the fall of 1798 was the exterior completed. (By this time Washington had ended his presidency and John Adams had succeeded to the office.) Rather than use marble, which was expensive and very difficult to transport long distances, the walls were made of gray sandstone, cut from the Aquia quarries in Virginia. They were painted to seal them from the weather; white was chosen probably so the building would resemble marble. (The story that it was first painted white to cover the stains of the British-set fire of 1814 is closely held but nonetheless a myth.) The substitution of sandstone for marble has had one marked advantage in the years since: With periodic new coats of paint, the White House has to this day maintained an almost luminescent appearance. (Occasionally the usually quadrennial painting is neglected, as it was during World War II.)

When the eighteenth century passed into the nineteenth, the building was finally ready to be moved into, although the un-built staircases, flooring yet to be laid, and a lack of interior plaster and window glass would make life in it somewhat trying. On November 1, 1800, President John Adams and his wife, Abigail, arrived to take up residence in the few habitable rooms.

Water closets hadn't yet been installed, so a smart new three-holer was quickly put up for the First Family in the backyard. The Adamses brought their own meager furniture to the entirely unfurnished "palace."

The stories about the difficulties endured by Abigail—hanging the laundry out to dry in the East Room and so on—are true, but she and her husband didn't have to put up with the discomfort for long. Adams lost the election that month, and the second President and his wife were out of the White House the following March.

The new occupant was a widower, Thomas Jefferson. He made the politically expedient decision that whatever official building efforts were to be made would best be spent on the totally inadequate Capitol, then going up at the other end of Pennsylvania Avenue. A much-needed well was dug on the mansion's grounds, however, since the water supply coming from a nearby brook had become contaminated. By the beginning of his second term Jefferson was ready to shift the emphasis back to the White House.

The first additions he made were the two loggias extending from either side of the mansion, which when finished contained storage space and additional privies. He had the south grounds leveled to improve the view of the Potomac off in the middle distance; the two hillocks visible to tourists today through the fence around the south grounds are the mounds of heaped-up earth removed at the time.

The President's attention then turned to Hoban's planned porticoes, or columned porches. (In William Ryan and Desmond Guinness's architectural history of the White House, the authors surmise that both the north and south porticoes as built were actually designed by Jefferson himself.) Good intentions aside, by the time he left the presidency in 1809 no work on the porticoes had been done, although the interior of the house itself was completed and fairly comfortably furnished. Jefferson's appointment to serve as the new architect of the White House and Capitol (and successor to Hoban), Benjamin Henry Latrobe, stayed on during the next President's first term, acting mainly as James and Dolley Madison's interior decorator. (There are, however, no inside views of the White House prior to 1814; even the precise placement of the interior walls is unknown.)

The first great blow to the mansion came in Madison's second term, on August 24, 1814, during the so-called War of 1812. The President's home along with the Capitol was burned by the British invaders directly at the order of their commanding officer, Rear Admiral George Cockburn. Everything in the house was destroyed except the portrait of George Washington, which Dolley Madison had taken off the wall and hidden in a nearby farmhouse. (It was not, however, cut out of the frame as the persistent legend would have it; the frame was broken away, and the canvas rolled up.) The walls of the building were left standing only because of a fortunate thunderstorm, even though the rainwater on the hot sandstone caused massive cracks. Cockburn and his invaders departed Washington the same night.

The Madisons lived temporarily in the Octagon House—still standing today—when they returned to the capital. Although Congress was hesitant about maintaining the federal government in Washington, it eventually decided to do so, and funds were provided to restore the two burned buildings. Hoban, recalled to supervise the repair work on the President's home, had to take down most of the walls because of the fire damage, with the result that the better part of today's White House walls date from 1817, the year the building was reconstructed.

The six-columned semicircular south portico was built around the bow of the south front at this time, though Hoban's original plan to carry the portico across the entire south front wasn't carried out. The new colonnaded porch had graceful flying staircases on either side winding down to the lawn; the ground-level center door gave access to what was then merely a basement. (Because of the slope in the White House site, this floor on the north side of the building is below the level of the north lawn.) What is today the center window of the main-floor Blue Room bow was then and for the remainder of the century a French door serving as the main south entrance to the mansion.

In keeping with the leisurely manner in which the house was built, the south portico took seven years to finish, being completed just as Madison's successor, James Monroe, was ending his second term. A year after the portico on the south side was finished, Congress appropriated funds to build one on the north side. The familiar entrance with four columns on the front and two on each side forming a porte cochere became the main state entrance; it was completed in 1829, the year John Quincy Adams turned the White House over to Andrew Jackson. The mansion itself was then fully built and looked to the casual observer very much as it does today. The last significant exterior change would come in 1947, and for the President who ordered it there would be political hell to pay.

Until the major interior structural alterations of 1902 the greater part of the changes to the White House were the result of progress in modern technology. The first central heating system to supplement the twenty-nine fireplaces was installed in 1837 and was expanded to nearly every room in the house by 1847. President James Polk bought the first "refrigerator" in 1845, paying $25 for it. Gas lamps replaced oil lamps in 1848, compliments of the Washington Gas Light Company. The first stoves to replace the open-hearth fireplaces for cooking came in the early 1850s. In the middle of that decade a President finally got a plumbed bathtub and toilet. An elevator was installed in 1882. Electric lights replaced the gas ones in 1889.

The first of the hideous conservatories and greenhouses which would be attached to the west end of the White House on top of Jefferson's elegant service colonnade was put up in 1857; the last of these excrescences wouldn't be removed until the end of the century. Victorians loved rooms crammed with great huge potted plants, and it was then considered the height of indulgence to have one's very own glass houses in which to grow them, an immoderation which led to the inside of the White House's looking like a rain forest by the end of the century.

The east service colonnade built during Jefferson's second term was demolished in 1869, and in its place a small portico was put up outside the East Room windows, with a formal landscaped walk cascading down to the Treasury Building. A new street—East Executive Avenue—was cut through to run between the Treasury and the east entrance of the White House.

During the last century Presidents spent as little time as possible at the White House during the summer months. The nearby Tiber Creek was a breeding ground for mosquitoes, and on hot nights they would envelop the low-lying buildings. In 1881 Mrs. James Garfield was bitten by one of these resident pests and as a result came down with malaria. As if the mosquitoes weren't plague enough, rats, mice, moths, cockroaches, and millions of black ants infested the mansion. Many Presidents continued to conduct business there during the day but spent nights at higher ground elsewhere in the District. Grover Cleveland actually established a summer White House a few miles from the real one; the area around it, now one of the wealthiest neighborhoods in Washington, is named in honor of his summers there, Cleveland Park. The Tiber Creek was eventually made into a canal and disappeared entirely in the 1870s by being paved over.

In the 1890s there were serious studies under way to relocate the President's home elsewhere in the city, leaving the White House to serve solely as the executive offices, a function then rapidly overtaking the building's living spaces. Plans were made to build a new mansion on Sixteenth Street, north of the White House. One of the proposed sites is today's Meridian Hill Park, a few blocks north on the thoroughfare that was then the center of the city's diplomatic and fashionable life.

Failing that scheme, Mrs. Benjamin Harrison had still more plans drawn to enlarge the White House itself. Considering the era, it's not surprising that the proposed "extended" mansion was an eclectic jumble. Two encircling wings matched the original style of the building, but dainty Victorian glass and cast-iron cupolas were stuck on each roof. The fourth and enclosing wing was, naturally, another greenhouse. The plan was defeated more for political reasons than for aesthetic ones. The next occupant, Grover Cleveland, tried another scheme, only marginally less ugly. His plan involved nearly identical "new" White Houses at angles to each end of the original. One was to be for social functions, the other for offices; the real one was to be left as the completely private home of the President. One White House is uniquely beautiful; three wouldn't be. Cleveland's scheme omitted the cupolas, but Congress still quashed the idea.

There was to be one more attempt to disfigure the President's home. At the turn of the century two beaux arts wings were devised for cither end of the classical building. Cupolas were back. The plan was condemned by the prestigious American Institute of Architects, putting a deserved end to it.

But it was clear that something had to be done about restoring the mansion to a residence from the office building it had become, which was the motivation for all the above scheming. Part of the first (state) floor (which had no living space for the First Family except for the private dining room) and half of the second floor were being used as the President's executive offices. The ground floor was merely a cellar and bereft of living space, and the attic was used only for servants' and storage rooms. Official callers would sometimes wander past the First Lady's boudoir, an invasion which not surprisingly infuriated presidential families. When Teddy Roosevelt and his large family moved into the White House in 1901, the overcrowding had finally reached a point where the problem could no longer be tolerated.

It was decided to construct a new office wing at the end of the west colonnade, long since buried under conservatories and greenhouses. ("Smash the glass houses," Teddy ordered.) It would be called the Executive Office Building—today's West Wing—and would at last permit all office work to be separated from the White House itself. The new building, attached to the mansion by a loggia, was theoretically designed to be "temporary" since it was thought that any major outbuildings would detract from the beauty of the central mansion and that someday executive offices would be built elsewhere.

Because the mansion itself was in very poor structural condition owing to the many and usually careless alterations made to it over ten decades, a decision was also made to rebuild a great part of the interior at the same time the office building was going up. Roosevelt and his family went to live in a house on Lafayette Park, a move which must have been difficult for a man who so obviously relished the glory of living in the country's chief residence and which probably accounts for his insistence upon having the work completed in a period of a little more than four months.

While all the construction was going on, a new east portico was also built to replace the 1869 portico which had in turn replaced Jefferson's loggia. This time an arcade over the original loggia was built, and a pavilion attached to the end of it to contain a porte cochere and a vestibule in which large groups of people entering the building from the east side could be corralled. The old basement, now more elegantly renamed the ground floor, was remodeled into a proper floor of reception rooms in place of the workrooms to which it had been given over to for the entirety of the nineteenth century.

The interior of the White House was extensively rebuilt. Many of the worst alterations and "improvements" of the Presidents of the Gilded Age were swept away, and the classical decor which replaced them was generally much more in keeping with Hoban's original ideas about what the house should look like. Even so, some aesthetic mistakes were made, notably the Jacobean-style State Dining Room with its dark paneling and moose heads stuck all around the walls—heads which, by the way, were bought from a New York taxidermist for $2,000, not bagged by TR himself. Little thought was given to the servants' safety on the attic floor. The attic stairs were removed, and it was reachable only by elevator—a dandy arrangement in case of fire.

In 1909 President William Howard Taft remodeled the "temporary" West Wing into a permanent addition and in doing so nearly doubled its size. In it a new "oval office" was built for the President. Mrs. Woodrow Wilson started using part of the servants' space in the mansion's attic for family bedrooms a few years later. (No servants live at the White House today, although senior employees occasionally stay overnight.) Two administrations later the Calvin Coolidges reroofed the White House and took the opportunity to turn Mrs. Wilson's improved attic into a real third floor (nearly undetectable from ground level), complete with a new "sky parlor" over the south front bow. The President and Mrs. Coolidge stayed in Cissy Patterson's mansion on Dupont Circle while the rebuilding was going on; it was there that they received Colonel Charles A. Lindbergh in 1927, returning from his historic flight to Paris.

During Franklin and Eleanor Roosevelt's years in the White

House significant changes were made in the two wings. The executive offices in the West Wing were enlarged, and the President's private office was moved to a choicer spot in the building's southeast corner. The office was again built in an oval shape and now opened onto the loggia leading to the mansion. The basement was converted into office space, and it was extended out under the south lawn with a light well sunk in the center to illuminate the lower floor. The street separating the wing from the old State-Navy-War Building, West Executive Avenue, was still a public thoroughfare (although not officially a part of the Washington street system as it was considered within the federal reservation), and traffic flowed within a few yards of the Oval Office itself. American schoolchildren chipped in pennies to pay for a swimming pool for the polio-stricken President; it was built in the loggia connecting the West Wing to the mansion. Shortly after World War II began, the pavilion at the end of the east loggia was enlarged into an office building nearly as big as the West Wing; it was to be used primarily by the First Lady and her staff. A bomb shelter was built directly under it, the modern necessity for residences of chiefs of state. (A larger bomb shelter has since been built under the level of the mansion's new lower basement.) The new wing cost $65,196, a figure that today seems remarkably trim and precise in an era that has become acclimated to government budget items rounded off to the nearest million dollars.

Both East and West Executive avenues were closed for the duration of the war, as were public tours of the White House itself. (A further wartime security measure recommended by the Army was to paint the White House black, but Roosevelt vetoed the idea.) Today West Executive Avenue is still sealed at both ends for security reasons as a result of a permanent wartime executive order of Roosevelt. Highly unlikely ever to be reopened, it now serves as a parking lot for the West Wing and Executive Office Building staffs.

Shortly after World War II ended, Harry Truman made the last major alteration to the mansion's exterior, one that caused a huge press uproar and was strongly condemned by the advisory Fine Arts Commission. The President wanted a simple balcony installed outside the second-floor center bow room (then used as his private study) of the south façade, right between the columns and the windows. The press loved to criticize Truman's personal foibles, and they predictably jumped all over him for his proposed balcony. Since Harry Truman generally got what he wanted, the balcony was built—a distinctly nonclassical intrusion on an otherwise pristinely classical façade. The President himself thought it made the White House look better—he said it needed something to break the "skinny perpendicular lines of the columns." The Truman balcony remains in place today, although air conditioning pretty much obviates the reason the President wanted it built in the first place.

What Clement Conger, today's White House curator and chairman of the mansion's Fine Arts Committee, calls the "second greatest vandalization of the White House, exceeded only by the burning by the British in 1814," was the next travail to which the tired and patched-up old building was subjected. In early 1948 Margaret Truman noticed the East Room chandelier sway when a marine color guard marched across the floor during a ceremony; later one of the legs on her piano broke through her sitting-room floor. The commissioner of public buildings looked into the situation at the President's urgent request and to no one's surprise reported the mansion unsafe to live in. Beams had been cut through to install service pipes and wiring with no thought given to the load they were supporting; the 180-ton third floor with its tile roof was too heavy for the walls to support; and the clay footings were compressing, causing the building to sink.

Some consideration was given to razing the entire White House and starting over from scratch. But it was eventually decided—in the cause of "historical continuity"—merely to gut the building, rebuild the inside, and leave the newly strengthened and underpinned original walls standing. The interior was to be supported by a new steel frame; the outer walls would no longer be load-bearing. To today's world, accustomed to expert architectural restoration capabilities, this solution sounds historically unforgivable. But in the cultural miasma of the late 1940s, few voices were heard in opposition to the plan.

Fortunately it was the Trumans who were the tenants of the White House when it began to fall apart in earnest. It's hard to imagine another President, *or* another First Lady, voluntarily giving up the executive mansion for three and a half years—from Thanksgiving 1948 to March 27, 1952, all but the last year of Truman's second term. The President, his wife, Bess, and their daughter, Margaret, moved across the street to Blair House for the duration of the $5,761,000 construction job. Actually the publicity-shy Bess Truman was said to prefer the smaller and more private home to the White House, although the President was anxious to get the work done and move back in.

As Truman was crossing Pennsylvania Avenue on his way to work in the Oval Office on the morning the excavating began, he noticed a large Colonial-style swinging sign had been erected in front of the White House by the contractor as an advertisement for his firm. The President was furious at what he considered a gross impertinence and ordered its instant removal. But Truman had no reservations about selling bits and pieces of the rubble taken from the mansion. For $1 plus shipping charges, the memorabilia collector received one brick; for $100, he got enough "to build a fireplace." About 30,000 of these souvenir packages were sent out.

Because the new foundations were twenty feet deeper than the original footings, the freshly excavated area provided for two subbasements in which storage and laundry rooms and a servants' dining room, as well as wiring, plumbing, telephone lines, and air-conditioning systems, were installed. (Sophisticated air and water filtration systems have since been added as security measures against the introduction of poisons or gases into the White House.) The digging extended under the north portico and lawn to house air-conditioning compressors and shops.

The 1817 floor plans were adhered to in the rebuilding of the interiors of the ground, first, and second floors. Running ice water was installed, as were duplicate water supply lines and more than 2,000 electrical plugs and switches. The third story was refurbished, but the well-constructed steel floor built for the Coolidges in 1927 remained; additional bedrooms were built, and the sky parlor became the new sun room. Truman had plans to turn the West Wing into a far larger office building but was stopped because of the understandable concern that it would overshadow the mansion itself.

The most recent changes to the White House complex have involved the two wings. In 1969 Richard Nixon floored over the pool (which is still buried, chrome-plated ladders and all, waiting to be uncovered by some future restorers) to provide space for the press corps, which up to that time had been using the area that now serves as the West Wing's lobby. A new formal portico and driveway were added to the north side of the wing, also by Nixon. Solar collectors have recently been placed on the building's roof. Finally, a new visitor's entrance pavilion, scheduled to be opened in 1983, is being built just south of the east portico.

So there it is, sitting on the edge of a definitely nonpresidential neighborhood. Two or three blocks to the east, anyone can easily find whatever variety of stimulant, depressant, or other mind-altering substance his particular needs might call for. Porno bookshops and all manner of prostitutes are busy within the same perimeter. The old downtown shopping district immediately to the east of the White House has crumbled into a blighted shadow of its once-proud self, with little sign that it will ever regain its former eminence in the nation's capital.

But within the intricate security arrangements guarding the presidential compound is one of the most elegant and elaborate executive establishments in the world. Probably the only residence of a head of state with an ordinary street address (10 Downing Street is *not* the residence of a head of state), it is also the only such executive home in the world which is open free of charge to the public.

More than 1,500,000 tourists troop through the White House every year—an average of 6,000 each day. There are summer days when that many must be turned away. The vast majority of these tourists get the ordinary, nonexclusive public view of the mansion between 10:00 A.M. and noon every Tuesday through Saturday. The line usually stretches down from the East Executive Avenue entrance gate and around the curve of the south grounds. The wait far exceeds the time actually spent touring the mansion, which in midsummer can be as little as ten minutes but averages about half an hour. A much smaller but not inconsiderable group see the mansion on the so-called congressional, or VIP, tour starting at 8:30 A.M. Each congressman and senator has a weekly allotment of ten or twenty tickets (given to any of their constituents who write and ask for them) for this better (and longer—about forty-five minutes) view of the inside of the President's home. The public tour folks are herded through in great clumps, without a tour guide to identify the sights or an opportunity to stop and take it all in. The favored VIP tourists are also taken through in clumps, albeit smaller ones, but they have the added attraction of a slightly saccharine narration explaining where they are and what they're seeing. The narrator-guides are members of the Uniformed Division of the Secret Service who have volunteered for this temporary duty. The latter group also gets to see some of the ground-floor rooms not entered on the regular tours.

One of the first and most-lasting impressions received by the first-time visitor to the White House is just how small it is: stately, gracious, beautiful—but small. In spite of its status as residence of the head of state of the richest nation on earth and its importance as the symbol of the executive branch of that nation's government, the residence portion of the three-building complex is easily overshadowed by other, more imposing statements of architectural grandeur in Washington's monument-dotted center. The mansion contains 132 rooms on the four floors, including 18 bathrooms and lavatories and 50 or so storage and utility spaces. The state floor—that seen by the majority of the tourists—has only six principal rooms, but they form the heart of the nation's ceremonial life.

A convenient way to describe the interior of the White House is to take you on a room-by-room tour from the ground up, preceded by the East Wing and ending with the executive offices in the West Wing.

The President's House sits in its own private park, with Pennsylvania Avenue to the north, East and South Executive avenues to the east and south, State Place to the southwest, and Seventeenth Street to the west. Before 1942, West Executive Avenue divided it from the Old Executive Office Building to the west; that street is now a parking lot, and the Old EOB itself is today a part of the White House compound, enclosed by a fence and permanently off limits to the public.

The East Executive Avenue gate, directly across the street from the neoclassical Treasury Building, is the public entrance and serves as the starting point for all the tours.* A short flight of steps up past a guardpost, a pathway leads to the East Wing lobby doors. It's difficult to overstate the transformation in this area before and after noon on tour days. When the public is being taken through, the beauty of the paneled lobby and graceful colonnade overlooking the Jacqueline Kennedy Garden is subliminated to a throng in the usual undress of tourists, in summer months many wearing shorts and T-shirts. One day a touching vignette took place in the midst of the clusters of expectant sightseers: the distraught young wife of a congressman was told that this crowd *did* constitute her "congressional" tour. Having thought the name of her scheduled tour implied something exclusively for her and other such privileged persons, she was angrily telephoning her husband's office, trying to arrange for the exclusivity she apparently felt was her due. There are, in fact, authentically exclusive VIP tours of the White House every now and again, but the VIP generally stands for "very important philanthropist," the kind who is a potential donor to the White House Preservation Fund.

After tour hours the lobby takes on a tranquil appearance. Squadrons of cleaners appear to restore the floors to their usual gleam, a scene repeated all over the mansion as well. The restraining cordons are removed, and the metal-detecting device is dismantled until the next day. Putting one of these airport types

---

* The much-needed new Visitors' Entrance Pavilion will replace this entrance as the starting point for public tours. Built to resemble a Palladian garden pavilion, with floor-to-ceiling French windows and doors decorated with grillwork, it was designed by Warren Hardwicke. When completed, the building will expedite the daily flow of visitors through the security check, as well as allow as much of the security equipment as possible to be concealed.

of apparatus in the country's first home was resisted as long as possible for the obvious reason that it's an appalling symbol of the nation's mounting lawlessness. Nevertheless, after the March 1981 attempt on the President's life, the device was installed anyway. Its opponents were right about the symbolism—one gets a sinking feeling having to run a gauntlet of security devices and unsmiling guards to see the President's home. What's equally depressing is the realization that it's probably going to be this way for keeps, that there's no justification to think that any day soon the metal detector and army of guards can be taken away.

The East Wing is a two-story rectangular building built at a right angle to the colonnade that leads to the mansion. Traditionally the East Wing has been the First Lady's territory, as the West Wing has been the President's. Most of it is taken up by offices; the White House theater is located on the first floor (the often prerelease films shown to the First Family are provided without charge by their producing studios). Probably *the* prominent feature of the lobby is the large guards' station which serves as a sort of traffic control center for the wing. A door off the foyer leads to a carpeted staircase that ascends to the second-floor offices of Mrs. Reagan's chief of staff and the White House social secretary.

Just past the East Wing lobby is the Regency-style Garden Room, which is actually a part of the colonnade connecting the mansion to the wing. This is where the ubiquitous item of Washington touristiana is housed—the souvenir shop. Just outside the Garden Room on the south grounds is the Jacqueline Kennedy Garden (referred to as the *East* Garden by Pat Nixon), named in her predecessor's honor by Lady Bird Johnson in 1965. First Ladies use it as an informal reception area when weather allows.

Starting at the Garden Room, the colonnade leads to the East Foyer just inside the entrance to the ground floor of the mansion proper. An enclosed passageway running the length of the colonnade is lined with large windows of handmade glass. A series of display cases contains all sorts of White House memorabilia; recent color glossies of the Reagans are interspersed among the cases.

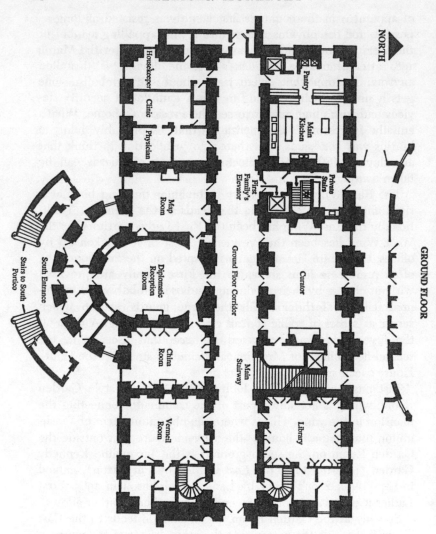

Finally, inside the mansion itself is the Ground Floor Corridor, a passageway extending the entire length of the building. Before the 1902 Roosevelt remodeling, the ground floor was simply a damp and cluttered basement, filled with service rooms, heating mains, and air ducts disfiguring the architecturally beautiful groined ceiling. Constantly rotting wooden slats covered the tile floors. The kitchen workers kept up a running battle with rats, a problem not entirely solved even today. The Roosevelt remodeling turned this "cellar" into a proper formal floor, today heavily used for many official functions.

The corridor's walls are covered with marble, and a red carpet runs the length of the cleanly elegant hall. During tour hours a pair of tall red screens are placed midway in the corridor, shielding the First Family as they enter and leave the White House through the Map Room and the Diplomatic Reception Room. Off the opposite end of the corridor (the west end) are the kitchens and storerooms, the domain of a small army of cooks and domestic servants. Behind a locked door just across a passageway from the kitchen, a one-time pantry has been converted into a wine cellar; the collection in the temperature-controlled (58-degree) nook is today down to a few dozen bottles.

A tradition has developed since the 1902 remodeling that the Ground Floor Corridor's walls are lined solely with portraits of the First Ladies, those of the last two flanking either side of the entrance to the center Diplomatic Reception Room. That of Jacqueline Kennedy, a hauntingly beautiful portrait by Aaron Shikler, is the most striking object in the entire corridor. A painting of Pat Nixon joined those of the other First Ladies in the autumn of 1981. (Since nearly all the paintings and many of the pieces of furniture in the White House are periodically shifted around, it's impossible for a guide to the placement of the works of art to stay current for any length of time.)

The Library is the first room on the right as one enters the Ground Floor Corridor from the colonnade. Tourists can only look into it from its roped-off doorway. The space, a laundry room before 1902, had been used as the gentlemen's anteroom before the Franklin Roosevelts turned it into a library in 1937. The first permanent books for the White House weren't bought until 1850, when Millard Fillmore started buying authors by the yard. Since then American publishing houses have kept the wall shelves filled free of charge. Some of the timbers torn out of the

White House during the Truman rebuilding were used to construct the Library, as well as several other of the ground-floor
rooms. Mrs. Gerald Ford completely refurbished the room in
1976, replacing some of the reproduction furniture with authentic late Federal period Duncan Phyfe pieces and repainting the
ivory walls a soft gray. It's unlikely that the presidential family
uses the room for its library purposes very often; it generally
serves as a small reception chamber and for serving tea to ambassadorial parties coming to present credentials to the President.

Directly across the hall from the Library is the first of a range
of four rooms (the last three interconnecting): the Vermeil
Room—Harry Truman's billiards room and now named for the
priceless collection displayed in it (vermeil is silver that has
been gilded, or coated with a thin layer of gold). The collection
was bequeathed in one lump to the White House in 1956 by
Margaret Thompson Biddle and is still occasionally used for
official entertaining. During large receptions or state dinners, the
room serves as a women's coatroom. A Monet—"Morning on the
Seine"—over the mantel was the gift of the Kennedy family to
the mansion shortly after the President's assassination. Reportedly friends of the Kennedys aren't too happy about its placement in what amounts to a part-time women's lounge.

Next to the Vermeil Room is the China Room, the Presidential
Collection Room, where Ellen Wilson first gathered for display
representative pieces of all the existing sets of White House
china. Relatively little furniture is placed in the room so that
tourists can see the display cases full of gold-edged and multicolored dishes as closely as possible. The outstanding picture is
a full-length Howard Chandler Christy portrait of Grace Coolidge, painted the day her husband was to have sat for the artist
but was too preoccupied with the then-breaking Teapot Dome
scandal, the Watergate of the twenties.

The most distinctive architectural feature of the mansion is
the three elliptical, or oval, rooms, one above the other on the
south front. That on the ground floor, called the Diplomatic Reception Room, is the next of the south side rooms on the corri-

dor. It's hard to imagine this elegantly beautiful salon, directly in the center of the mansion's south front, as the boiler room throughout the nineteenth century. A door leads into a short passageway opening onto the south lawn; the room serves as the building's major entryway for invited guests. The modern restoration of the President's home really began here when in 1960 Mamie Eisenhower initiated its transformation from a fairly undistinguished space into a white and gold Federal drawing room recalling the early nineteenth-century origins of the White House. Mamie's cream walls have been replaced with a striking panoramic wallpaper above the wainscoting; the cornerless room is perfect for displaying the murallike scenes based on early engravings of American life. Franklin Roosevelt broadcast his fireside chats from in front of the mantel on the east side of the room.

The last of the four principal south side rooms is the Map Room, so named because FDR used it as a situation room during World War II. Since its 1970 redecoration it has been a reception room and serves as the men's coatroom during large gatherings in the mansion. It is furnished in American Chippendale.

The remaining rooms on the ground floor are used by the housekeeper, the doctor, and the curator. The office-*cum*-workroom of Clement Conger, the present curator, is directly across the corridor from the Diplomatic Reception Room. His desk sits in front of the original ovens, used for cooking before the first stoves were installed a century ago.

There are three primary means of access to the state floor: an elevator and a private staircase, between the kitchens and Conger's office, and the Main Stairway, between the curator's office and the Library. These marble stairs, covered with a red and gold runner, ascend to the state floor's Entrance Hall, the ceremonial receiving area for greeting distinguished visitors. Directly across the Entrance Hall from the Main Stairway is the chief usher's small office. An armed guard is now on permanent duty in the Entrance Hall. Double glass and bronze doors open onto the north portico.

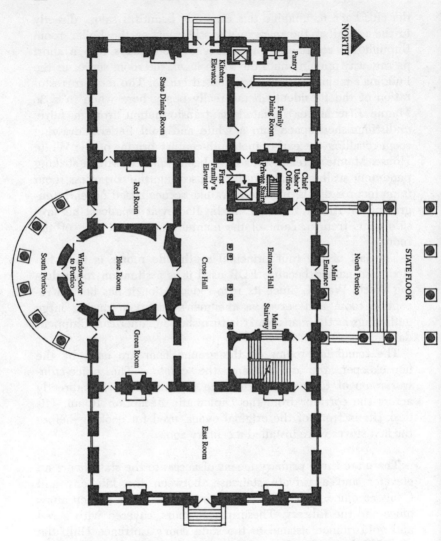

The Entrance Hall is separated from the Cross Hall by six Doric columns, the inner four set in pairs. The Cross Hall is the central bisecting corridor of the state floor—five of the six principal rooms open off it. (The Main Stairway, which continues up to the second—private—floor, opened into the Cross Hall before the Truman renovation; it was then repositioned to open onto the Entrance Hall and thus be visible to entering guests.) The most magnificent chandeliers in the mansion—made of English Adams-style cut glass—hang in the Cross Hall. Just as recent First Ladies' portraits line the Ground Floor Corridor, those of recent Presidents are traditionally displayed in the Cross Hall. The new (and extremely flattering) Alexander Clayton portrait of Richard Nixon recently supplanted that of Lyndon Johnson on the wall just outside the East Room.

To most visitors, it comes as a surprise that the state floor contains only six principal rooms, and only one of these has anything like palatial proportions. Five of them are open to the public; only the now misnamed Family Dining Room is closed to tourists. Directly ahead from the Entrance Hall are three formal drawing rooms, named for the prime colors in their decor—the Blue, Red, and Green rooms. (They correspond exactly to the Diplomatic Reception Room, Map Room, and China Room on the floor below.)

Until the 1902 rebuilding of much of the White House the south entrance to the mansion was through the French doors opening off the Blue Room onto the south portico. Probably the most elegantly proportioned room in the White House (the ceilings are considerably higher than in the otherwise-identically-shaped rooms above and below it), the Blue Room was an object of some controversy regarding its latest decoration scheme. Once known as the Elliptical Saloon, it was used as an office by FDR when the West Wing was being renovated in 1934. Three presidential daughters (Monroe's, Tyler's, and Wilson's), one presidential son (John Quincy Adams's), and one President himself (Grover Cleveland) have been married in the Blue Room.

It is today furnished in the French Empire style, as it was during the presidency of James Monroe. Several of the original Monroe pieces of furniture made by the French cabinetmaker Bellangé have been located and returned to the room. Portraits of President Monroe and his First Lady look down on "their" room from positions flanking the fireplace.

From its first blue decor in 1837, the room has gone from 1860s steamboat Gothic, replete with an enormous ugly chandelier, to Tiffany's busywork of the Chester Arthur presidency. In 1902 it became Empire again, the walls covered in dark blue silk with heavy matching draperies. It stayed pretty much this way after the Truman rebuilding and all through the Eisenhower years. Mamie used only yellow flowers in the room—the gold and blue motif gave the chamber a luxurious appearance.

In 1962 French interior designer and a member of the famous Jansen decorating firm of Paris Stéphane Boudin redecorated the room at Jacqueline Kennedy's instigation. In what curator Clement Conger considers today to have been an "incorrect" design scheme, Boudin's work resulted in striped satin-covered walls in two tones of cream, with a blue-trimmed valance surrounding the room, all set off with blue draperies. Conger refers to it as it was then as Boudin's boudoir. Jacqueline Kennedy, on the other hand, remembers it as her finest contribution to the White House. The curator's reasoning is that the President's House— specifically that of a mansion of the first quarter of the nineteenth century in which the owner had "all the money and all the taste in the world"—should reflect American, not French, taste.

In 1971 Conger and Pat Nixon set about undoing Boudin's work, and today the Blue Room is "correct," according to Conger's guidelines. The fabric on the walls was replaced with a pale greenish beige paper with a polychromed classical frieze around the top and at the bottom above the wainscoting. The draperies are blue, the swags gold, and the thousands of intricate tassels—each taking a worker a full day to make—gold and blue.

The center "window" looking down the Ellipse and across the Mall to the Jefferson Memorial is actually a concealed door opening onto the south portico; the sash raises, and the wainscoting swings away like a gate. The opposite center door opens onto the Cross Hall; positioned above the entrance on the hall side is the presidential seal, with the American and presidential flags on standards flanking it. Inside the Blue Room on either side are two sets of doors, those on the east connecting with the Green Room, the pair on the west going into the Red Room.

Smaller than the Blue Room, these two identically proportioned parlors are also used mainly for receptions and small teas. The more striking of the two is Nancy Reagan's favorite, the Red Room. By the standards of a residence of a head of state, the American Empire-style (1810–1830) room is almost intimate. It was once known as the Washington Room because of the famous Gilbert Stuart portrait of the first President that hung there. President Rutherford B. Hayes took the oath of office in the cozy little chamber late on a Saturday night, March 3, 1877–the regular inaugural day fell on a Sunday, and impiety was not to be courted. It was here that President and Mrs. Jimmy Carter received President-Elect and Mrs. Ronald Reagan on the morning of inauguration day 1981.

With the 1952 reopening of the mansion, the room's walls were covered in a deep cherry red patterned wallpaper. The hotel type of furniture from New York's B. Altman & Company ordered by Bess Truman gave the room an undistinguished appearance, but Mrs. Kennedy's 1962 redecoration transformed it to an American Empire look, which was continued with Pat Nixon's further major redecoration in 1971. As with most of the work carried out under Mrs. Nixon's direction, the primary emphasis was on upgrading the quality and authenticity of the furnishings—the basic motifs of these state rooms still owe their inspiration to Jacqueline Kennedy Onassis.

The White House's most beautiful painting hangs in the Red Room. The 1842 Henry Inman portrait of President Martin Van Buren's daughter-in-law, Angelica Singleton Van Buren, reminiscent of Franz Winterhalter's portrayals of the British royal family, hangs above the white marble mantel. Within the portrait the artist painted a small bust of Van Buren; the same marble sculpture is displayed on a bracket cornice a few feet from the painting, making for a striking historical union.

The third of the three state drawing rooms (and the most richly furnished) is the Green Room. Today decorated in Sheraton, or American classical, style, it was once used by Thomas Jefferson for small dinner parties and later as a cardroom by the Monroes; it has most often served as a small reception parlor in the years since. The 1950s saw the same sort of heavy-patterned wallpaper that was found in the Red Room, together with an official-looking rug woven with the presidential seal—the entire decade was big on presidential emblems, eagles, and such, worked into as many corners of the White House as possible.

This was the first room furnished by the Fine Arts Committee in 1961; it was refurbished by Mrs. Nixon in 1971. The green watered silk fabric on the walls perfectly sets off the sumptuous Sheraton furnishings. The windows (one of which is a window-door like that in the Blue Room, opening onto the south portico) are covered with coral and beige draperies, green swags (again edged with the wonderfully intricate, labor-intensive tassels found in most of the state rooms), and gilt cornices. The green Turkish Hereke rug is a rarity: Because green is the color of Mohammed's turban, Moslems are reluctant to walk on the color, thus relatively few rugs of that kind have been made.

One of the finest and most graceful furniture groupings in the mansion is set along the Green Room's west wall, below the historic David Martin portrait of Benjamin Franklin. A Duncan Phyfe settee is flanked by two drop-leaf library tables, each set with antique covered cachepots and crystal and silver oil lamps. Facing the settee is a wonderful little mahogany sofa table with clover-leaf ends and Sheraton chairs at either side. The tall silver coffee urn on the sofa table once belonged to John Adams. A masterpiece he considered one of his "most prized possessions," the urn is supported by a pair of French silver candlesticks bought by future president Madison from future president Monroe in 1803. Such are the countless historical associations found in almost every corner of the President's home.

If the White House had a throne room, the East Room would be it. It has seen everything from Abigail Adams's wet knickers hanging out on lines to dry to Pablo Casals holding a distinguished audience in thrall, from Alice Roosevelt's wedding to John Kennedy's lying in state. Until recently it served as a roller rink for Amy Carter and friends. The East Room—perhaps the commonplace name is fitting for a republican residence of state —is the White House's all-purpose room. It looks very much as the first Roosevelt decorated it at the turn of the century, but some simplifying of its details was done when the Truman renovators put it back together a half century later: The twenty-two-foot-high ceiling moldings and rosettes were made less fussy, the three Bohemian cut-glass chandeliers refashioned in a less ornate and ponderous manner (and dimmers were first installed on them), and almost all the furniture was removed, leaving only a piano and a few benches between the gold-draperied and corniced windows.

At 45 feet by 87½ feet, the room fills the eastern end of the state floor from north to south. With walls painted in an off-white shade the only major piece of furniture in the room is an elaborately decorated Steinway grand piano, presented to the mansion in 1938. On the east wall, facing visitors coming in through any of the four doorways—two from the Green Room, one from behind the Main Stairway, and the main entrance from the Cross Hall—are two full-length portraits of George and Martha Washington. The former, probably the most famous painting in the Western Hemisphere, is the only certain object in the White House from before the 1814 fire. The picture is a copy of the original Gilbert Stuart made for William Bingham of Philadelphia. Some refer to it as the "teapot" Washington because the President's pose suggests the handle and spout of a teapot. It has never been determined for certain whether Stuart himself actually painted the copy. In any event, Dolley Madison had it removed only hours before the British arrived and destroyed the building. The flanking portrait of Martha was not painted from life but was commissioned 100 years after her death to balance that of her husband.

At the opposite end of the Cross Hall is the State Dining Room, corresponding to the East Room in width, but a bit less than two-thirds its length. Before 1902, besides being considerably smaller, it was turned on the opposite axis; the staircase at the west end of the Cross Hall was removed, and the space added to the State Dining Room's north end. A dark-paneled room until the Truman reconstruction, it was then painted light celadon green, and a black marble mantel replaced the Roosevelt buffalo-head model. The new silver chandelier and sconces shone softly over state dinners where as many as 110 guests were served at a horseshoe-shaped table. To fit in an extra 30 guests, Mamie Eisenhower devised an E-shaped table seating 140.

Today small round tables, each seating 8, are usually used for state dinners; the new style is altogether less banquetlike and more cheerful.

When Jackie Kennedy went to work on the room, it was repainted white, and the silver chandelier and sconces were gilded. (When Mamie Eisenhower first saw the results of Jackie's work on the silver, she let out a low but justifiable moan —they did, in fact, look better when they were silver.) The black mantel was again replaced, this time with a reproduction of its white buffalo-head predecessor. There are five doors off the room: Two lead into the Red Room, one into the Cross Hall, another in the northwest corner into a butler's pantry, and the last into the state floor's final principal room and the only one not open to the public, the Family Dining Room.

Right up through the beginning of the Kennedy residency, the Family Dining Room really did serve as the First Family's private dining room. Jackie found it awkward to feed her children on the state floor, however, and had one of the second-floor bedroom suites converted into a new private dining room and small kitchen-pantry. Today the Family Dining Room is used mostly as a supper room and for presidential business breakfasts; its finest feature is the segmented vaulted ceiling, the only one of its kind in the White House.

Stuck in the northwest corner of the state floor next to the Family Dining Room is a small butler's pantry serving both dining rooms opening off it. An automatic dumbwaiter brings food up from the kitchens below. The passenger elevator in the pantry serves all but the second floor.

The last bit of the state floor is the area between the Entrance Hall and the Family Dining Room (corresponding to the Main Stairway space on the other side of the Entrance Hall). The chief usher's office, entered from the Entrance Hall, takes up about half the space; the other half, entered through the Cross Hall just ahead of the State Dining Room entrance, is a small lobby housing the private presidential stairway and elevator. Truman wanted the original elevator put back in 1952 but was told that modern machinery wasn't compatible with it, so it was sent off to the Smithsonian. Mamie Eisenhower was rather possessive of this elevator. She once had to wait while a servant was using it and immediately gave orders to the chief usher that this was *her* elevator and not to be used by anyone else. (Presumably her husband was exempted from the decree.) There was absolutely nothing shy or hesitant about Mamie in her role as mistress of the house.

The state floor of the White House is as much a museum as it is a living space—the ratio of sightseers to private invited guests is about 30 to 1. But in ascending to the second floor, one leaves this semipublic grandeur for the entirely private beauty of the "family quarters," the name used to officially designate the real presidential living areas—two floors with thirty-five rooms, sixteen baths, and sixty closets.

In reality, the First Family can't exactly call the entire second floor home—the floor's eastern end is designated as semistate rooms, although the Main Stairway leading up to it is closed to any wandering tourists. The floor is traversed from east to west by a corridor extending the length of the house, and is broken into three principal areas: the East and West Sitting halls and the Center Hall, as well as the smaller Stair Hall between the East and Center halls. The Stair Hall, at the top of the Main Stairway, is enclosed with locked sliding doors on either side. Lady Bird Johnson managed to lock herself out one night after a state dinner. Dressed in her bathrobe, she drew herself up, sauntered down the stairs, and, with the cleaning staff staring at her, crossed the main hall and got back up to her bedroom on the elevator.

The East Sitting Hall (which has a ramp up its two-foot incline to accommodate the extra ceiling height of the East Room directly below) is decorated in gold and white. It has the feeling of a formal sitting room, which is the function it serves for the Queens' Suite and the Lincoln Suite off either side of it. By far the most striking ornament in the area is the lovely Palladian double-arched fanlight window overlooking the East Wing and the Treasury Building.

Before the West Wing was built, this end of the floor served as the President's official offices, and solid doors had to be in-

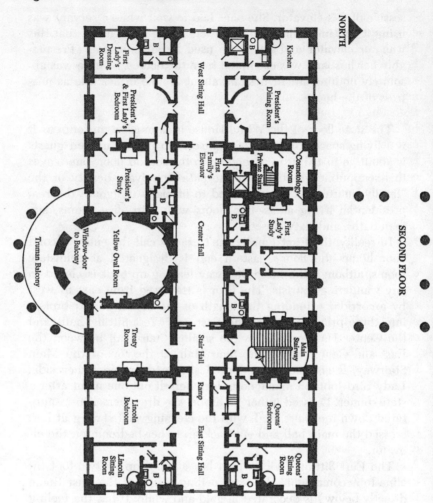

stalled in the Center Hall to shield the First Family's private apartments. Until Blair House became the exclusive presidential guesthouse in the 1950s, visiting heads of state were quartered in the two suites off either side of the East Sitting Hall. Both suites are now used by private guests of the presidential family; the Prince of Wales and Princess Anne used the rooms as the "personal" guests of the Nixons in 1970.

The bedroom formerly used by male state visitors is the Lincoln Bedroom, so named not because it was actually where Abraham Lincoln slept when he lived in the White House, but because it has been furnished with artifacts associated with his tenure in the mansion. The room was used by Lincoln for Cabinet meetings and as an office; in it he signed the Emancipation Proclamation, but only after flexing his handshake-swollen hand for several minutes so his signature wouldn't look "weak or uncertain" on the historic document. The ornate and massive dark rosewood bedstead in the room was bought by Mary Todd Lincoln but probably was never used by her husband; Theodore Roosevelt and Woodrow Wilson slept on it during their White House years, though. All the remaining furniture is mid-Victorian.

Next door, in the southeast corner of the floor, is the Lincoln Sitting Room, also furnished in the Victorian style, the decor dating from the Kennedy years. In front of the window overlooking the south grounds is a small desk made by Hoban and recently returned to the White House. The room is interconnected with the Lincoln Bedroom; the suite's bathroom is off the sitting room.

Richard Nixon used the room as a sort of private hideaway. Playing his Mantovani records on the stereo, the President would hole up in it for hours. It was here that he and Secretary of State Henry Kissinger reportedly got down on the rug to pray together shortly before the end of his beleaguered presidency; forty-eight hours later he handed the secretary his resignation letter in the same room.

Directly across the East Sitting Hall from the Lincoln Suite is the Queens' Suite, composed also of a bedroom (called the Rose Room until the mid-sixties) and a sitting room. (These four rooms together with the sitting hall correspond to the East Room on the state floor directly below.) The suite is named for the queens who have stayed in it over the last four decades— Wilhelmina and Juliana of the Netherlands, Frederika of Greece, and Queen Mother Elizabeth and Elizabeth II of Great Britain. As a princess the latter presented a seventeenth-century trumeau to the White House, a gift of her father, King George VI; the floral painting and mirror framed together in gilt today hang over the mantel in the bedroom. The room, with its carved American Sheraton canopy bed, was refurbished by Betty Ford in 1976.

A small sitting room is connected to the bedroom through an inside door. Basically unchanged since the Kennedy years, the blue and white neoclassical furnishings make a strong contrast with its connecting bedroom. A Roman Catholic mass was once said in the room—for the first birthday of Patrick Lyndon Nugent, Lyndon Johnson's first grandchild. The suite is often used today—as is the Lincoln Suite—by personal friends of the Reagans, and its use is one of the greatest honors the First Family can bestow on its guests.

At the top of the Stair Hall, and corresponding to the Green Room below, is the Treaty Room, called the Monroe Room until it was renamed during the Kennedy administration. On Winston Churchill's frequent and lengthy wartime visits to Roosevelt, he used it as his personal situation room (he slept in the Queens' Bedroom). Two famous treaties signed in the room—that ending the war with Spain by William McKinley in 1898 and the Nuclear Test Ban Treaty by her husband in 1963—prompted Mrs. Kennedy to give it its new name during her renovation. The furnishings are Victorian, as is the wallpaper with its geometric border, identical to that in the Peterson House room a few blocks to the east in which Lincoln died. A small half bath is connected to it in the curved wall space formed by the Yellow Oval Room next door.

Treated as a room, albeit a windowless one, the Center Hall is a white and gold area enhanced with several French and American impressionist paintings, including the work of one of America's finest painters, Childe Hassam. The primary function of the Center Hall is to serve as an anteroom to the Yellow Oval Room overlooking the south grounds. Mrs. Reagan's 1981 redecoration had a striking effect on the Center Hall. An enormous 150-year-old English octagonal partners' desk, donated to the White House by the Jules Steins during the Kennedy years and retrieved from storage, is in the center of the hall, dividing it into a sort of double drawing room. Comfortable furniture grouped in small seating areas has for the first time given the area the warmth and cheerfulness of a family living space.

The most formal of the private presidential apartments, the Yellow Oval Room (jokingly called the Standing Room by Betty Ford because of its largely ceremonial uses) is decorated with French and American antiques in the Louis XVI style, but now modified by Nancy Reagan with comfortable sofas and chairs for easier conversation. Used as a drawing room off and on throughout the White House's history, it has also served as a bedroom for John Quincy Adams, a breakfast room for the Lincoln family, an office for Grover Cleveland and Benjamin Harrison, and from 1933 to 1961 as a study by FDR, Truman, and Eisenhower. Jacqueline Kennedy returned it to its use as a formal salon, a function it has maintained since. At state dinners today the President and First Lady meet with their guests of honor in the Yellow Oval Room, exchange gifts, and get ready for the formalities downstairs. The door on the west side of the room connects directly with the President's study; a blind door on the other side, no longer used, connects with the Treaty Room. Access to the famous Truman balcony is through the window-door in this room.

The balcony itself provides a breathtaking panorama across the south grounds to the Mall. With a slate tile floor, it is pleasantly furnished with white wrought-iron furniture fitted with plump beige cushions. Planted geraniums give it the ambience of a garden. Small white spotlights around the inside of the portico ceiling provide soft illumination for evenings spent relaxing on the terracelike balcony.

Off the north side of the Center Hall is another set of rooms—two bedroom-and-bath suites facing Pennsylvania Avenue under the eaves of the north portico and used by members of the First Family. One of the two larger rooms was Amy Carter's bedroom, the other her playroom, and Nancy Reagan has today modified one of the rooms to serve as her office. Reflecting her elegant taste, the personal study is strié-painted in pale green with white details. Silver-framed family photographs fill the shelved wall recesses; a portrait of Britain's queen mother, whom the First Lady met while in England for the Prince of Wales's wedding, tops a small table. One wall is nearly covered by twenty-five framed wild flower prints artfully arranged in a perfect square. The view from the window looks straight up Sixteenth Street, with only the guy chains supporting the huge lantern under the portico marring the vista.

The "cosmetology room" (as Mrs. Reagan calls the beauty salon) next door is filled with $8,000 worth of beauty equipment and new furniture donated by the beauty industry. What had been Eisenhower's painting room was first turned into a hairdressing salon by Pat Nixon; Rosalynn Carter had plans to renovate it but left the job for her successor. All the hairdressing equipment can be folded away into the wall when not being used to do the First Lady's hair, leaving it as a small sitting room. The beauty equipment is not, by the way, used by White House staff members.

The last room off the south side of the Center Hall before the archway into the West Sitting Hall is the President's study. Inside its door is a small hall, with a bathroom to the left and a connecting inside passageway to the Reagans' bedroom on the right. Used by the President as a more private working office away from the formalities of the West Wing, the room is furnished mainly with pieces from the First Family's Pacific Palisades home: The partners' desk with its silver firehorn lamp was in the bedroom of their California home; the chairs and a lamp, in the den. As with all the private rooms of the White House, desk tops, bookshelves, and end tables are covered with family photographs. On the desk is Reagan's famous little cast brass plaque reading: "There is no limit to what man can do or where he can go if he doesn't mind who gets the credit."

The West Sitting Hall has served as the primary second-floor "living room" for the last several presidential families. The space is larger than, but otherwise similar to, the East Sitting Hall; the great fan window overlooking the West Wing and the Old Executive Office Building forms the principal architectural element. Until the west grand staircase was removed in 1902, the area was merely an elaborate stair landing. Today, with a partition with sliding doors between it and the Center Hall, it has the look of a room, but little of a room's sense of privacy. Doors leading off to chambers on either side still remind visitors that it's a hallway, and the view 168 feet down to the east end of the floor is fairly forbidding. Until the Franklin Roosevelts moved in a half century ago, it was furnished with wicker arranged on a checkerboard-patterned grass rug in the sort of indoor garden setting popular in the twenties and thirties. The Truman renovation put a fifties hotel veneer on it, with chintz-covered sofas and a television set built into the wall and enclosed by a door and latch that made it look like an icebox; a painting now covers the old opening.

When the Reagans first entered the West Sitting Hall in the late afternoon of inauguration day, they found it already decorated for them with their old furniture from Pacific Palisades, a move designed to make them feel at home as quickly as possible. The two opposing red and white sofas and matching easy chairs fill the west end of the sitting hall under the enormous window. The rest of the mostly Truman era furniture has been replaced with pieces long hidden away in storage (the White House storage warehouse is at Fort Washington, a short distance south of Washington), now repaired and refurbished. The walls are peach with white wainscoting. Tables are covered with antique blue and white porcelain, a gift to Nancy Reagan from her mother.

Rooms used by the President, his wife, and their children for various purposes naturally change from one administration to another. Usually in the past the First Lady used the two-room suite in the southwest corner off the West Hall as her bedroom and dressing room or study; the current President's study next door generally served as the President's bedroom. Now the larger of these two rooms is the Reagans' bedroom. Lavishly redecorated for the First Couple by Ted Graber, it is today a richly elegant room the walls of which are covered with a pale Chinese hand-painted wallpaper, blending into a light beige carpet, the whole overlooked by an antique crystal chandelier. The marble columned fireplace, designed by Latrobe, has a mantel topped with an ornate profusion of bibelots. The couple share a king-size bed. The smaller room next door in the southwest corner is Nancy Reagan's dressing room, with a connecting bath;

the two windows look out onto the south grounds and over the West Wing.

In the northwest corner of the floor is the President's Dining Room, actually the First Family's private dining room and today used by the Reagans generally only for breakfast. (Dinner for the couple when alone—a rare occurrence—is served on trays in the President's study, Mr. Reagan sometimes already in his pajamas and robe.) What was once Margaret Truman's bedroom, then Mamie Eisenhower's mother's room was converted by Jacqueline Kennedy into a superbly decorated dining room, with an unusual inside bowed wall. The wallpaper in the room has had a checkered past, one that has caused considerable problems for Curator Conger. Called "Scenic America" and printed by the Alsatian firm of Jean Zuber et Cie in 1834, the Kennedy-installed mural didn't suit Betty Ford's taste ("too busy"), and it was removed at her orders. Rosalynn Carter had it put right back up. "Fortunately it's on linen," said Conger, "so it can be rolled up and stored, but still it's hard on it." The Reagans have left it in place.

Mrs. Kennedy had a functional little kitchen and pantry and dumbwaiter installed in what had been the small connecting dressing room in the corner of the floor. The First Family's private meals are prepared in it now.

The least known part of the White House is the entirely private third floor, architecturally shielded from ground view so as not to damage the lines of Hoban's two-story house. An ornamental balustrade almost encircles the roof line, broken only by the peak of the north portico. A promenade runs the same course around the third floor, part of it glassed in. The third floor covers about 80 percent of the second floor.

What was simply an attic until Grace Coolidge decided to claim part of it in 1927 for her family's use is today the mansion's most secluded living space for the presidential family. Mrs. Coolidge's sky parlor, Mamie's sun room, today's solarium juts off the floor onto the top of the south portico, and a series of utility and storage rooms are enclosed within the sloping eaves over the north portico. The rest of the floor is taken up by guest rooms and suites used by family members and their private guests. All the Ford and Carter children (except Amy, whose room was on the second floor) had more or less permanently reserved suites on the third floor.

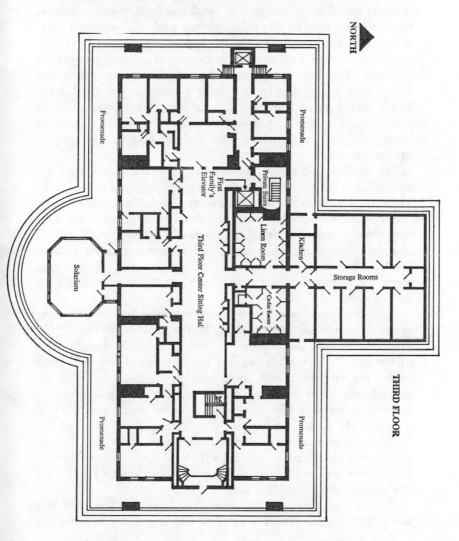

NORTH

THIRD FLOOR

Promenade

Promenade

Promenade

Promenade

Solarium

Third Floor Center Sitting Hall

First Family's Elevator

Private Stairs

Linen Room

Cedar Room

Kitchen

Storage Rooms

Much of the structure of the third floor was saved when the building was gutted in 1949, but it had never been particularly prepossessing in appearance. During the Truman days a porcelain drinking fountain was affixed to the wall in the main corridor as though it were a YMCA. Bess picked out some casual bamboo furniture to put on the linoleum floor in the solarium; the fabric she used for the valances was evidently meant to coordinate with her husband's ties. Ike and Mamie changed very little. Finally, Jackie Kennedy put her decorating talent to work on the area. The first guest room she refurbished in the White House was one of the small corner rooms on the third floor, which then became known as the Empire Guest Room after its predominant style of furnishings. A bed for the room, one which supposedly had belonged to John Quincy Adams, was lent by the Smithsonian.

The third-floor corridor, corresponding to the combined Center Hall and Stair Hall below, is today officially called the Third Floor Center Sitting Hall. Mrs. Reagan and Mr. Graber totally transformed it from what had been simply a large awkward hallway into a beautiful drawing room. Gilt sconces and crystal chandeliers now light the area, and bookshelves with trompe l'oeil pediments line its walls. It serves primarily as a sitting room and library for the guests staying in the surrounding bedroom suites.

Since the Nixon presidency the octagonal solarium (which is reached by an inclined corridor in the middle of the Sitting Hall's south wall; the solarium is three feet above the elevation of the rest of the third floor) has become one of the most used rooms for Presidents and their families to relax in. With its magnificent views in three directions, the informal retreat is today a center of family conversation, casual meals, and fun and games. (The small kitchen off the Sitting Hall, installed for FDR's aide and alter ego Louis Howe, was often used by the Carters for their Sunday evening suppers.) Most recently the solarium was set up as Ronald Reagan's convalescent room after the attempted assassination.

On the roof above the solarium the American flag now flies every day. Before World War II it was lowered whenever the

President drove out the mansion's gates, but Roosevelt changed the custom soon after Pearl Harbor.

The third and last structural element of the White House is the West Wing, the building of which in 1902 allowed the mansion to become a livable home for the presidential family. The wing's Reception Room—sometimes called the Visitors Lobby —is, like the mansion, filled with American antique furniture and paintings. Just inside the small foyer is a receptionist's desk, the only "official"-looking piece of furniture in a room otherwise resembling an early-nineteenth-century drawing room. Overhead is a multi-armed brass chandelier. One of the most luxurious touches is the profusion of brass door hardware— latches, lockboxes, and handles, all gleamingly polished. Worthington Whittredge's arresting 1868 painting "Crossing of the River Platte" hangs next to a 200-year-old English library bookcase. Aside from all the wonderful things to look at, half the fun of being there is waiting to see who's going to come in the door next—very often, it can be expected to be someone who will be seen on the evening news.

Doors open off either end of the Reception Room. That on the west end, guarded by a Uniformed Secret Service officer, leads to the offices of two of the President's chief advisers, James Baker and Edwin Meese; the door at the east end, oddly without a guard, goes through to the Oval Office and Cabinet Room area.

The most notable decorations in the wing's corridors are the many framed color photographs of the President and his wife. Taken by White House photographer Michael Evans, the candid photos of the first couple at their ranch, Camp David, and various places around the White House and its grounds also line the walls of the East Wing and the east loggia traversed by tourists on their daily rounds.

The three major West Wing rooms are on the east side of the building, two looking out onto the grounds (the Cabinet Room and the Oval Office) and the inside Roosevelt Room. The latter is the major staff meeting room, named for both Presidents Roosevelt, whose portraits hang on either side of its west wall.

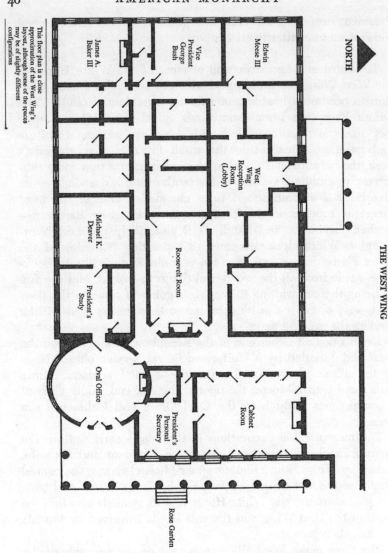

This floor plan is a close approximation of the West Wing's layout, although some of the spaces may be of slightly different configurations

NORTH

THE WEST WING

Edwin Meese III

Vice President George Bush

James A. Baker III

West Wing Reception Room (Lobby)

Roosevelt Room

Michael K. Deaver

President's Study

Oral Office

Cabinet Room

President's Personal Secretary

Rose Garden

Reagan's top aides meet in the large room—known as the Fish Room in earlier days because FDR kept an aquarium there—at seven thirty each morning to brief senior members of the West Wing staff. When the President is having discussions with a head of state in the Oval Office, his foreign guest's chief advisers meet simultaneously with his top aides in the Roosevelt Room. A marble-manteled fireplace at the end of the long conference table warms the room on winter days.

The Cabinet Room looks like a slightly larger and somewhat more elaborate version of the Roosevelt Room, but it is enhanced by the beauty of French doors opening onto the Rose Garden. Richard Nixon bought the long mahogany pedestal conference table in 1970; it is today customarily topped with a large crystal jar full of Jelly Bellies, the presidential sweetmeat currently in favor. (It's considered polite to leave the coconut ones for Mr. Reagan.) The leather armchairs around the table for each Cabinet member are almost, but not quite, identical. Each officer's name is engraved on a brass plate on the back of his chair, and the chair is taken by the Cabinet member when he leaves office. (This is, incidentally, the only furniture that can ever be removed from White House ownership.) The President's chair, centered on the east side of the table with its back to the French doors, is a couple of inches taller than any of the others.

One of the diverting little customs that accrues to incoming Presidents is to designate three presidential portraits to hang in the Cabinet Room. At the stroke of noon on January 20, 1981—the instant Ronald Reagan became President—two of the three Carter choices came down. Lincoln remained, but Jefferson and Truman—the latter evidently too symbolic of populist excesses—were removed. Reagan's choices were Dwight Eisenhower and the supply sider's patron saint, Calvin Coolidge. Unfortunately there wasn't an appropriately sized portrait of Coolidge available, and the official White House portrait by Charles Hopkinson, hanging in the East Foyer, couldn't be moved, so the industrious staffers scrambled around until they found one at the American Antiquarian Society in Worcester, Massachusetts. The society graciously agreed to lend it for the new President's pleasure and whatever political inspiration it might provide.

Wherever the President is can legitimately be called the center of power in the Western world, and a great part of the time that place is the West Wing's Oval Office. The character of this room has changed dramatically from the thrift-shop clutter of

Franklin Roosevelt and Truman's utilitarian drabness—General Services Administration (GSA) sofas, maroon velvet draperies, brown window shades looking like a school superintendent's office. Eisenhower painted the walls moss green and furnished it with no-nonsense general officer's quarters furniture, which was later replaced with the more congenial arrangement clearly evidencing Jackie Kennedy's touch—white linen-covered settees forming a conversation area in front of the fireplace, an innovation retained by each President since. Johnson's only memorable addition to the room was that famous six-foot-long triple television set, allowing him to see and enjoy himself on all three networks at the same time. Nixon got a new rug, an overly bright electric blue one with the gold seal of the presidency woven into its center, constantly reminding the occupant who he was. Ten flags on standards stood behind his desk. Ford's personal touch was a big Plexiglas globe.

Ronald Reagan has continued to use the massive desk with the presidential carved seal on its kick panel, a desk at which several of his predecessors toiled. It was made from the timbers of the wrecked British ship HMS *Resolute* in 1880 and presented by Queen Victoria to her fellow head of state, President Rutherford B. Hayes. Jacqueline Kennedy dug it out of many years' storage for her husband's use.

Seeing the Oval Office in photographs doesn't in any measure do justice to the real impression it makes on the first-time visitor. It's a surprisingly large room, seemingly made more so by its lack of corners, which is brightened by a bank of French doors and windows overlooking the White House grounds on the south and east. (The windows are made of a practically indestructible bulletproof glass.) The ceiling is recessed with a ring of diffused light around its crown (John Hersey called the room an "egg of light"); in the ceiling's center the presidential seal is set in low relief. The doors have crisply elegant pediments over them, and the French windows are topped with deeply incised lunettes—concave shell-shaped recesses. The fireplace opposite the President's desk has a splendidly proportioned Ionic-columned marble mantel framing the hearth. Oriental ginger jars top the mantelpiece. Mrs. Reagan has covered the facing couches in a red-and-white-striped light yellow fabric and purchased new chairs for the office; big scheffleras are planted in Chinese cachepots, and a grandfather clock stands against the wall near the fireplace. Behind the desk are the American flag and the President's personal flag on black and gold standards.

Just outside the office an arcaded terrace leads to the west colonnade, which also serves as the President's route home from the office every evening. The passage along the colonnade is not, as is its counterpart in the East Wing, covered; Jackie Kennedy tried without success to have it enclosed with a glass screen.

Between the Oval Office and the Cabinet Room is a small room for the President's secretary, more often titled in these sexually tense times something along the lines of "personal assistant." (Reagan's secretary is called just that, however.) On the other side of the Oval Office is another small room that acts as an informal hideaway/study for the President; assistant Mike Deaver's office connects with it directly. Three other large offices at the other end of the floor are tenanted by Ed Meese, Jim Baker, and the Vice President.

On the top floor are the relatively more mundane offices, albeit still occupied by ranking members of the President's staff. The West Wing basement contains a tiny one-chair barbershop manned by first barber Milton Pitts (haircuts are fifteen dollars), as well as the canteen and the Executive Dining Room, both run by the Navy as official messes; status involved in the use of the latter is dynamite. More about that later.

Originally the grounds for the President's home were meant to cover an eighty-acre area, taking in what is today Lafayette Park and the Ellipse. In 1800 the present grounds were marked off, and by John Quincy Adams's presidency in 1825 finally had a fence built around them. In 1849 the swamplike south grounds were drained; two years later landscape designer Andrew Jackson Downing laid out a new design for the property, most of which survives today. During Ulysses S. Grant's administration East and West Executive avenues were cut through, defining the mansion on either side.

Today the White House sits on an enclosed eighteen-acre site (not counting the Old Executive Office Building), the largest parcel in central Washington. The parklike setting is cut into two areas, known as the north and south grounds, with the mansion and its two wings the axis dividing them. There are eight gateways to the grounds, as well as the entryway through the Old EOB. The main approach to the more formal north portico entrance is a curving driveway making an arc beginning and ending on Pennsylvania Avenue. The semicircle encloses a low round fountain spurting up a single jet of water and flower beds on the spot where a statue of Thomas Jefferson stood for thirty-five years of the nineteenth century. Television news reporters ("White House correspondents") videotape their nightly reports from this lawn; more news is generated from it than from anywhere else on earth. Banks of electronic plug-in devices—audio, video, and telephone—are permanently embedded in the ground for the convenience of the media crews.

Constant demonstrations, as well as sit-ins and sleep-ins, are staged along the north fence. The outer perimeter of the fence serves as a bulletin board for numerous hand-lettered signs, generally espousing either metaphysical or revolutionary causes, sometimes both. (An example, leaning against the fence: "I suspect all revolutionaries' main motivation is love.") Their caretakers live in sleeping bags on the sidewalk. The north grounds were closed to the public in the 1930s, although tourists leave the mansion today through the north entrance and are thus permitted the pleasure of strolling down the driveway on their way out through the northeast gate.

The White House's southern approach is through a gateway on East Executive Avenue, and it is the usual route used by the First Family; a driveway leads to the Diplomatic Reception Room entrance. The south grounds are closed to the public except on very few occasions: the annual Easter egg "rolling" and two weekends every year, when the gardens are shown, attracting between 6,000 and 8,000 visitors on each of the four days. The 1981 weekend opening started two hours after President Reagan returned home to convalesce after his hospitalization for his gunshot wound. Tourists mingled nonchalantly with SWAT

teams, electronically equipped security guards, and other uniformed guardians of the First Family's safety.

Thickets of flowering bushes and small copses of trees hide
the President's Walk in the south grounds. Surrounded by tulips
is a round fountain with nine jets plashing around the clock. A
swimming pool (built for Jerry Ford) and tennis courts have
been recessed into this elysian setting. Set on a low patch of
ground, they are so well camouflaged by shrubbery and trees as
to be undetectable by the public scrutinizing the grounds
through the fence running along the southern perimeter. The
tennis courts were witness to a tragic episode in their history:
Calvin Coolidge's son developed a blister on his right big toe
while volleying with his younger brother; inflammation of the
bone marrow set in, and he died six weeks later at Walter Reed
Hospital, his parents at his side.

Loudspeakers have been installed at short intervals along the
fence; a taped message tells tourists the story of the grounds.
Most of the great variety of trees have plaques affixed to them,
crediting the Presidents during whose terms they were planted.
Nixon planted a California giant sequoia, but it died. Its replacement won't grow straight.

The two named flower gardens are in the lees of either wing:
the Rose Garden, serving as an outdoor reception area for the
President, and the Jacqueline Kennedy Garden, frequently used
by the President's wife for the same purpose. Two memorable
grand occasions held in the Rose Garden were the 1971 Tricia
Nixon-Edward Cox nuptials (the only outdoor wedding ever
held at the White House) and the 1976 state dinner for Britain's
queen. The garden was first planted with roses by Ellen Wilson
in 1913; Mrs. Paul Mellon redesigned it at President Kennedy's
request in 1962. Jimmy Carter would sometimes stop there on
his way back to the mansion after work to pick a rose for
Rosalynn.

II

Presidential Court

PEOPLE IN THE
WHITE HOUSE

Subordination tends greatly to human happiness.
SAMUEL JOHNSON

EAST SIDE

WHITE HOUSE TERRITORIALITY splits with a sharp distinction between that considered the President's turf in the West Wing and the area where First Ladies since Eleanor Roosevelt have held sway in the East Wing. Since the mansion itself is controlled by direction ultimately emanating from the First Lady, we'll include it here along with the east side establishment.

The nerve center of the social side of presidential life is centered on the second floor of the East Wing, amid surroundings little reminiscent of the antique-laden grace of the mansion or the West Wing. Nancy Reagan's "office building" is a no-non-sense beehive of hell-bent-for-election activity, constantly in the thick of planning up to a half dozen daily social events revolving around the President's and First Lady's lives.

During the first year of the Reagan administration Mrs. Reagan's staff was headed by forty-year-old Peter McCoy, the former president of the Southern California-based auction house of Sotheby Parke Bernet and an old friend of the President's wife; in December 1981 McCoy was promoted to the new position of undersecretary of commerce for travel and tourism, and early in January 1982 James Rosebush was chosen to replace him. Rosebush's full title is Deputy Assistant to the President and Director of Staff for the First Lady, the order of the two parts being a formal indication that his first duty is still to the President and planning the President's social life. Since a First Lady assumes management of the social side of executive life, his real day-to-day job is to function as Nancy Reagan's manager and run her staff of thirteen (down from Rosalynn Carter's twenty-three-member staff, which was twice as large as Lady Bird Johnson's, Pat Nixon's, or Betty Ford's) with its annual budget of $600,000.

The thirty-two-year-old native of Flint, Michigan, had been a special assistant to the President in charge of the White House's "private sector initiative program"—the effort to get private enterprise to help support social programs—when Mike Deaver picked him to replace McCoy. Rosebush's promotional abilities and his exceedingly trim good looks, always a key factor with Mrs. Reagan, led to his promotion.

Rosebush's first chore each morning is an eight o'clock West Wing meeting with the President's big three—Ed Meese, Jim Baker, and Mike Deaver; Deaver is Rosebush's nominal boss. After coordinating the President's and First Lady's schedules, the young chief of staff is likely to spend the remainder of his day planning Nancy Reagan's day and helping her through the social events crammed into it. Besides his $55,387 salary, one of the perks of his position is a large sunny office on the East Wing's second floor.

Another of the perks of presidential employment is immortality in the form of an appearance in *Doonesbury*. Muffie Brandon made it, surely a highlight in her long Washington career. James Rosebush's chief subordinate—officially Social Secretary to the White House and the latest in a succession of social secretaries since the first was hired by Teddy Roosevelt—Mabel Hobart Brandon has long been an influential capital social fixture. The forty-six-year-old Brandon known universally around Washington as well as at the White House as Muffie, is a tall, beautifully dressed and groomed, extremely efficient career woman kept very busy by a demanding and important job. People—especially important dignitaries—don't expect to see any lapses in the intricate social quadrille at the President's home. Making sure they don't is Muffie's job.

A 1957 graduate of Smith College (Nancy Reagan and Barbara Bush are fellow alumnae), Mabel Brandon comes from what can fairly be described as Washington's establishment. She got the job of social secretary after seventy other hopefuls were interviewed, a selection process that was more complicated than that for most of the Cabinet officers.

Brandon plans, or at least has a hand in, every social function that involves or is related to the First Lady or the White House itself. Though James Rosebush is responsible for scheduling Nancy Reagan's time and seeing that she gets to where she has to be at the time she has to be there, Brandon prepares guest lists and invitations, acts as protocol intermediary with the State Department, functions as the military aides' supervisor, and oversees the countless and intricate elements involved in state entertaining.

Brandon's second-floor East Wing office—gray walls, white woodwork, beige carpet—is the center of the wing's controlled chaos, with lots of on-the-fly instructions about "Mrs. Reagan's schedule" charging the atmosphere. It's wise to arrive well in advance of an appointment with her, since a call from the First Lady in the mansion's living quarters will send her flying. Her personal staff consists of a secretary and an assistant who is housed in a smaller version of Brandon's well-appointed office. After leaving her desk to conduct an interview on the small sofa in the corner, the social secretary explained how she and her staff prepare line-by-line "scenarios" of all social events, guidelines that show what's supposed to be done every minute of the official day. She emphasized that the "absence of ground rules or a game plan for the job requires constant improvisation"—within the sharply defined rules of protocol, of course. She thinks of herself as a "floating cannon," shooting out ideas and suggestions. By general consent, White House hospitality under the Reagans has been superb, an indication that Muffie Brandon is coming up with the right ideas.*

Two other major activities connected with the First Lady are carried on in the East Wing. One is the Correspondence Center. Recent First Ladies have received a weekly average of 2,000 letters and 500 invitations to various events at which their presence would add invaluable cachet. Nancy Reagan's correspondence staff answers these queries on white bond topped with the legend "The White House"; her personal notepaper is similar but is further embellished with the presidential seal embossed at the top. The envelopes are also marked simply "The White House." As with letters to the British royal family, correspondence from personal friends of Nancy Reagan is denoted with a special code by the sender on the envelope so they can be sent directly to the First Lady unopened.

The White House Visitors Center is headed by Carol McCain, who has the responsibility of allocating the relatively precious few VIP White House tour tickets to congressional offices as well as arranging the special public events such as the annual Easter egg roll (only children or adults in the company of children are permitted to attend) and the south lawn arrival ceremonies for visiting heads of state to which guests are invited. In case you're wondering how somebody gets a job like McCain's, she worked for Ronald and Nancy Reagan in both his 1976 and 1980 campaigns, taking care of scheduling and advance duties for Mrs. Reagan on the latter campaign. Her reward was the job she holds today, one considered very much a plum. A lesson hard learned early in her new position was not to

* (In April 1983, Gahl Lee Hodges, twenty-nine-year-old assistant chief of protocol at the State Department, succeeded Mrs. Brandon, who resigned to open a Washington, D.C., office for an international public relations firm.)

cross congressmen. New York Democrat Thomas Downey requested and was refused sixty-five tour tickets for Boy Scouts
from his local district; he claimed unfair treatment when not
only did he not get them, but his regular weekly allotment of
four tickets was mysteriously canceled. McCain wrote it off as a
"misunderstanding" but is now careful to check more closely to
whom she's refusing tickets.

Although the West and East wings have traditionally been in
sharp conflict, the former regarding the latter with a certain
amount of condescension, the mansion itself has been neutral
ground. Deemed to be within the First Lady's sphere of
influence, its staff is far less prone to winds of political change
than that of either wing. Many of the ranking mansion personnel
have seen several administrations come and go, adjusting to the
desires of one President and First Lady, knowing full well that
the next presidential couple will change all the old rules and ini-
tiate new ways of running the country's first home.

There are eighty-five full-time domestic employees in the Executive Residence (the official name of the mansion, to distinguish it from the two wings). The man who runs the domestic
staff is Rex Scouten, officially chief usher, unofficially general
manager. Famous for his closed-mouth discretion when it comes
to his knowledge of the presidential families' lives, he first came
to the White House more than thirty years ago as a member of
the Secret Service. The position of chief usher is a Civil Service
job and has the same kind of job description all such jobs have.
In Scouten's case, it calls for a person of seemingly endless
talents:

> subject only to the general direction of the President of the
> United States, serves as general manager of the Executive Man-
> sion, including the administrative, fiscal, and personnel functions
> involved in the operation and management of the mansion and
> the grounds; responsible for preparation and justification of
> budget estimates, as well as the direction and supervision of all
> mansion employees, including all hiring and firing; serves as the
> White House receptionist and as such is responsible for receiving
> and caring for all personal and official guests of the president and

first lady; arranges all official entertainments, receptions, dinners in the mansion, as well as the procurement of all food; makes personal appointments for the president and first lady; is responsible for answering all correspondence regarding the mansion; and, finally, is completely responsible for the efficient operation, cleanliness and maintenance of the 132 rooms, containing 1,600,000 cubic feet of space, of the mansion.

In short, just about everything but ushering.

Under Scouten comes a whole raft of domestic employees who cater exclusively to the First Family's wishes (as Nancy Reagan put it on *60 Minutes,* "it takes getting used to—anything you want—boom!") and who keep the White House in immaculate order—sometimes a Herculean effort, especially after a typical summer's day of 6,000 tourists going through the building. They include underbutlers, housekeepers and maids, doormen, plumbers, carpenters, electricians, even a florist—all technically Park Service employees (except for Scouten and his four assistant ushers, paid out of a special White House budget annually appropriated to the President).

Probably the most visible employee under the chief usher's supervision is the White House chef, Henry Haller. Haller's domain includes not only the restaurant-size kitchen on the west end of the ground floor but also the small second-floor kitchen where the First Family's meals are prepared and the staff kitchen and dining room in the basement.

Since René Verdon turned the White House into an American Maxim's for the Kennedys, presidential food has become a good deal more simplified. Both Johnson and Nixon were famous for their unpretentious (some would say appalling lack of) taste where food was concerned; the former's knowledge of sauces was said to end with ketchup. Haller, who came to the White House under the Johnsons, takes pains to ensure that food served to the President "doesn't distract him—he has enough problems as it is." The chef has complete authority to buy the best food available on the market; the presidential family more often than not has guests at meals, and first-class cuisine is a foregone conclusion.

The subject of food in the executive establishment is hemmed in by some of the most stringent of the many security arrangements which surround the President and his family. Where the food is bought, how it's transported to the kitchens, what security arrangements are employed to protect its safety all are highly classified White House secrets.

The main kitchen, a huge space fitted with stainless steel and white enamel counters, sinks, and cabinets as well as a number of storerooms used for various purposes, is a cook's dream. The all-electric kitchen can turn out thousands of cookies for a reception or a five-course state dinner for 100 guests as efficiently as whipping up a bowl of cottage cheese and ketchup. A historic touch is the Madonna of the Kitchen, a small ceramic plaque Mamie Eisenhower hung on one side of the pantry cabinets.

Contrary to the popular notion that the President gets everything at the White House free, he, in fact, pays for his and his family's food out of his own pocket—but not, however, for the salaries of the staff that cooks it. Haller sends a bill to the State Department's entertainment fund for state dinners and to the President's political party's national committee for any kind of partisan political function. Allocating barrels of potatoes and sides of beef this way can make for some fairly complicated bookkeeping.

Haller, a Swiss native, has some typically Swiss commonsense rules about food service at the White House. "I don't ever want to be a fat, sloppy chef, and I go on that principle in serving dinners. The best thing is for people to leave the table saying, 'I could have eaten a little more, but I won't do it.'" A unique rule applies to Haller's kitchen: Where in most cases the chef rules the roost, here it's the President whose whim is law. There were times when Franklin Roosevelt couldn't get what he wanted out of some uppity domestic staff members, but that is *not* the case today. Haller says, "Here it is the President who gives the orders . . . you just make the best of it."

"Early Statler" was the accurate description Jacqueline Kennedy's friends say she applied to the White House after Mamie Eisenhower took the First Lady-to-be on a tour of what would shortly be her new home a few weeks after the November 1960 election. Except for a token start at redecoration in the Diplomatic Reception Room, the White House looked very much at the end of the Eisenhowers' eight years as it had at the beginning—which is to say, like a high-class hotel. The reproduction "antique" furniture the Trumans had bought by the carload to fill the house after its reconstruction was a faithful reflection of the fifties: ersatz, dull, and comfy. Jacqueline Kennedy, herself anything but dull, was appalled at the interior of the most famous house in the world, and a lifetime in the American aristocracy gave her the undoubting willpower to start the process that would transform the White House's interior into one of the finest collections of early-nineteenth-century Americana in the country.

Her husband got the ball rolling by passing the first of the laws aimed at achieving this end; in 1961 new statutes declared that "furniture of historic or artistic interest" in the mansion—today considered every stick of furniture and furnishings—becomes the "inalienable" property of the building and can never be sold or given away except to be lent to or stored in the Smithsonian Institution for anything not currently being used. (Less than 5 percent of the "important items" are not currently in use, according to Chief Usher Scouten.) This put an end to the repeat of past instances of incoming First Families selling off cartloads of furnishings used by their predecessors and no longer considered "fashionable"; President Arthur stripped the mansion of twenty-four loads of valuable and historic furniture this way.

The Kennedy redecoration involved most of the rooms on the state and second floors of the building. To help in what she called a "serious historical endeavor"—not a mere redecoration scheme—the First Lady created a Fine Arts Committee for the White House, with the late Henry Du Pont, a founder of the Winterthur Museum in Delaware, as its chairman; Lorraine Pearce became the first White House curator at the same time. What Jackie Kennedy, Du Pont, and Pearce ended up with was a strongly French-influenced look reflecting the taste of the decorator (really an "interior architect," as Mrs. Onassis later referred to him), Stéphane Boudin.

When her husband came to the presidency in 1963, Lady Bird Johnson found herself reluctant to alter what Jackie Kennedy had wrought. At the time popular approval for the Kennedy contribution to the White House was at its peak; there was very little popular resentment about the cost of beautifying the President's home, as there would be two decades later. Camelot had been the nation's pride.

Early in the Johnson years the President signed an executive order establishing the Commission for the Preservation of the White House, ostensibly a way to keep the Kennedy restoration from ever being reversed by some President and/or First Lady with less than Kennedy-like taste. Of course, the commission's members were chosen by the President and served at his pleasure and could always be changed by any future President to reflect his and his wife's preferences. By the time the Nixons came to the executive mansion in 1969, the years and millions of tourists and hundreds of thousands of invited guests had taken a prodigious toll on the place. With no backup furnishings, little money, and Pat Nixon's initial reluctance to change the status quo, the White House degenerated into a state of tattiness bordering on its appearance at the end of the FDR years. Enter Clement E. Conger.

The man much of Washington calls the Grand Acquisitor has, more than any individual in its 200-year history, been responsible for what the White House has become—the repository and museum of one of the world's greatest collections of furniture, an unmatched showcase of the finest craftsmanship of the young United States. Since 1970 Conger's innate talent for tracking down rare antique museum-quality furnishings, and then cajoling them away from their owners for the greater glory of beautifying the country's chief residence, has made him indispensable to four successive First Ladies. The wonder is that serving in the White House is only half of his two-pronged career.

A unique characteristic of Clem Conger is how perfectly he combines an aura of aristocratic hauteur with a gleeful joy in what he does. Looking about fifteen years younger than his sixty-nine years, the patrician curator is a descendant of the founder of Alexandria, Virginia, and its only lord mayor, William Ramsay. Married to the daughter of a former chairman of General Dynamics Corporation, Conger today lives with his wife in the city his forebear founded. After serving as a staff officer to the Joint Chiefs of Staff during World War II and later in the military government in occupied Germany and in the Foreign Service, he was transferred to the Protocol Office at the State Department; by 1960 he was deputy chief of protocol.

One day in the course of his duties he was accompanying Mrs. Christian Herter, wife of the then secretary of state, on a tour of the new Diplomatic Reception Rooms on the top of the State Department's Foggy Bottom headquarters building. A reception was being planned for Queen Frederika of Greece, and Mrs. Herter was less than happy with the GSA-inspired decor of the rooms. Conger's volunteering on the spot to "fix up" the three main reception rooms led quickly to a new career—as curator of the Diplomatic Reception Rooms of the State Department.

While building the State Department's collection (described in Chapter VIII) in his spare time, Conger remained in his protocol post. But that came to an end the day in 1969 when he took President Nixon on a tour of his by now famous handiwork. Nixon said, "These rooms look better than the White House. How about coming over to help us?" Since James R. Ketchum, Pearce's replacement and curator since the Kennedy years, had just resigned, Conger was expropriated to start the second branch of his curatorial career. In a show of his usual fine sense of presidential prerogative, Nixon had his new curator's desk moved to the White House that afternoon.

With Conger's active collaboration, it didn't take Pat Nixon long to lose her timidity about tampering with Jackie Kennedy's work. In reality, Conger took the upper hand at this point in deciding how the White House's public rooms should look and hasn't relinquished it since.

Pat Nixon and Clem Conger first decorated the Green and Blue rooms, which were reopened to the public in 1971 and 1972 respectively. Conger—who calls himself an "advanced amateur," alluding to his lack of formal academic training in the field of antique furnishings and decoration—also worked on the ground-floor Map Room and the Red Room at the time, although these changes weren't so dramatically different from what Mrs. Kennedy had done with them.

Since the Nixon redecoration—Conger himself credits Pat Nixon with the greatest influence on today's White House, saying, "More was done during her years to upgrade the White House furnishings than at any time in history"—design changes to the state and semistate rooms have been relatively minor. Succeeding First Ladies have wanted to move paintings around and buy a few pieces here and there, but today's tourists see essentially what Pat Nixon left in 1974.

Betty Ford, who had a thing about yellow, was able to indulge her love for it in the President's Dining Room and in the third-floor solarium. When Rosalynn Carter arrived, she changed the President's Dining Room again, and her private decorator, Wayne Dean, repainted the "awful" solarium from brilliant yellow to an off white. Now Nancy Reagan has *her* private decorator, too, and some of the controversy surrounding the social aspects of the Reagan presidency are indirectly tied to him. Predictably the hubbub concerned money and the lavish spending thereof.

Every time the White House changes occupants, the new crew gets an automatic $50,000 to redecorate the family quarters to suit itself. Since $50,000 will barely pay for the curtains these days, the President can also dip into part of the $3,100,000 annual general maintenance and repair budget (which includes the cost of entertaining) to supplement the $50,000, but not to the point where the maintenance of the public portions of the building would suffer. When the Reagans let it be known that there just wasn't enough money to do up the second and third floors as they would like them to be done up, the "private sector" took over. In no time at all, $822,641 was raised to help out, with donors such as Frank and Barbara Sinatra kicking in $10,000. The press sniffed a good story, what with the President's budget cuts threatening a whole range of social programs.

But things didn't really come unglued until Nancy Reagan's press secretary gave out the news that the First Lady had ordered a new set of official china at a price of $209,508. Even though there hadn't been a new and complete set of china since the Truman years (the $80,028 Johnson china was merely an "augmentation" to that the Trumans had bought, according to the President; ironically, the $80,028 in 1968 dollars comes to just about $200,000 in 1982 dollars), and, further, even though the Lenox company was selling the china to the White House at cost (it "couldn't begin to estimate a retail value"), cries of out-raged fury rose out of the land. When it had first become known that Mrs. Reagan wanted the new china, money for it was given as a specific bequest to the White House from the Knapp Foun-dation of Maryland. (The money was in addition to the $822,641 already collected, although technically the funds for the china come out of the total—more than $1 million—that was collected and is controlled and disbursed by the White House Historical Association.) The 4,732-piece set, averaging $952 for each of the 19-piece place settings, consists of fish plates, finger bowls, bouil-lon cups, soup cups and stands, demitasses, and berry bowls along with the more mundane pieces. In addition to the place settings, 60 extra demitasse cups and saucers and 72 large plat-ters were ordered.

It's understandable that Nancy Reagan should want to leave something of herself in the White House for the sake of posterity (the rim of the china is painted in a shade called Nancy red), but the already white-hot wrath of the press was further hot-tened up at the tidings that the Reagans had ordered a new set of *personal* china to be used in the private apartments upstairs and presumably to be taken with them when they leave. The Carters had wanted to make the White House a gift of personal china for the First Family's private use, but their successors po-litely declined the proffered 700-piece set of Japanese-made stoneware, called Rosalynn. Even the White House admitted the timing of the new purchase was "unfortunate." The twenty-four place settings of the private china—to be named Nancy—were made by Boehm. The price of the hand-painted and mono-grammed dishes is a secret, but Boehm said a less expensive ver-sion would be available to the public for around $150 per place setting, "something affordable so people can buy a setting every other month or so."

As anybody must do who lives in a position at which potshots are so easily taken, Nancy Reagan quickly learned to take the criticism in stride. At the $200-per-plate Alfred E. Smith Memorial Dinner in New York, she asked her audience if it had heard of her latest project, the "Nancy Reagan Home for Wayward China," at which she received wildly approving applause. A postscript to the china story: Shortly before the new state china was to be finished, the Lenox plant in New Jersey was hit by fire, but as reported by the local police, "Nancy's china made it through."

One of the sad realities of life even as it affects the White House is the enormous cost of even the most minor acquisitions. From his jumbled combined office and workroom off the Ground Floor Corridor, Clem Conger directs a financial operation the Rothschilds might approve. When one considers that the new overdraperies in the State Dining Room cost about $130,000, or that $60,000 was paid for the alternate rug for the Green Room, and that none of these moneys come out of public funds, it's obvious that Conger has to be fairly skillful to do the financial orchestrating that makes it all possible. The comparatively little criticism that the curator has been subjected to has been for the unorthodox manner in which much of the furnishings are paid for. Some pieces are given by bequests, permitting their owners to deduct 50 percent of the value off their income taxes since the federal government is the donee. In other cases, owners sell their prized possessions to the White House. But most are bought by Conger directly from sales and auction rooms; the curator is considered one of the harder people to outbid at the auctions of the really good stuff. The money to pay for them comes from cash donations and the proceeds of wills in which the White House Preservation Society is a benefactor. Sometimes a generous-minded donor gives a sum of money meant to purchase a specific piece that has been picked up by Conger. In other instances money is taken out of this general fund to buy things that have been lent to the White House. (Only rarely have lent pieces been reclaimed by their owners, by the way.)

There's little problem in finding uses for the funds given to the White House. Pat Nixon's redecoration cost (in early 1970s

dollars) $485,000 for the Green Room, $292,000 for the Blue
Room, and $170,000 for the Red Room. On a tour through the
major rooms Conger casually pointed out new acquisitions costing hundreds of thousands of dollars. The purchase, restoration,
and repairing of picture frames come to $30,000 a year. Compar-
atively little-known early American paintings now sometimes
cost a half million dollars. The upholstery in the Diplomatic Reception Room has to be replaced every six months—part of the
$400,000 upholstery and drapery bill. Conger has replaced nine-
teen reproduction chandeliers with exceedingly valuable authentic ones; likewise, every fireplace tool in the house. He admitted
it would be almost impossible to put the same collection together today because of the inflated prices on early American
furnishings.

The Reagan redecorating carried out under interior designer
Ted Graber's direction which occupied most of 1981 involved
extensive work on the private second and third floors, but most
of the nearly $800,000 went into the repair of old furnishings
that had been collecting dust in the White House storeroom and
the refinishing of 33 mahogany doors (out of 412 in the mansion) and the floors in twenty-four rooms. Ten rooms, seven
closets, and eight bathrooms got new wall coverings, while
twenty-one other rooms were repainted. Endless yards of carpets
and curtains that had in many rooms become actually tattered
were replaced. Some of the money went for repairs and acid-
etching cleaning of the marble floors on the state floor. The
funds also paid for cleaning all twenty-nine of the White
House's fireplaces.

Sales of guidebooks by the White House Historical Association and royalties on the presidential medals struck by the
Franklin Mint have helped, but the lion's share of the nearly
$10,000,000 Conger has raised for the refurbishing of the execu-
tive mansion has come from private bequests. If it has sometimes taken gentle arm twisting of affluent prospective donors, at
least the motivation has been sincere. The White House isn't
now and never has been merely one family's home, but, instead,
one shared by every American. Thanks in large measure to the

incumbent curator, it is now one of the most beautiful state residences in the world.

WEST SIDE

Few would argue with the assertion that more history is made in the West Wing of the White House than any other single place in the world. Housing all this history making is a building that cost $65,000 when Teddy Roosevelt first had it "temporarily" constructed at the turn of the century. A warren of carefully defined and jealously guarded power centers, the West Wing is packed to bursting with a presidential staff that well understands the inexpressible importance of being right in the middle of where almost everything of American presidential consequence originates.

After an appointed visitor enters the northwest gate and is checked off the roster of expected callers by a guard using the central computer and his handy cathode-ray tube terminal (asking his birth date to make sure he's really who he says he is), he proceeds on his own on a pleasant and heady little walk up the driveway to the wing's north portico entrance. Entering the gracefully furnished, spacious Visitors Lobby is like stepping into another, far quieter world. An unfortunate reminder of the outside world, though, is the purposeful-looking armed guard stationed in the otherwise-elegant room. Except for the guard, the only person present is a well-groomed, soft-spoken receptionist who interrupts a sotto voce phone conversation courteously to ring the new presidential assistant for media relations. A former San Francisco television news anchorperson, Karna Small Stringer had until the day before our meeting been assistant press secretary on the merry-go-round of presidential staff appointments. Now a liaison person between the administration and the news media, she had agreed to provide a guided tour through the President's office building.

There are 322 full-time White House office personnel (plus the 15 in the East Wing) officially listed in the Office of Personnel Management. Like almost everything else in government, the number keeps growing, but as quietly as the administration can manage it. (The total operating budget was $18.9 million for 1982.) Some of these people are located in the two presidential outbuildings, the Old and New Executive Office buildings. Those who work in the West Wing are, with few exceptions, the people who really make the executive office run.

During the Eisenhower years the credentialed visitor had very little trouble getting to the Oval Office. What then served as the lobby was directly outside the President's elliptical office. To find it from the lobby today, you have to make four turns, open two closed doors, and go down four hallways. At the junction in the corridor outside the President's office is the duty station of another of the ubiquitous uniformed guards. The door into the sanctum sanctorum is left open when the President is away, but a theater type of velvet rope is put across it so that West Wing visitors can't actually step inside the room.

Adjacent to the Oval Office is that of Kathleen Osborne, who is formally titled Personal Secretary to the President. Helene von Damm, Reagan's secretary for many years, including the eight spent in Sacramento, was promoted late in 1981 to director of presidential personnel, with the rank of deputy assistant to the President; she consequently moved over to the Old EOB next door. (In mid-1982, von Damm was again advanced in rank, this time to assistant to the President for presidential personnel, and in early 1983, she was appointed ambassador to her native Austria.) Ms. Osborne, von Damm's assistant in Sacramento for three years, later worked as Mrs. Reagan's secretary. While serving as Reagan's secretary, von Damm held the rank of special assistant; Osborne, at this writing, does not. Still, being manager of the President's office, she's in a position of not inconsiderable authority—handling Reagan's personal phone calls, arranging his papers, supervising the steno pool. The duties are those of any secretary, but when the boss is the President of the United States, otherwise-routine matters automatically become affairs of state.

Before we go on, it might be helpful to explain the various titles used in the White House Office, which is the official name for the West Wing. There are several levels of assistant, the generic rank for the President's top levels of personal aides, and by definition those who help him directly with whatever duties or problems he chooses to assign them. The special assistants are the lowest rung of this category, about eighteen people in jobs ranging from such amorphous duties as policy development and special support services to more specific tasks like director of advance office and scheduling. Some are sort of free agents, just called special assistant without a specific portfolio.

The next step up is the deputy assistant, about sixteen slightly more important functionaries who carry out major staff duties; few at this level ever become household names, though. Deputy assistant titles run the gamut from such convolutions as Deputy Assistant to the President and Assistant to the Deputy Chief of Staff to Deputy Assistant to the President and Director of the Office of Cabinet Administration.

There is now one holder of the title of Deputy Counselor to the President, a slightly more prestigious level one half step up from deputy assistant.

The highest level—assistant to the President—is where the substantive policy making is carried out. Staff shake-outs here are fairly common occurrences; as of early 1982, the twelve holders of this title include everyone from the President's chief of staff and his deputy through the press secretary.

At the top of the heap is counselor to the President—a rank now held only by Ed Meese. He is also the only Reagan aide to be given Cabinet rank. His salary is the same as the twelve assistants, but the higher title was meant to specify clearly Meese's status and his authority to function as an equal with the heads of the executive departments.

Even though some people within each category are obviously more powerful or important than others, each of these major classifications carries one salary for all persons in it: special assistant, $50,112; deputy assistant, $55,387; assistant, $60,663. (The latter is the same as that earned by U.S. senators and representatives.) Thus, it frequently happens that subordinates are paid the same salary as their bosses.

Recent Presidents have had slightly different permutations of these staff titles, the only constant being the trend upward in their numbers and gradations of grandness. In Herbert Hoover's last year in the White House, he got along with three "secretaries"—all male. They were paid $10,000 a year, a salary in 1932 signifying substantial and important duties. (Vice President Charles Curtis made $15,000 at the time.) The President also then had three "clerks," two receiving $7,600 a year, the other $5,600. That was it as far as titled assistants went.

Even during World War II Franklin Roosevelt had only a handful of aides who would rank with any of today's assistants. LBJ turned the corner on levels of titles, though, with a range beginning to approach the majestic diversity of today's designations. Richard Nixon wasn't one to be outdone by *anyone* as far as Machiavellian title games were concerned and his staff constantly jockeyed for the increased status that came from minute title enhancements. Finally, Ford got really modern with a counsel to the President, two counselors to the President, seven assistants to the President, two deputy assistants to the President, one special consultant to the President, nine special assistants to the President, four associate counsels to the President, one executive assistant to the counselor to the President, an aide to the President, as well as a whole raft of lesser staff factotums.

For all his talk of "cutting government down to size," Jimmy Carter quickly exempted his own office from any such thing. His dozen or so degrees of assistants and associates and directors made Nixon's staff seem in comparison like that of a Third World state.

Reagan's own staff "enhancing," to borrow a euphemism his aides use when they mean something has gone up (like taxes) or gotten bigger (like the federal deficit), has had the effect of cutting down the average size of his West Wing staff's offices. In Eisenhower's day the average space per person was 125 square feet; today it's 70 square feet. This battling for space, according to Public Administration Professor Howard McCurdy makes for "insecurity" for staff members and "difficulties in communications" for just about everybody. Since it's unlikely that anyone is going to contemplate actually cutting down the size of the staff, the professor thinks the answer is to rebuild the West Wing.

For all its turf tensions and overcrowding—not to mention the ominous presence of a battalion of uniformed armed guards—working in the West Wing is not without its pleasures. In the larger sense, being at the center and fount of power is, of course, the greatest attraction. But there are also certain fleshly rewards as a part of West Wing life. The clublike Executive Dining Room in the basement, run by the Navy and open to about forty members of the President's staff, is one of the nicer perks as well as being the scene of a good deal of order pecking. (The adjacent mess with some sixty-eight members, also run by the Navy, is for lower levels of West Wing staff.) The later one's assigned dining time, the higher one is in terms of power—which is to say, one's closeness to the President, who is the well from which this and all other White House honors spring. Betty Ford's press secretary, Sheila Rabb Weidenfeld, considered it a minor social coup when she was formally notified that her lunch hour had been set back from noon to 1:00 P.M., a tangible mark of her increased status. Reagan not only has undone Carter's born-again exclusion of spirits from the Dining Room (California wines are now quite the most fashionable lunchtime drink) but has also halted his predecessor's creeping democratization regarding who was entitled to use it.

Navy stewards serve lunch in this most exclusive of settings at bargain-basement prices. For staff eating alone, there's a single large round table; its lazy Susan is filled with relishes, crackers, bread and butter, and, until recently, peanut butter. There are no prices on the menus—bills come at the end of the month.

Directly across the hall from the mess is the Situation Room, the President's intelligence command center. Built by Kennedy in 1961 after the Bay of Pigs disaster, it has conference areas with lead-lined walls to prevent any possible (presumably) Soviet-inspired bugging. Intelligence information is funneled into the room from the State and Defense departments as well as the Central Intelligence Agency and National Security Council. During the Vietnam War it was very nearly a full-time office for Lyndon Johnson.

Seldom far away from the President is the man who makes sure the chief executive is never without instant medical care.

Dr. Daniel Ruge, a sixty-three-year-old neurosurgeon, replaced Rear Admiral William Lukash, who had filled the position of White House physician for the fourteen years prior to 1981. Reared on a Nebraska farm, Ruge was chosen partly because of his associations with Mrs. Reagan's stepfather, Dr. Loyal Davis, with whom he had practiced medicine in Chicago for twenty years. One of the responsibilities that goes with the job is learning to live a private life at the constant call of the President; a White House signal phone at Dr. Ruge's home ensures his instant availability.

Another nonpolitical shadow of the President is Michael Evans, a man whose job is most concerned with posterity. The official White House photographer as well as official personal photographer to the President, Evans heads a West Wing operation with a $300,000 annual budget. The main mission of the White House Photographic Office (a part of the Press Office) is to record for history the story of the administration and, while doing so, to make sure that its chief history maker looks good. It has long been evident that the public perception of the President can be manipulated by the photographs released by the White House. FDR and the press had a tacit agreement that photographs of him would downplay his paralysis as much as possible; consequently, many Americans didn't realize the extent of his disability. But it wasn't until Lyndon Johnson first gave the title of Personal Photographer to the President to Yoichi Okamoto that the position became institutionalized in the executive office. Johnson gave Okamoto extraordinary liberty to photograph him whenever and wherever he chose, and as a result, a recorded photographic history of the Vietnam War's mark on the conduct of the presidency makes today's viewers almost tangibly aware of the feeling of those tragic years in the White House.

Richard Nixon wasn't as free and open to his personal photographer, Ollie Atkins. Atkins referred to most of his photographs as "grips and grins"—posed photos of his boss with Oval Office visitors. This lack of access was another factor which isolated the Nixon presidency, insulating it from public view and, perhaps, a more sympathetic understanding which might have averted the paranoia leading to Watergate.

The most widely publicized of the White House photographers was David Hume Kennerly, whose relationship to Gerald Ford was unusually close; Sheila Rabb Weidenfeld called it almost one of surrogate father to son. The talented young Pulitzer prizewinner (for his photos of the Vietnam War) even spent weekends with the First Family at Camp David and at their private weekend chalet in Vail, Colorado.

Jimmy Carter didn't appoint a personal photographer, perhaps reasoning that it was merely another symbol of the growing monarchial nature of the presidency with which he had pledged to do battle. For whatever reason, the loss is major as far as history is concerned.

Michael Evans has proved to have the same kind of access to Reagan that Okamoto and Kennerly had to their bosses. Not only are his photographs of the First Family a main source of decoration in the White House, at Camp David, and on *Air Force One,* but far more important, they will provide a boon to future researchers of the Reagan years. All pointedly show the President being presidential, which was, of course, the intent when they were taken. Evans was with the President during the March 1981 assassination attempt but was not among the several who took pictures of it. In a *New York Times* interview he said that the reason was that he's "probably too close now; if I had been an outsider, I would have attempted to take pictures."

Back up on the main floor of the wing is the office of the press secretary. The Press Office is responsible for the "White House News Summary," a daily ten-to-fifteen-page compendium of issues and events involving the President or the White House. Available to newspeople, it also has a circulation of some 400 administration officials and presidential aides from the Cabinet down. In addition to the "News Summary," the Press Office is the source of the White House News Service, which is used by small radio stations without major wire service capabilities. The stations can call into an automated answering device for a tape of the President or a Cabinet officer giving a message explaining the administration's position on various issues. The service is used by about 500 stations daily.

Under Acting Press Secretary Larry Speakes (a deputy assistant to the President), many of the 1,400 or so newspeople regularly accredited to the White House are briefed daily on the President's actions or plans. The beat is considered a highly important one for reporters—those representing the electronic media, especially the major television networks, often are promoted to anchor positions.

As of the spring of 1983, the Press Office is still technically under Press Secretary James Brady, grievously wounded in the March 1981 assassination attempt on the President, but whose job Reagan ordered left open pending his recovery. Larry Speakes, as his deputy, has served as de facto press secretary since the shooting. In charge of the White House Communications Office is the assistant to the President for communications, David Gergen.

Anyone in a position to decide what information the President will read is in a position of a good deal of potential power. Under the Reagan presidency that position has been shared by two dissimilar men in their thirties who are all but unknown to the public, but who provide the President with most of the written information he gets—summarizing vast amounts of memorandums, reports, statistics, and options for him to ponder.

Richard Darman and Craig Fuller have titles that don't accurately describe their real jobs. Thirty-eight-year-old Darman, a Harvard M.B.A. who serves as deputy to the chief of staff, White House staff secretary and coordinator of the Legislative Strategy Group, reports to the White House chief of staff, James Baker. Fuller, eight years younger, a Southern Californian educated at UCLA, titled Assistant to the President for Cabinet Affairs, is under Ed Meese. In keeping with the same responsibility split as their bosses, Darman handles basically White House internal matters, while Fuller takes Cabinet affairs. Darman serves as a pipeline between the President and the areas of the White House supervised by Baker—political strategy, legislative lobbying, personnel appointments, public liaison, intergovernmental affairs, the press office, and the legal staff. Fuller's duties follow those Meese oversees: the Cabinet and domestic policy planning. But both have the same ultimate function—to prepare the President to make decisions based on a précis of information and options. Ideally their own personalities shouldn't enter into the matter; practically anybody in such positions would have a nearly impossible job in masking his own views or preferences. Thereby comes the clout of their jobs—in deciding how much emphasis to give competing views or options, whose views are to be heard, and even *when* Reagan is presented with pertinent information. "We're in a position to either really screw things up or be a constructive influence," Darman understated the situation in a *Los Angeles Times* interview.

At the top of the White House power pyramid stands a quadrivirate of courtiers guarding the doors to the Oval Office. Joining what was originally a triumvirate a year after Reagan entered the White House was his old and close friend William P. Clark. The replacement for National Security adviser Richard Allen took the job on the condition that he would, unlike his predecessor, have unlimited access to the President. Such access by an aide is and always has been in Washington a pearl of great price, one that put Clark on the highest rung of the White House power ladder. The other three top aides are Edwin Meese III, counselor to the President, James A. Baker III, chief of staff and assistant to the President, and Michael K. Deaver, deputy chief of staff and assistant to the President. The rectangle is not exactly equal-sided—according to the source, Meese and Baker are a little more equal than Deaver, and Clark may now outrank them all. But combined, they're the equivalent in the Reagan administration of Haldeman-Ehrlichman or Jordan-Powell, public figures futilely trying not to be, a (sometimes) co-operative team whose goal it is to make its man a success. So close are they to each other and to the President that they rotate attending Reagan on his vacations in the manner of ladies-in-waiting to the British queen. Another sign of their value to Reagan is the fact that all now have their own Secret Service agents assigned to them, the first time in White House history that presidential aides have been routinely protected by the Se-cret Service. (They're also the only aides with door-to-door lim-ousine service.)

Deaver is the most *personally* indispensable of the President's advisers. One associate says, "He knows what Ronald Reagan is thinking before Ronald Reagan does." Among Deaver's duties as deputy chief of staff (a position nominally subordinate to Baker, but the President is in reality Deaver's only boss), he is in charge of the White House military aides, the travel office, and the First Lady's East Wing staff. One of the prime sources of Deaver's authority is his personally close relationship with Nancy Reagan, who has by far the greatest access to and influence over the President, according to White House insiders. (Her influence is said to be more in telling her husband what she thinks of people than of issues.)

Deaver's office may not be the biggest of those occupied by the Big Four, but if nearness to the President is the chief criterion in determining power in the White House, there is no one nearer except Reagan's secretary—only the President's small study separates Deaver's office from the Oval Office. Centered in the elegantly decorated office, Deaver's desk is most easily within the President's beckoning, something that happens often every working day. During his many sessions with the President, Deaver also exercises a privilege with Reagan that supposedly only Nancy Reagan and Nevada Senator Paul Laxalt (one of the President's oldest political allies) share: the ability and the willingness to talk back, even—rarely—to shout back. Deaver's least-known and probably least-important duty at the White House is serving as Reagan's "wine administrator" and architect of the President's "California wine policy."

James A. Baker III has the appearance of an *éminence grise* to the President—the buttoned-down, polished, everything-in-order aide conjuring up images of Cardinal Richelieu. But the fifty-one-year-old, supremely efficient chief of staff is one of the few of Reagan's highest aides who has had a political career independent of his boss. His duties relate mainly to the administration of the presidency itself, rather than to the executive departments. Reporting directly to the President, he oversees congressional lobbying, the Press Office, speech writers, and working with special interests groups.

Baker's large southwest corner office in the West Wing—the same one occupied in the past by Bob Haldeman and Hamilton

Jordan—is the scene of the daily 7:30 A.M. (an hour when the boss is still in bed) breakfast meeting with Deaver and Meese. Baker's tidiness in mind and body (Nancy Reagan, one of Baker's strongest supporters, is said to like the way he "looks, smells, and acts") is probably the reason Reagan named him, rather than his older associate Ed Meese, chief of staff. Others credit his rapid rise in the President's eyes with the fact that Baker is a man of inherited wealth, a hugely successful law practice, and high-level contacts from his days as undersecretary of commerce—in other words, more of an equal than the other aides who have made Reagan's career their career.

So sure is Baker of his authority that he is publicly and clearly seen to seemingly be giving orders to the President. While boarding the helicopter for his weekend sojourn at Camp David, Reagan kept answering the questions shouted at him by the reporters on the scene. Baker finally said to the President, audible to the television microphones, "We've gotta go!" One can imagine the fate of any aide taking the same liberty with Lyndon Johnson.

Reagan's granting of Cabinet status to an aide is unprecedented in White House history. Edwin Meese, the aide the press initially dubbed "deputy President" is an affable (his own self-description), courteous, and easy-to-approach man who wields considerable substantive decision-making power in the Reagan White House. Housed in the last of the corner offices—the other three corners are occupied by Baker, the President, and the Cabinet Room—fifty-one-year-old Meese acts as a "keeper of the philosophical flame" for the administration, the most intrinsically conservative of Reagan's top aides and the man whose thinking can almost be guaranteed to reflect his boss's views.

More likely to be seen socially in the mansion with their wives than officially in the West Wing, the Reagan kitchen cabinet is still a political force of some influence. The term "kitchen cabinet" refers to the (usually) small bodies of informal presidential advisers, generally men who aren't themselves holding public office. It was first used to describe a group of Andrew Jackson's friends on whom the President relied—the "kitchen" designation presumably signifying his and their reputation for unpolished manners. Reagan's group may be known for a lot of things, but *not* for unpolished manners, that and their substantial bank accounts being an area of commonality, along with their old, close, and politically valuable ties with the President.

In a way, Reagan has been another investment for these men, and good businessmen that they are, they probably expect some kind of return on their investment. But to date there has been no evidence that any of them has the President beholden to him in any political sense beyond a shared philosophical desire to turn the country in a more conservative direction. The Reagan kitchen cabinet acts far more as courtiers to an impressively courtlike White House than it does as backstage political manipulators.

III

Presidential Hospitality

ENTERTAINING AT THE WHITE HOUSE

A guest never forgets the host who has treated him kindly.

HOMER

WHEN IT BEGAN, White House hospitality was characterized by forms far more royal than republican. John and Abigail Adams had few precedents to guide them on how to conduct social functions at the new executive residence during their brief four-month tenancy, so they took the understandable course of imitating European court behavior. Mrs. Adams regularly received her guests while seated in the upstairs oval room, crimson curtains at her back, the President in knee breeches and silver buckles at her side, his hair powdered, majestically bowing to the assembled court. These weekly levees had been an innovation of George and Martha Washington, who had held them in

Philadelphia with the then Vice President and Mrs. Adams taking the roles of crown prince and princess.

Fortunately—and, in hindsight, remarkably—for the republican future of the country, the next President swept away many of the royal ways of doing things. The course set by Thomas Jefferson has been the basic model which governs presidential entertaining to this day—a combination of dignity and respect for the nation with a new freedom which would allow a far broader mix of the citizenry to enjoy the head of state's hospitality than would be thinkable in any European kingdom.

As it is the nature of any palace of a monarch, so it is with the Executive Mansion, that its primary purpose—after providing a roof over the head of state's head—is to serve as a place of entertainment. Balls, dinners, receptions, luncheons, teas, stag parties—these are the gatherings at which the President honors a wide range of his fellow citizens with a coveted invitation to the nation's chief residence. But the preeminent fete at the President's home is the state dinner. Under the Reagans these events have come to be spectacularly glittering evenings that for all but the most blasé guests will remain memories lasting a lifetime. Describing the planning and details of these dinners—an average of one takes place every month—gives a better understanding of how social life is carried out at the White House.

State dinners are the official and most elaborate entertainment that is given to state visitors. Not all visits by foreign heads of state rank as state visits. Only one such visit during each administration by a given individual is classified as a state visit; others by the same leader count as private visits. If a country changes its head of state, the new leader's visit to Washington—even if it occurs during the same administration as that of his predecessor —may be another state visit. On the other hand, not all foreign heads of government are entitled to have their visits classified as state visits; to be such, a head of government has also to be head of state, such as the American President. Calls by prime ministers (premiers, chancellors, etc.) can be ranked only as official visits, and thus the dinners given for them are classified as official dinners. The fact is that there isn't a great deal of difference between a state visit and an official visit as far as the social effects of the call are concerned; one minor distinction is that heads of government only receive nineteen-gun salutes at the welcoming ceremonies on the White House lawn, while heads of state get an extra two shots. In this country the prestigious twenty-one-gun salute supposedly commemorates the year 1776, and the salutes are sometimes fired 1-7-7-6.

State or official visits are usually conducted on a similar time frame—the visitors spend two days in Washington and sometimes several more seeing other parts of the country. The days in the capital are likely to include two private meetings with the President, a White House dinner, perhaps a luncheon given by the secretary of state, and a return dinner for the President at the visitor's embassy. These ground rules are flexible, but the idea is to treat all such visitors, whether from nuclear superpowers or vest-pocket principalities, pretty much equally.

Whether it's going to be a state visit or an official visit, planning starts early, as much as eight weeks before the guest is due to arrive. After a foreign leader has responded to a formal invitation from the President to visit this country, possible dates are negotiated. (The official fiction is observed that the foreign leader is the personal guest of the President and the First Lady acting in their roles as the country's first host and first hostess.) The invitation itself is accepted through diplomatic channels, and a mutually acceptable date is worked out, again through the State Department. This can involve sometimes ticklish planning to be certain that other visits or business on either side don't impede, that nobody's national holiday is impinged on, that the principals are not being threatened with coups, and so on.

The dates settled, serious planning can be gotten down to. Nancy Reagan takes personal charge of the two biggest items for the state dinners: the guest list and the menu. Official Washington attaches an enormous degree of importance to an invitation to a state dinner, possibly more than to any other kind of social function, presidential or otherwise. (A summons to dine privately with the First Family or to one of the rare White House weddings may be its only serious competition.) Proposed

invitees come from a number of sources, including the top presidential aides in the West Wing, Congress (Jack Kennedy
insisted that congressional invitations be equally divided between Democrats and Republicans), the Cabinet, the State Department, and even suggestions from the guests of honor of persons they would especially like to meet or see again. Mrs.
Reagan has of recent limited the number of these dinners to 96,
rather than pack the State Dining Room to bursting with the 120
or more it will hold. Aides say the limitation "keeps people's
elbows from falling into their neighbor's soup."

Guest lists for Reagan state dinners always include a healthy
sprinkling of the President's old Hollywood friends. The Frank
Sinatras (Sinatra is the quasi-official "entertainment coordinator"
for the Reagans; his first job was to round up performers for the
state dinner honoring Jordan's King Hussein), the Bob Hopes,
and the Charlton Hestons can be expected to elicit a frisson of
excitement from even the most sophisticated of old Washington
grandees. (The Carters were just as big on show business people
at their functions; only then the stars were likely to have names
like Willie Nelson or Loretta Lynn.) Congressional leaders and
industrial magnates as well as Nobel prizewinners and people
from the arts—publishing, writing, the theater—round out the
lists. Usually the invitations include an ethnic matchmate or two
—Senator Sam Hayakawa for a dinner for the Japanese prime
minister, Omar Sharif (who failed to show up) for a dinner for
Anwar Sadat. Even Curator Clem Conger gets into the act—
some of the major donors of furnishings and art objects to the
White House are occasionally included on the guest rosters. Social Secretary Muffie Brandon says that she's compiling a book
of names of eligible invitees and that when the final decisions
for a dinner are made, "there is usually some tough negotiating"
—but the First Lady's word is the last one. The invitations go
out about a week before the dinner.

The menu is another item of considerable importance, one
which, if not carefully planned, can be potentially embarrassing.
As is true of any host, it's thoughtful to be considerate of your
guests' likes and dislikes; unlike the case with other hosts, to do
otherwise can put a pall over festivities which are designed

solely to cement and/or improve relations between this country and that of the guests of honor. The White House has been given a list of things the visitor can't (because of religion) or won't (because of a personal dislike) eat. No pork for Jewish or Moslem visitors, no seafood for the queen of England, no alcohol for teetotalers, and so on.

Chef Henry Haller does the working out of a menu—something on the chic side, but now only four courses, down from the six or seven (too fattening today) served for state dinners through the Hoover administration. (The all-time gourmandizer was President Grant, who thought nothing of putting out twenty-nine courses for a visiting potentate.) The Franklin Roosevelts finally pared the feasting down to less formidable limits.

Haller will consult with Mrs. Reagan and make any changes on her advice. The First Lady may have a sample meal of the menu made beforehand so she can try everything out; at one of her dinners this resulted in the elimination of a sauce from a soufflé and the addition of mint to the rack of lamb—much nicer. Jackie Kennedy used to send her chef, René Verdon, little illustrated notes showing the outline of a canapé she wanted served so he could make each precisely that size.

Guest list and menu decided, countless other details can be gotten down to. Muffie Brandon and her people prepare their "scenario"—the line-by-line guideline for the dinner, listing everything that has to be done every second from the time the guests of honor leave their official quarters at Blair House for the short drive to the White House until they depart at the end of the evening from the north portico.

Down in the basement below the ground-floor kitchens, full-size florist refrigerators are presided over by the White House floral director, Dottie Temple. The flower room, jammed with vases, baskets, and miles of multicolored ribbons, turns out the dozens of bouquets required for the dinner. Assisted by professional florists and volunteers, Mrs. Temple follows Nancy Reagan's lead in the choice of flowers and colors. Gone are Mamie Eisenhower's pink roses, pink snapdragons, and pink carnations. Now guests are likely to find a spray of papyrus and water lilies, or small potted trees, or massed cymbidium orchids with Free-sias, ivy, and fern fronds, the whole set off with Spanish moss and polished river rocks strewn (artfully) around the table. None of these elaborately ingenuous creations is simple; it often takes up to a full day for the floral director and her assistants to do the flowers for a state dinner.

Calligrapher John Scarfone's office is in the East Wing. The beautiful place cards and menu cards of gilt-edged heavy white stock with the gold presidential seal are turned into small works of art with the addition of Scarfone's flowingly elegant calligraphy. Place cards for the host and hostess are marked "The President" and "Mrs. Reagan"; cards for the guests of honor read, for example, "The President of the United Mexican States" and "Mrs. López Portillo" or "Her Majesty the Queen" and "His Royal Highness the Duke of Edinburgh." The cards are almost always taken home by the guests as souvenirs, rare mementos of an evening passed at the very pinnacle of America's social life.

The White House maître d' (the title was changed from chief butler during FDR's presidency) and de facto sommelier John Ficklin, Sr., presides over the serving of the wines and the selection of the glasses for every course and for the ceremonial toasts. Each place setting has four stemmed wineglasses for the evening's wines, vintages which run along lines set by the President and Mrs. Reagan. Naturally the wines in this administration are from California. An attempt is made to serve wines appropriate for each guest of honor. For German Chancellor Helmut Schmidt, California wines made from German grape varieties were chosen—a Balverne Healdsburger and a Johannisberg Riesling. But for the François Mitterrand dinner, a French wine was served—a Château d'Yquem, the first French wine served in the Reagan White House. From time to time, as for the visit of the Prince of Wales, the President himself will ask for specific wines. For that occasion his favorite 1970 Cabernet Sauvignon was served. The First Couple sometimes sample several wines for state dinners, working out the final choices with Ficklin and "wine administrator" Mike Deaver.

Table settings are Nancy Reagan's most personal contribution to the evening. Even though Clem Conger complains that the

State Dining Room set up with a dozen round tables makes it look "nightclubby," the Kennedy-originated mode has remained the Reagans' favorite. Mrs. Reagan chooses floor-length cloths in rich fabrics for the tables, ranging from rose-colored and patterned lace over silk moiré or white organdy shadow work to dramatically luxurious, heavy dark green watered silk. For the first time in many years each guest is now served on matching china. The sterling flatware has an edge of tiny beading; the knife handles are made of mother-of-pearl. One of Dottie Temple's floral arrangements is centered on each of the twelve tables, as are tall white tapers in silver candlesticks. Small silver dishes hold salt, matches, cigarettes, and foil-wrapped chocolate and champagne wafers. The familiar gold wooden chairs with off white cushions surround the tables. With the State Dining Room's massive gilded chandelier turned low, the scene is one of sumptuous splendor.

The dinner is usually scheduled for the day the guest arrives in Washington. The ceremony officially greeting the visitors was for decades held at Union Station or one of the Washington area airports, and because there was a welcoming parade down Pennsylvania Avenue, the average Washingtonian could feel at least a small part of these momentous goings-on. By the early 1960s it had become impossible to scare up enough people to make a decent showing on the sidewalks, so in late 1962 John Kennedy for the first time held the welcoming ceremony on the White House grounds; Ahmed Ben Bella of Algeria was the guest of honor. Sadly, security considerations would mitigate against any more such parades today, making it a certainty that the south lawn ceremony has become a permanent part of the capital's social scene.

On the day of the arrival several dozen invited guests have assembled on the lawn to witness the ceremony. The guest of honor is brought to the grounds in a limousine from the airport, and after a short speech of welcome by the President and then his own return remarks, he is driven off to Blair House to wash up for the greater festivities to come. During the shah and empress of Iran's state visit to the Carter White House, demon-

strators on South Executive Avenue bordering the grounds as a
token of their untoward feelings for the honored guests set
off tear gas bombs, the unpleasant fumes of which drifted north
a few yards to the First Couple. Most of the participants, including Empress Farah, were forced to wipe their eyes, but the shah
stoically refused to acknowledge the irritation.

For the evening's main event, the guests start arriving shortly
after seven, their cars rolling into the south grounds through the
East Executive Avenue gate, where the passengers alight in
front of the Diplomatic Reception Room entrance. Many have
their own limousines, but for those who don't and would like
others to think they do, Washington's fifty-seven limousine rental
agencies are available to take care of their needs. Muffie Brandon greets each invitee as he enters the door, and invitations are
checked under ultraviolet light to guard against any forgery-
minded gate-crashers. The guests proceed straight through the
brightly lit room, across the Ground Floor Corridor, and up the
Main Stairway.

At the top of the stairs an aide announces each guest's name,
primarily for the benefit of the assembled press pool and photographers. It it's somebody hot, pencils and shutters fly. All the
guests are handed small cards, letting them know where they're
supposed to sit at dinner; they're then directed into the East
Room, where musicians—perhaps a flutist and a harpist—play
music designed not to be noticed. Here everybody can have a
cocktail (reinstated after the wine-and-punch Carter years) and
wait for the principals to show up.

In the meantime, the stars of the evening—theirs and ours—
are each about ready to set the major events in motion. A call is
made to Blair House to coordinate the motorcade of the guests
of honor to the White House, a distance of some several hundred feet, taking about two minutes. Walking would make more
sense, from the aspect of energy conservation, but of course, that
wouldn't do. For the official dinner of the Japanese prime
minister, seven cars were required for this hegira—one with
Prime Minister Zenko Suzuki and his wife; another with the Japanese foreign minister, chief of protocol Leonore "Lee" Annen-

berg, and an interpreter; another with the Japanese ambassador to the United States and his wife and the American ambassador to Japan (former Senate Majority Leader Mike Mansfield) and his wife; and the other four with members of the prime minister's entourage.

When the call signifying President and Mrs. Reagan's readiness is made, the presidential couple leave the family quarters, elevator down to the state floor, walk outside the main entrance, and wait at the north portico, where—ideally and usually—the guest of honor's limo is just pulling up. It all goes like clockwork most of the time.

After diplomatically effusive greetings, embraces, and whatnot, the Reagans and their chief guests (in the Japanese case, the Suzukis, Foreign Minister Masayoshi Ito, both ambassadors and their wives, and the protocol chief, whose job it is to oil the gears should they start to grind) proceed back up the elevator (the press people have a "photo opportunity" during this little walk) to the Yellow Oval Room. The aides making up the higher-ranking part of the Japanese party were taken into the Red Room for cocktails; the lower-ranking members were driven straight from Blair House to another White House entrance, where—for the first time—they now have their own little dinner party together with their U.S. titular counterparts in a ground-floor room set up like a junior version of the State Dining Room.

Back upstairs in the Yellow Oval Room, the principals have about ten minutes to have a quick drink, exchange gifts, and brace themselves for the ceremonies to come. The gift giving, which has all the spontaneity of income taxes, is really only an exercise in diplomatic good manners. More on that later.

At seven forty the members of the presidential group leave the Yellow Oval Room, take a right and then a left in the hallway toward the Main Stairway, all the while preceded by a military color team the officer in charge of which has formally requested and been formally granted by the President permission to secure the colors (flags). At the foot of the Main Stairway the color team divides, and the four principals stand and have their picture taken, the best-known moment of these state occasions as far as the public is concerned.

The color team still leading the way, the two couples march toward the East Room; when the doors are thrown open, the band strikes up "Hail to the Chief" (Jack Kennedy said the old Gaelic melody, first played for President Tyler in 1844, was his favorite tune), the assemblage probably all getting goose bumps simultaneously. The color team divides, and the two national leaders and their spouses step between them, thus forming the receiving line, along which the entire congregation will now pass. A military "whispering" aide standing in the background murmurs the name to an "introducing" aide, who gives each person's name to the President and his wife, who then shake hands and present their guest to the guests of honor. It's not considered good manners, by the way, to strike up a conversation with the principals; a lot of people have to be gotten through. If the President wishes to have a little talk, though, that's okay. Just in case there are any Chatty Cathys, a "pulling-off" aide is standing at the end of the receiving line, ready to nudge the offender along his way.

As the guests pass down the line, they leave the East Room and stroll down the Cross Hall, past military aides standing at semiattention in dress uniforms, and into the State Dining Room at the opposite end of the corridor. After a decorous scramble for seats the principals come in, and everybody gets down to the theoretical reason they're there—to have dinner.

At roughly five minutes to eight, dinner begins. A small legion of specially hired temporary waiters (all of whom have been subjected to rigorous security checks) fans out to start serving the four courses—maybe lobster Bellevue (franglais dishes are popular now), followed by a roulade of veal farcie, then perhaps a watercress salad, topped off by a fresh peach cardinal or, Nancy Reagan's favorite, small hot soufflés. By the way, second helpings are never offered at formal dinners.

After the dessert the toasts are made, first by the President, then by the guest of honor. Toasts are not a simple little ceremony of rising to one's feet, murmuring, "Cheers," and drinking up. They've turned into an occasion for assuring each other of mutual fidelity—or sometimes for dropping diplomatic clunkers, like the time Anwar Sadat included in a toast his view that the

Palestine Liberation Organization, an outfit generally regarded in official Washington as a pack of jackals, should be an accepted part of the Middle East peace negotiations. When something like this happens, our President can only sit there and act as though it's a wonderful idea. Lyndon Johnson once got the shah's formal title—Shananshah—mixed up in his toast, lifting his glass to the "Sha Sha Shah." The Aryan king of kings got back at him, though, by returning a gracious little tribute to his good friend "LBG."

As soon as the two leaders have finished their toasts, the entire party passes into the adjoining Red Room and its two connecting parlors, the Blue and Green rooms. There are particularly tight clusters around the President and his guests of honor and any movie stars who happen to be present. Henry Kissinger, when in attendance, also attracts a sizable court. At this time the junior staff members, who have just finished their dinner downstairs, come upstairs to join the main party for coffee. Everybody now stands around chatting happily about how wonderful it all is. (During the Carter years one might find oneself chatting with Amy after dinner.)

Until the early sixties the group was sexually segregated at this after-dinner coffee, the men in the Green Room with their cigars, the ladies in the Red Room. After about a half hour of socializing the President and the male guests would head for the Blue Room; an aide in the corridor would signal what was happening to the First Lady, who would then lead her group in the same direction. The men were supposed to match up with their dinner partners again, and everybody would then march down the Cross Hall to the East Room for the "musicale."

At most state dinners today a B group is invited to join the A group after dinner for the entertainment. They arrive at about nine thirty and wait in the Diplomatic Reception Room, the China Room, and the Library, where refreshments are served to them. Now they get to come up to the state floor to join the others.

Just as the B people are coming up the stairs, the rest of the party has moved into the East Room, which has been transformed into a sort of minitheater. In 1965 Rebekah Harkness gave a portable stage (designed by Jo Mielziner) to the White House to be used for East Room performances such as small ballets and musical theater presentations. The cleverly designed aluminum apparatus (which takes up a third of the room and requires a full day to set up and another to take down) matches the decor, pilasters, and ceiling decorations of the room, making it look like a permanent part of the architecture when it's in place at the north end of the room. Dancers have to be careful not to leap too high or they run the risk of banging into one of the chandeliers. If the performance is to be a solo act, a smaller platform is set up on the east side of the room.

What were the simple musicales of the Eisenhower days (when Fred Waring and his Pennsylvanians were very likely to be the evening's entertainment) have evolved into sophisticated productions. Jackie Kennedy invited some of the world's major classical artists to perform—an invitation coveted in the world of show business. (Artists perform without a fee; the honor of entertaining the President and his guests is considered compensation enough. The honor is eagerly sought by dozens of performers—or their agents—who offer their services every year.) The evening in 1961 when Pablo Casals played for the visit of the governor of Puerto Rico was one of the most famous in White House history. (Casals had vowed never to perform in a country that recognized Franco, but made an exception for Kennedy because of his great respect for the young President.) Richard Nixon had the entire Broadway musical 1776 performed in 1970 on George Washington's birthday. Betty Ford invited the company she had once studied with, New York's Martha Graham dancers; afterward she persuaded her husband to join her and the dancers on the stage for a little improvising. Reagan artists have run from pianists Arthur Gold and Robert Fizdale to singers Shirley Verrett, Robert Goulet, and Dinah Shore, the latter for Menachem Begin's 1981 visit. The star performers are always invited to the dinner itself, while the supporting entertainers are offered a light supper in their dressing rooms.

After the entertainment and the introduction of the performers to the guests of honor, the honorees are escorted to the north portico by the President and the First Lady, tucked into their limousine, and sent back the short distance to Blair House. This is the signal for the hair to be let down, so to speak. The United States Marine Band Dance Ensemble, brightly uniformed in scarlet tunics, is set up in the corner of the Entrance Hall, and the marble floors of the hall and the Cross Hall take on the appearance of a chic supper club. The Reagans usually lead off the dancing, preferably to something like familiar Cole Porter melodies. Cutting in is perfectably acceptable. Mrs. Reagan will probably have a hard time prying the President off the dance floor, but before long they ascend the Main Stairway—which is not, however, an indication the evening is necessarily ending for the rest of the guests. Many stay and dance into the early hours of the morning, nourished by waiters mingling through the group with trays of champagne and small pastries.

Finally, the last of the guests leave, and the state and ground floors are turned over to a platoon of cleaning men and women, anxious to get the place back in shape for the thousands of tourists who will be seeing a scrubbed and shiny mansion in just a few hours.

One of the factors which give state dinners their unmatchable ambience is the small group of men and women whose full-time job is to be professional military and naval officers, but whose temporary assignment (not exceeding four years) is duty as White House social aides. The thirty-six-member contingent, representing bachelor officers of all five branches of the armed services, is under the direction of the senior military aide to the President for the social aide program, Lieutenant Colonel Jose Muratti. The assistant social secretary admits "we couldn't run the White House without them."

The duties of the aides are as varied as the official functions which they are assigned to attend: directing traffic at state dinners ("guiding guests with dignity and ease and without confusion"), laying wreaths for the President, working on receiving lines, dancing with forlorn guests, chatting at receptions; once an aide even helped Britain's queen mother squeeze her over-generous evening dress through a White House door. Their mingling is work, however, and not play; aides aren't allowed to eat or drink anything until the "gloves off" signal from Muffie Brandon is given near the end of the evening. The degree of formality of their uniforms is determined by the function or how the President dresses. Female aides wear long dress-uniform skirts for formal evening affairs.

Only since the Eisenhower years have the aides been other than senior officers; now all are company or lower field grades. One aide from the fifties, Major Gerald Hall, who served during both the Truman and Eisenhower administrations, remembers an orientation tea and tour of the White House given for the aides by Harry and Bess Truman. The President specially pointed out a portrait of James Monroe which he swore had his daughter Margaret's nose, figuring that must prove a "family connection." The First Lady, homespun as any ever to fill the role, told the group of young officers how she had fixed up a chest at the end of a guest bed in anticipation of a visit by Holland's stately Queen Wilhelmina, "just in case her feet stick out over the end."

The Eisenhower years were a little more difficult because of a more demanding First Lady. Hall remembers that Mamie didn't want any footprints on the red carpet in the Entrance Hall when the guests of honor were due to arrive, so he and his fellow aides had to jump across. Her redemption was the annual Christmas party for the aides on the second floor, when gifts from the First Couple included hairbrushes, knives, and other useful and personal items. The President was strict in his demand that they not capitalize on their White House connection; they were never to accept invitations to outside events as White House aides. The reason was primarily to ensure that nothing they said or did could be construed as giving any kind of official presidential sanction.

In the fifties rules which are still in force were developed: Aides must never cluster or congregate by themselves but, instead, remain dispersed among the guests; except when seated in the State Dining Room, the President and First Lady should always be accompanied by an aide, close enough to answer requests but far enough away so as not to appear to be eavesdropping; and very important, aides must remember even the finest points of protocol—for example, in the British army, a brigadier is *not* a general officer and is never announced as one, as well as other such slight but socially weighty marginalia.

State dinners may be the most sumptuous events at the President's House, but they by no means constitute the bulk of the entertaining. Until 1960 the *official* White House social schedule was carried out on an unvarying annual basis: Starting in the early weeks of November and lasting until Lent, a series of great formal events filled the calendar, comprising the President and First Lady's "season." First came two diplomatic dinners, held on successive nights, at which the Washington ambassadorial corps had their one yearly opportunity to dine with the man to whom they were officially accredited. Two weeks or so later a Cabinet dinner was held, followed by a large military reception, the Supreme Court dinner, and a judicial reception. The First Couple had a three- or four-week respite to attend to their own Christmas festivities, and then starting in early January would come the last four functions: a congressional reception, the Vice President's dinner, the speaker's dinner, and a diplomatic reception. With minor exceptions, this schedule was carried out year after year.

Since the Kennedy administration the social calendar has been extended from the old winter season to a year-around basis. What had been the unvarying round of annual dinners and receptions is no longer held on the same basis. Kennedy initially switched the diplomatic dinners to late-afternoon parties, and then Nixon changed them to a regional geographical basis—first entertaining Latin and Organization of American States ambassadors, then the Asian and Middle Eastern people. He never got around to the Europeans. Ford and Carter cut the official evenings even further. The Reagans recently hosted two black-tie diplomatic dinners in the East Room, which, because of the size of Washington's ambassadorial corps, were held on subsequent Thursday evenings, with 140 guests at each. The First Couple does not plan to reactivate the Vice President's or speaker's dinners, nor are any of the old receptions planned, except for a large Christmas tour of the White House for the military. The

Supreme Court has been the recipient of a Reagan luncheon, and Congress is received at an annual Christmas party.

The biggest category of social activity is the receptions, ranging from intimate teas given by the First Lady—today very often in the Yellow Oval Room—to the huge congressional receptions. When Mrs. Reagan receives small groups on the second floor—a single honor for those invited since they have a chance to see the private living quarters—guests are escorted from the Diplomatic Reception Room to the elevator and taken up to the family's private apartments. Larger gatherings—clubs, charity organizations, and so on—are held on the state floor, usually in one or more of the drawing rooms.

One of the innovations most often remembered from the Nixon years—with varying degrees of approval, usually depending on one's political coloration—was the Sunday worship service in the East Room. Beginning shortly after his 1969 inauguration, about 350 guests were invited on alternate Sundays to the "interdenominational" (but usually controversial) quasi-church services. Predictably the issue of separation of church and state was a constant theme in the press regarding the short-lived innovation. More successful were the Nixon "evenings of entertainment"—musical festivities to which a large cross section of official Washington was invited to hear performers like Bob Hope or Duke Ellington.

Dinner dances are a popular—and, in the Reagan administration, elegant—form of White House entertainment. Officially private and off the record, they're usually held in honor of close friends or for some special occasion, such as the memorable one given by Mrs. Reagan for her husband's seventieth birthday a few weeks after he took office. Far more chic and formal than in recent administrations, the format can vary from a sit-down dinner in the State Dining Room to the kind of party given for the state governors in which the first floor was turned into a sort of super supper club with tables set up in the Green, Blue, and Red rooms and dancers floating freely in and out of the Cross Hall dance floor.

The Reagans have private but very soigné gatherings once or twice a month, with as few as eight and as many as thirty guests, from the kitchen cabinet group of close friends to such old Hollywood chums as Pat O'Brien and Jimmy Cagney. The format is typically a dinner followed by a first-run movie in the sixty-five-seat East Wing theater. No longer is it permissible, as it was in the Carter administration, for single invitees to bring a date to White House social events; the possibility of a guest's bringing someone not "acceptable" is a risk not to be courted.

Many of the state visits entail state luncheons in addition to the more publicized dinners; luncheons are also a regular part of the official working visits, a notch in precedence below state visits. The tone of a luncheon is more business-oriented than the dinners. For example, a luncheon given for the South Korean president and his wife was attended by a bevy of military, diplomatic, business, and congressional leaders involved in issues directly relating to Korean business or economics. The spouses arrive separately, with the head of state first meeting with the President in the Oval Office, the wife coming an hour or so later to have prelunch sherry with the First Lady in the Red Room; the Vice President's wife is usually included as well. If an interpreter is needed, this prelunch chat usually turns out to be only a fairly stiff exchange of banalities.

Unquestionably the superevent at the White House, one on the magnitude of a coronation, is the wedding of a presidential daughter (sons never seem to get married there). There have only been two (plus a third reception) in recent years: those of Lynda Bird Johnson in 1967 and Tricia Nixon in 1971. The second Johnson daughter, Luci Baines, was married in 1966 at the National Shrine, but the postnuptial celebrations were held at the White House. All turned into national media spectacles for a public eager to share vicariously the grandeur of presidential life-style.

For Luci Johnson's reception, the state floor became a bower of pink and white carnations, roses and rubrum lilies, nicotiana and lavender. A white canopy covered the then new Jacqueline Kennedy Garden, through which the guests passed on their way to the Blue Room and its receiving line. The seven-tiered cake, a gift from Senator and Mrs. Birch Bayh, was cut in the State Dining Room.

Sixteen months later Luci's older sister, Lynda Bird, was married to Marine Captain Charles Robb (now governor of Virginia) in a ceremony in the East Room. The bridegroom had met the bride during the course of his duties as a social aide in the mansion. The wedding was covered by 500 members of the news media.

The social high point of the Nixon presidency was the June 1971 wedding of his elder daughter, Tricia, to law student Edward Finch Cox, son of a socially prominent New York family. It was also the only wedding ever held on the White House grounds. An open wrought-iron pavilion covered the altar, set up in the Rose Garden outside the Oval Office—400 guests sat among the masses of roses and baby's breath. The reception given in the mansion was the scene of one of the rare dances the President and his wife shared in the White House. They two-stepped to the music of the Army Strings rather than to the more traditional Marine Band—the President wanted to give a little morale boost to the Army, which at the time was suffering great indignities as a result of the war in Southeast Asia.

The arrival of any member of the British royal family at the White House is sure to be treated as an event of stellar magnitude. The first time a reigning British monarch was the guest of any American President was when King George VI and his wife, Queen Elizabeth, came to see the Roosevelts in 1939. After the standard Washington formalities (during which the king stayed in the Lincoln Bedroom and the queen in the Rose Room; since they were just down the hall from the Roosevelts, screens were used to help separate the royal from the presidential quarters), the President and First Lady took the king and queen to the Roosevelts' home at Hyde Park, New York, where the most noteworthy tidings were that everybody ate hot dogs. It probably wasn't terribly amusing for the royal couple—especially with a battery of newsreel cameras recording every dribble of mustard —but Americans loved it, "proving" that European monarchs much enjoyed the simple egalitarian pleasures of life as it was lived on the President's manorial estate.

As a princess Britain's Queen Elizabeth II stayed with the Trumans at Blair House for several days in 1951. The President's deaf mother-in-law, Madge Wallace, lived in an upstairs bedroom; Truman delighted in bringing the princess and her husband up to meet her, shouting as they got there, "Mother, I've brought Princess Elizabeth to meet you!" Winston Churchill had just been voted back into power, and Mrs. Wallace told the princess how glad she was "that your father's been reelected."

In November 1954 the queen mother was the Eisenhowers' houseguest, staying for the second time in the Rose Room Suite (now the Queens' Bedroom Suite). A gala dinner was held, with a list of invitees that included a good chunk of the American power structure of the era. (See appendix III.)

Queen Elizabeth II made her second visit—a state visit this time—in October 1957, the last time a state visitor stayed in the White House. The queen and Prince Philip's visit was the one such social call President Eisenhower, who wasn't especially fond of such visits, said he was sorry to see end.

In the summer of 1970 the third generation of the royal family visited, although this time on a private basis. The Prince of Wales and his sister, Princess Anne, were officially the houseguests not of the Nixons but of their daughters, staying, as had their parents and grandparents, on the east end of the second floor. (Since this was not an official visit in the diplomatic meaning of the term, the Nixons were able to allow the pair to stay in the mansion without giving offense to other official visitors.) Long before the much heralded visit a number of columnists had Charles all but engaged to Nixon's pert elder daughter. In fact, Tricia's parents themselves didn't miss an opportunity to pair her off with Charles, sending them on a day trip to Mount Vernon, on a tour of the Capitol, to a baseball game, at which co-host and keen sportswriter David Eisenhower explained the rules to the foreign guests, and finally to a "young people's" dinner dance in the White House. Charles was able to take the publicity surrounding the visit in stride, but his sister didn't prove to be as even-tempered.

The latest British royal visitor was the queen again, hers and Philip's third stay in Washington. Having arrived for the bicentennial celebrations in the summer of 1976, the sovereign and her consort were entertained at a lavish state dinner given by the Fords. The reception line was formed on the south grounds outside the Diplomatic Reception Room entrance. An alfresco dinner was served under a canvas marquee, with Julia Child giving a blow-by-blow description for public television viewers (except during the actual eating, of course; the queen won't chew on camera). The redoubtable Mrs. Child tried to get a sample plateful sent to the set where she was doing her describing—she naturally thought she could give her viewers a better idea of the sort of things served to monarchs and presidents if she could have sampled the lobster and other delicacies ("How can I tell the viewers what it tastes like if I can't eat it?")—but the White House chef mysteriously turned her down.

One of the more solidly established rituals practiced at White House state dinners is the formal exchange of gifts between the President and his chief guest in the Yellow Oval Room. After the foreign leader and his wife (or her husband, in Britain's case) have been escorted by the President and First Lady up to the private second-floor quarters, the exchange begins. The visitors give the presidential couple usually quite lavish gifts, but ones which they know can't be kept personally. The First Couple in turn give their guests something, also fairly pricy. The guests are allowed to *keep* their gifts.

What led to this strange state of affairs was the perception on Congress's part that government officials are susceptible to being bribed by foreign governments if they're allowed to keep all the largess given to them in the official course of their duties. Accordingly a law was passed in 1966 requiring such officials—including the President—to turn over to the General Services Administration (GSA) all gifts with a value in excess of $50. The law was amended in 1977, upping the limit to $100 (really a net loss with inflation figured in) and providing for a $10,000 fine for anyone caught not doing so.

What happens to all these presents? The treasures given to the President and First Lady may be used for the duration of his term and, after he has stepped down, are turned over to the government, later to be put on display in his presidential library. Other government officials' gifts, handled by another branch of the GSA, are treated differently. In 1981, for the first time since the collection began fifteen years earlier, the accumulation of baubles was first offered to various museums and government agencies for display purposes. The law requires that they eventually be put up for public auction, but only after they have been offered back to the original donee for "fair market value." Very few of the donees bought any of "their" gifts back—how many people, after all, really need a silver espresso set complete with incense burner (a gift from Kuwait to Secretary of State William Rogers) or a $25,000 diamond necklace (from the Saudi defense minister to Mrs. Harold Brown, the wife of Jimmy Carter's defense secretary)? The public auction of these gifts is naturally a relatively sensitive issue, but according to the Protocol Department—the people charged with handling the subpresidential largess—"it's made clear to foreign governments that we have no option." In any event, Henry Kissinger (the all-time winner in the number of gifts received) *did* buy back a very nice $4,800 diamond necklace that Pakistan had given to him.

All the Carter gifts are now in the GSA storehouse, awaiting a Carter library for their eventual final resting place. There was a minor agitation when Rosalynn kept a $1,400 four-strand pearl necklace given her by the Friendship Force International, which was incorrectly listed as a gift from a foreign government. The law covers only gifts from such governments, which the Atlanta-based "non-governmental people-to-people organization" isn't. Mrs. Carter had it reclassified when she found the error. "Nonacceptance would," said the White House, "cause embarrassment to the donor."

As for the state gifts given in the name of the American people to foreign leaders and other dignitaries, gifts usually personally chosen by the President and First Lady, Steuben glass of New York has been a favorite since Harry and Bess Truman sent a magnificent engraved crystal bowl to Princess Elizabeth when she married in 1947; the Nixons later sent Princess Anne a gift of Steuben—four candleholders with gold cups and a flared bowl supported by four gold eagles on a malachite base—for her 1973 wedding. The British royal family was again enriched with Steuben when the Prince of Wales married Lady Diana Spencer in July 1981. This time, designer Zevi Blum and engraver Roland Erlacher created an elliptical crystal bowl surmounted by a carved arcade of Richard Lion-Heart and seventy of his nobles preparing to disembark on their rampage through the Middle East. "It is," notes the company, "limited to a single example."

IV

Presidential Outposts

BLAIR HOUSE
CAMP DAVID • OLD EOB

Camp David is the best thing about the White House.
BETTY FORD

UNTIL FRANKLIN ROOSEVELT'S ERA and its enormous increase in both the size of the executive establishment and the lavishness of presidential perquisites, the functions filled by Blair House, Camp David, and the Old Executive Office Building were met by the White House itself: Visitors—state and official guests—stayed on the second floor, Presidents routinely spent their weekends at home, and business functions were carried out in the West Wing. The modern presidency has long since outgrown such limitations. To lodge the nation's highest-ranking guests and their entourages, to provide a constantly spotlit President with respite from the glare, and to house the overflow from the exploding White House staff, these three presidential outposts were made a part of the executive institution. None is open to the public; rarely are they even described. All, however, are fascinating extensions of presidential pomp, privilege, grandeur, and power.

BLAIR HOUSE

If you cross the street directly in front of the White House, turn left, and walk a few dozen feet to 1651 Pennsylvania Avenue, you'll be in front of one of the most extraordinary houses in America. Long before assuming its present role, it was the setting for exceptional men and history-making events, a salon frequented by Presidents, and a window on the cockpit of government from nearly the beginning of the capital's history. Before it came into the possession of the federal government in 1942, Blair House had been visited by six Presidents and fourteen Vice Presidents and had at various times been the home of another President, a postmaster general, and six Cabinet officers. Today it is a splendid (if somewhat frayed at the edges) repository of some of the finest American art and furniture, in terms of beauty and history a fitting and harmonious extension to the executive mansion of which it serves as the state guesthouse.

The only thing daunting about climbing the few steps under a canvas canopy to ring the front bell is knowing the significance of the house you're about to enter. There's nothing to stop a stranger from going up to the gate and ringing the bell; presumably it won't be opened unless the caller has a likely-looking appearance and is expected. The security arrangements are subtle but more than adequate to protect the building from any untoward behavior.

The front of Blair House, a neat but ordinary four-story row house flanked by two similar buildings, is anything but prepossessing. Affixed to the black wrought-iron fence are five plaques, four explaining the nature and giving a bit of the history of the house, the fifth memorializing a man who died there thirty years ago in an incident that might have turned into a national tragedy.

Although the black and white marble parquet-floored entry hall is a small space, without a staircase, it has a tone that is quiet, unpretentious, private, and historic—an accurate preview of the rest of the house. The housekeeper shows the visitor into a nearby small waiting room, called the Lincoln Room. In what is probably the most historic room in Blair House, one's eyes easily wander over the Victorian furniture and wonderful old Civil War era lithographs and political cartoons lining the walls. Facing each other from opposite sides of the room are an oil painting of Robert E. Lee and the famous "beardless" portrait of Abraham Lincoln, signifying one of the most poignant encounters in the country's history, a meeting that took place in this room twelve decades ago.

The history of the house considerably antedates that Civil War eve meeting. What is today simply called Blair House is really three adjoined structures: the original Blair House, the Lee House on the west at 1653 Pennsylvania Avenue, and the much larger house on the corner to the east with its main entrance on Jackson Place facing Lafayette Park. Blair House itself was built in 1824 and thus for five years looked across the avenue at an austere White House still without its north portico. Built by Dr. Joseph Lovell (already a fourth-generation Harvard alumnus and later the first surgeon general of the Army), who had bought the lot in 1818 from Stephen Decatur, the two-story dwelling immediately became a social magnet in the raw capital, then with its wealthiest citizens living around Lafayette Park. The house was often used as a rendezvous by Andrew Jackson's kitchen cabinet. In 1836 it was sold on Lovell's death for $6,500 to Francis Blair, a former Kentuckian and the editor of the Washington *Globe*, the organ of the Jackson administration. Two more stories would be added by the next two generations of Blairs, the family that continued to occupy the house for a century.

The Lee House next door, finished two years before the Civil War began, was built to resemble the Federal-style Blair House rather than in the then popular and overornamented Victorian style. The house was Francis Blair's gift to his daughter Elizabeth, who had married Samuel Phillips Lee, a member of the

Stratford branch of the famous Lees of Virginia. Blair's new son-in-law was an admiral in the U.S. Navy and would soon leave to fight in the coming conflict. During his and his wife's wartime absence Andrew Johnson rented the house for a short time near the end of his vice presidency; he waited there during his first days as President for the widowed Mary Lincoln to vacate the White House.

Six days after Fort Sumter was fired on by southern secessionists, Robert E. Lee was called to Blair House from his pillared mansion across the Potomac in Arlington Heights. Colonel Lee was a distant cousin of Blair's son-in-law and one of the most respected officers in the U.S. Army; Lincoln wanted to offer the colonel the command of the Union Army to put down the southern insurrection. Francis Blair's son Montgomery, a close friend in whom Lincoln had great trust, communicated the offer for the President in the small room off the entry hall of Blair House. Lee's answer, which must have given great pain to a man who loved his country as much as he did, was to decline because of a greater love for his native Virginia, one of the seceding states. That afternoon Robert E. Lee rode across the river to Arlington for the last time, and in the night he left for Richmond, never to see his Arlington home again.

After the war the two houses continued to be centers of Washington's social life. Samuel and Elizabeth Lee's son, Blair Lee, a United State senator from Maryland, inherited Lee House and lived there until the federal government bought it—unfurnished, for a little more than $130,000—in December 1941. Meanwhile, Blair House, which Francis had given to his son Montgomery (who built the third floor) in 1853, was in turn inherited by Montgomery's son, Gist (who added the fourth floor). He was to live there all his life. At Gist's death the house was sold by the family to the government for $125,000, furnishings included. On October 29, 1942, the two houses became the official government guest quarters, passing into the permanent possession of the nation.

The Blair-Lee House was to become the first official home of President Truman, who lived there for several weeks following Franklin Roosevelt's death in April 1945, waiting for his predecessor's widow to vacate the White House. Three and a half years later the two houses were physically joined, with doors cut through at each level, enabling the combined residence to serve as the de facto executive mansion for a considerably longer period—from November 1948 until March 1952. (Prospect House, Navy Secretary James Forrestal's Georgetown home during World War II, was leased by the government and served as the temporary presidential guesthouse during these years.) It was in November 1950 that Truman was attacked by two Puerto Rican nationalists while he was living in the temporary residence. In the mid-1960s the third structure now forming part of the Blair House complex (bringing the total number of rooms to one hundred fifteen, encompassing forty-five thousand square feet of floor space) was purchased; the Jackson Place annex had for many years housed the Carnegie Endowment for International Peace. Even today it's not generally realized that this red-brick, typically Victorian building is part of the presidential guest complex.

Juliette Clagett McLennan: related to two of Washington's oldest and most socially prominent families, divorced with two children, a tall, striking woman who wears her blond hair arranged in a casual ponytail—is manager of Blair House. As you sit talking with her in the historic little Lincoln Room, your first thought might be how completely *American* she must seem to the endless parade of foreign dignitaries whose comfort and well-being are the absolute primary responsibility of her unique job. McLennan, a native Washingtonian—a minor distinction in the heavily transient city—is a member of the Clagett family of long-standing residence in the District; her mother was a Leiter, another name of some moment in the city. McLennan is offhand about her social connections: in reference to the relative antiquity of her socially rooted forebears, she says, "Being here first doesn't make them better." Working with press aide Jim Brady and his wife on the Reagan campaign made her known to the incoming administration, and her own social verve and background made her a candidate for the high-prestige and high-visibility job.

Judy McLennan's first day as manager of Blair House was something in the nature of a baptism under fire. It was March 30, 1981, and she had just flown back to Washington from a vacation, preparing to start her new job the following day. Instead, she was met at the airport with news of the assassination attempt earlier in the afternoon. In an understandably agitated state she was asked to go to Blair House immediately to take over receiving the Dutch prime minister, who had just arrived for an official visit. She got to the presidential guesthouse at ten fifty that night and, together with Vice President George Bush, accorded the Dutch visitor all the normal honors and attention due his rank—even in the absence of the President and the rest of the preoccupied White House staff. She now says of the episode, "I just had to pull through and do it—there wasn't any question."

Blair House is funded and run by the State Department's Protocol Division, and its official boss is the chief of protocol. Besides McLennan, the house employs an assistant manager, a housekeeper, two chambermaids, three housemen, a cook, and a laundress. (These rather quaint job titles seem somehow appropriate in the historic setting.) The General Services Administration maintains the complex, which is officially called the President's Guest House. Its use is authorized for heads of state and heads of government on state and official visits or on private working visits if a meeting with the President is scheduled. Cabinet-rank officers may request use of Blair House's facilities for functions which "help to promote United States foreign policy" (a secretary of commerce, for example, giving a dinner in honor of a visiting secretary or minister of commerce); when it is not occupied by foreign guests, Cabinet wives may use it for official entertaining of foreign visitors. The President can presumably add to these authorized categories. (The chief of protocol normally has final say on who gets to use Blair House.)

Blair House may also serve as the President-elect's local residence between election day and inauguration day. This latter role put the place squarely in the headlines after President-Elect and Mrs. Reagan stayed there before his inauguration. It was reported in "Ear," *The Washington Post* gossip column, that the

Carter people had bugged Blair House with hidden microphones during the Reagan stay and that this was the source of the story that Nancy Reagan had wished aloud that "the Carters would leave the White House early" so she could get in and start redecorating. Carter threatened to sue the paper unless the story was retracted and an apology made in print. Both were grudgingly done by the *Post*, and the former President dropped his plans for the suit.

On a tour of Blair House it's evident that there are three different houses connected to one another because of the change in moldings and ceilings and the duplication of the rooms, but the integration has been skillfully handled so as not to give visitors any sense of being in a misjoined patchwork. The arches and entryways between the rooms flow gracefully, and one is far more conscious of the sumptuousness of the house's contents than of its original status as separate buildings. Fortunately the floors of the Blair and Lee houses were level with each other, so no ramps or steps were necessary when they were joined. The Jackson Place addition doesn't really function equally with the rest of the house, partly because of its orientation to another street; it is reached by a long corridor, and its main entrance faces Lafayette Park rather than Pennsylvania Avenue.

The first floor of the original Blair House is made up of the entry hall, the small receiving room (the Lincoln Room), a spacious double drawing room, and a dining room. One of the many historic treasures in the front drawing room is a portrait of Alexander Baring, first Baron Ashburton, the British minister to Washington responsible for the treaty which settled the U.S.-Canadian boundary line in 1842. (The concord was signed in his home on the other side of Lafayette Park, now the rectory for St. John's Episcopal Church, the "Church of the Presidents.") Both drawing rooms are elegantly decorated with early American Federal-style furniture. To ensure the continued historical authenticity of the contents of these rooms, a professional curator, Mrs. Edward Stone, has been assigned by the White House curator's office the function of overseeing the furnishings and decoration.

The Blair dining room is called the Roosevelt Room; its table, stocked with finger sandwiches, cookies, tea, coffee, candy, and nuts, serves as a twenty-four-hour refreshment buffet during state visits. When official visitors are expected, the magnificent Blair silver is put on display. The day of my visit, the Thai ambassador was coming to discuss the arrangements for the upcoming official visit of his country's prime minister, and a large selection of the coffee and tea services, bonbon dishes, candlesticks, and tankards was gleaming handsomely against the highly polished mahogany table.

On the first floor the Blair and Lee sides join in their respective front drawing rooms. In what is called the Green Room on the Lee side, the camelback sofa, armchairs, and antique hand-painted Chinese wallpaper all are in soft shades of green. The Lee rooms have a slightly more Victorian cast than the earlier Federal-style Blair rooms. Photo opportunities for the press are given in the Green Room by most of the heads of state who stay as guests in the house.

Off the rear Lee drawing room are French doors leading onto a small private garden. Before Blair House had air conditioning installed in the 1950s, much of the summer entertaining was done here. Now the garden is overshadowed by the high-rise New Executive Office Building facing the Seventeenth Street side of the block.

The Lee dining room, bigger than its Blair counterpart, serves as the official formal dining room for the ranking members of the visiting delegation, including the "principal guest," as the delegation's head is called. The President sometimes attends small dinners with his visiting guests here in an informal setting relatively free from the constraints of White House state dinners; the secretary of state may be present on these occasions, and much of the real business of the visits is conducted around the table. The Chinese export china is original to the house. Lyndon Johnson's Cabinet members' wives made the grape-leaf-pattern needlepointed seats for the chairs.

The last of the ground-floor Lee rooms is a small study, corresponding to the Lincoln Room on the Blair side. Truman used the room as an office during his three-and-a-half-year tenancy.

More recently Menachem Begin filmed a television interview in it for the Israeli press.

The other end of Blair House—the Jackson Place extension—has a more workaday flavor than the Blair-Lee section. Off the long passage connecting it with the main part of the complex is a plain little room used by the Secret Service as its command post during state visits, during which times, McLennan said, it is usually jammed to bursting with security men and their apparatus. The principal Jackson Place ground-floor room now serves as the press room, a long Victorian double parlor where heads of state met with the open press before this increasingly chaotic practice was recently brought to a halt; Anwar Sadat held the last such press conference there. Today more controlled and genteel meetings with groups of editors have replaced the free-for-all press sessions.

The Jackson Place dining room is where meals are served to the nonranking members of the visiting delegation, as well as to our own Secret Service and protocol people. The table was a gift from Judy McLennan's parents, one used at her family home when she was growing up. "It gives me," the manager says, "a feeling of personal attachment to the house."

Running nearly the full length of the basement is a long kitchen-pantry, where nearly all meals for official guests are cooked. (Only kosher food—that served to Israeli visitors—is catered.) The Minton china filling the cupboards was a gift to the house from the Leiter family, McLennan's grandparents. A walk-in silver vault is at the east end of the pantry.

Upstairs are the private quarters for the principal guests, with the splendid Blair library a part of the head of state's suite. The library is used for high-level private conferences between visiting delegations and top American officials. Its deep cherry paneling and twelve-armed chandelier overlook a dark-red Savonnérie carpet made especially for the room. White bookshelves cover the walls below the red paneling.

There are two main bedroom suites. The head of state's bedroom is decorated with Eisenhower memorabilia, including the chair from the late President's West Point bedroom and an odd bedspread painted with scenes from his life. Next door is the more luxurious bedroom generally used by the wives of heads of state. Two other nearby suites are available for the members of the principal guest's entourage whom he wishes to have closest at hand during the visit. Eleven more bedrooms on the third and fourth floors are reserved for members of the official delegation.

Life for state visitors is made exceedingly pleasant during their stays at Blair House. The staff, whose main purpose is "to demonstrate the best and warmest American hospitality, down to the finest details," coddles them to whatever degree demanded. McLennan said that the smallest flaw can have an effect on the attitude of high-ranking foreign visitors in the conduct of their official talks—"the President or prime minister shouldn't have any nagging little unpleasantries on their minds." Exact dietary requirements are obtained from the visitor's embassy so toast can be made just so or eggs boiled rather than scrambled if that's how the guests want them.

Security arrangements are a somewhat more complex matter. The Secret Service provides the primary protection for the visiting head of state, but all sorts of additional security agencies get involved. The State Department's security people guard not only the visitor's spouse but also the foreign secretary if he's accompanying his boss. The Uniformed Secret Service is responsible for outside perimeter guard duty. If the chief guest's motorcade goes around Lafayette Park, the Park Service Police get in the act. The Metropolitan (District of Columbia) Police are in evidence pretty much everywhere else the visitors will go while they're in Washington. Of limited help to our legions of security forces is the large number of the head of state's own guards (necessary, however, since our President takes *his* own security people along when he goes abroad). The sidewalk along the entire block in front of Blair House is cleared of spectators during the visit, a move which automatically takes care of any nettlesome demonstrators; even on the other side of the avenue no buildup of pedestrians is allowed during the arrivals and departures of the visitors, times when long lines of sleek black limousines are generated in front of Blair House's marquee. Ordinary automobile traffic on Pennsylvania Avenue is still allowed, but it is anticipated that soon only buses will be permitted to pass in front of the house when it is occupied by state guests.

In mid-1982, the complex was temporarily closed after being declared a "safety hazard" for dangers ranging from falling light fixtures to a boiler that was close to exploding. Renovation plans include new wiring, heating, and air-conditioning systems, as well as improved security arrangements. Official guests are being housed elsewhere in the District while the repairs are made. The work is expected to be completed in late 1983.

Blair House may not represent the same scale of imperial luxe many of its official guests are used to at home, but the unpretentiously handsome house splendidly reflects the best of America's heritage as well as its warmest hospitality. Its unique purpose is well met.

CAMP DAVID

In what was her only memorable public statement, Tricia Nixon Cox best summed up the place she used as her honeymoon retreat: "It's like a resort hotel where you are the only guests." The object of her affection, Camp David, is a misnomer, though—there's very little camplike about it anymore. It's strictly first-class luxury plopped down on a mountaintop in the wildest part of north-central Maryland. The "cabins" are beautiful houses, the privacy is absolute, and the ambience suggests what it really is—the world's most genuinely exclusive resort.

Presidents have tried to escape Washington almost as long as the city has been in existence. The first to establish a permanent close-by escape hatch from the capital's miserable summer weather in general and the White House's swamplike setting in particular was Grover Cleveland. Restricted by the primitive transportation of the day and the need to be back to the office on Monday mornings, he could get only as far as the heights above Georgetown, today considered a close-in neighborhood. Still, it was several blessed degrees cooler than the edge of Foggy Bottom, where the White House sat scorching in the insect-bedeviled summers.

Herbert Hoover was able to acquire something more rustic and removed—a semiauthentic camp named for its location at the headwaters of Virginia's Rapidan River. The 164-acre hideaway, today renamed Camp Hoover in his honor and used as a weekend retreat by high-ranking federal officials (Walter Mondale was reported to be very fond of it, spending a number of weekends there with his family), was where Hoover met with Britain's Prime Minister Ramsay MacDonald to hammer out a naval treaty together.

Franklin Roosevelt spent one weekend at Camp Rapidan and then wouldn't have anything more to do with it; officials consequently began looking for a permanent nearby vacation spot more to the President's liking. Three locations were thought appropriate—two in Maryland and one in Virginia. In 1942 FDR himself chose what was to become today's Camp David.

Built in 1939 by the Civilian Conservation Corps and the Works Progress Administration and named Camp Hi-Catoctin after the 1,850-foot-high mountain on which it perches, it was conveniently near the White House—seventy miles, two hours by car—for the President to get away to quickly and quietly. Called Shangri-la by Roosevelt for the mythical Himalayan utopia in James Hilton's then popular novel Lost Horizon, it was at first pretty ramshackle by presidential standards. But Franklin Roosevelt genuinely enjoyed what he considered getting back to nature, or as close as any President can get, and the chief executive slept on a plain iron bed in a tiny bedroom the connecting bathroom door of which would never completely close. The President conducted much of the planning for World War II at his Shangri-la, often (five times) in the company of the British prime minister and his cogeneralissimo, Winston Churchill.

Harry Truman didn't much care for the place, possibly influenced by his daughter Margaret's active distaste for roughing it. But Eisenhower spent a considerable part of his presidency there, especially after his second heart attack. He and Mamie fixed it up in high-fifties taste and surroundings—backyard barbecues, a large flagstone terrace, lots of rattan furniture, and, of course, a putting green. The couple renamed it for their five-year-old grandson, and the President's political talks with Nikita Khrushchev in the seclusion of the retreat became popularly known as the Spirit of Camp David. (Ike said privately they were just good "bull sessions.")

Shortly before he was murdered, John Kennedy came to appreciate Camp David, something he hadn't done in the early part of his White House years. He and his wife were building their own luxurious hideaway called Atoka, near Middleburg in the Virginia horse country, but the President later concluded it was a waste of money when he had Camp David "for free." When Kennedy's successor, Lyndon Johnson, wasn't at his ranch, he preferred spending weekends where the action was—in the White House. As a consequence, he and Lady Bird were infrequent Camp David visitors.

The retreat stopped being in any way rustic and started resembling a full-fledged resort when Richard Nixon took a hankering to it after realizing what a wonderful place it was in which to escape the press. What has been called his sanctuary from reality took on ominous overtones and an air of mystery during his many visits there. More than any other chief executive, Nixon used Camp David as a refuge, making 120 trips to it during his five and a half years as President. He sometimes stayed as long as two weeks at a time, completely out of sight of the public and the press. His successor, Gerald Ford, wasn't nearly as enamored with it and stayed there relatively few times. Jimmy Carter, however, spent a majority of his presidential weekends at Camp David, finding it—like Richard Nixon—a tempting escape from the difficulties of life in the White House fishbowl. The major success of his administration—the accords between Israel and Egypt—was carried out at Camp David, with himself, Menachem Begin, and Anwar Sadat the chief players in the very-high-stakes game. Ronald Reagan is following in Carter's footsteps, spending almost all his free weekends at the retreat. The present First Couple's idea of a big time is to gather around the piano in the presidential cabin with close friends and sing old Broadway and Hollywood show tunes.

Where Franklin Roosevelt was driven in a two-hour car trip, modern Presidents can now helicopter the seventy miles between the White House south lawn and the landing pad at

Camp David in thirty minutes. Once they get there, they enter a vastly different world—not more luxurious than the White House but possessed of the greatest indulgence and rarest commodity for a chief executive and his family: privacy. Set in the middle of the 6,000-acre Catoctin Mountain Park northwest of Washington, the 143 acres of presidential grounds are surrounded by a razor-sharp barbed-wire double-steel fence inside a cleared no-man's-land strip, guarded by handpicked marines as well as Secret Service agents who periodically stage mock penetration exercises to test the defenses. It is further protected by sirens, spotlights, and radar and endowed with a massive air-raid shelter sunk 100 feet into the mountaintop, accessible by an elevator and designed to be the President's command post if Armageddon comes when he's at Camp David. A White House aide made an apt comparison: "It's the nearest thing in this country to a medieval castle and moat with foot guards."

The rough little cabin that served Roosevelt has grown into what is today called Aspen Lodge (all the buildings at Camp David are named after trees), an elegant building with four bedroom suites, a massive stone fireplace (in which Nixon kept a fire going even in the summer), and extensive oak paneling covering the walls. The living-room window has a magnificent panoramic view across the Catoctin Mountains, but one which can't be reciprocated—the house is blended in so perfectly with its setting that even high-powered telescopes can't penetrate its privacy. The ten other residential structures—with names like Birch Lodge (used by Nixon as an office) and Linden—all with fireplaces and bedroom suites, have hosted more than twenty heads of state. Two were specially enlarged for the Nixon daughters and their husbands.

Maintained by the National Park Service but operated by the Navy and staffed by about 100 Navy and Marine personnel, Camp David has recreational facilities that put Grossinger's in the shade: a sauna, two clay tennis courts, a one-hole three-tee golf course, a two-lane bowling alley, a stocked trout stream, skeet shooting, an archery range, badminton courts, movies—if it isn't there, it'll be installed. A free-form pool on the terrace below Aspen Lodge was put in by the Nixons; another of his innovations was a voice-activated tape-recording system in the presidential cabin.

The Navy mess can't compete with the White House kitchens, but it manages very nicely. First Families often spend the holidays at Camp David, digging into splendid Navy-prepared turkey dinners. The presidential garbage is hauled thirty miles away to a landfill.

There are all sorts of perks available to the President and his guests at the compound. An in-camp limousine service shuttles notables back and forth between buildings. Highly coveted jackets with sewn-on presidential emblems are provided to the guests. Golf carts are used for tooling around, except when it's snowing and the snowmobiles, sleds, and toboggans are brought out. Ronald Reagan has put his mark on the place: a stable designed to house eight horses in a fair amount of comfort. The National Park Service has reestablished several new riding trails which Nixon had paved over for his golf carts for the President and his guests' gratification.

Camp David is probably the most pleasant gift of the American taxpayer to the President. It costs millions of dollars each year to operate—an amount buried deeply in the federal budget —but its redeeming feature is that it serves as a legitimate retreat from the world's most intense job scrutiny. Only when the President uses it to elude reality has it carried less than desirable implications.

OLD EOB

His intention probably wasn't to do any favors for the staffers in the Old EOB, but Richard Nixon's little working office there did tend to alleviate their collective inferiority complex. The central definition of power in the executive establishment is influence with the President, which is usually synonymous with nearness to the person of the President. The result in most cases is that the occupant of the smallest cubicle in the West Wing takes power precedence over the holder of the most lavish suite in the other two Executive Office buildings. (Onetime White

House staffer and now Senator Daniel Moynihan chose a tiny West Wing cubbyhole over a large suite in the Old EOB on the ground that it meant he "could piss standing next to Haldeman in the same toilet," a succinct appraisal of White House territorial power gradations.) In his peripatetic wanderings Nixon became enamored of his little working office in the great gray Victorian pile a few hundred feet from his West Wing office. Every Wednesday was his private day there. No meetings, no photo opportunities, presumably no tape recorders—just him, thinking and writing, all the while lending invaluable cachet to all his junior aides in the neighboring offices who represented the overflow from the West Wing.

The object of the President's affection has been the recipient of first great admiration, later general derision, and today nostalgic sentimentality. Although the EOB is sadly sealed tightly to the public, which was allowed to wander freely through it until World War II, this reminder of a less threatening time, once the proud headquarters of three senior federal departments, is now a dowdy, slightly seedy annex to the real incubator of power next door in the West Wing.

Formally called the Old Executive Office Building—usually abbreviated to simply the EOB (the new EOB is a modern high rise around the corner behind Blair House)—it began its career in far grander circumstances than its current status would betoken. Construction of the new State, War, and Navy Building started in 1871, during the postbellum rococo-flavored administration of Ulysses S. Grant. Replacing the earlier buildings which had housed the three departments on the site immediately to the west of the White House grounds, it was the world's largest office building when it was finished, a status it maintained for many years. It possessed two and a half acres of corridors stretching two miles, 550 rooms, 6,000 gas jets lighting the ornate marble-walled offices and six grand spiraling staircases lit by fixtures weighing 800 pounds each—nothing had been done in half measures. The south wing, the first completed, was originally the State Department; soon thereafter the east wing was finished for the Navy, and the War Department moved into the north wing. The west wing—along Seventeenth Street—was the last to be completed. It's still possible to identify which rooms were assigned to the three departments; their respective emblems were molded onto the bronze doorknobs.

Thousands of visitors came to see the splendid new office palace, in its first decades a prime Washington tourist attraction. Baedeker gave the place one of his coveted stars in his guidebook, helpfully noting for the British traveler that "the State Department corresponds to the Foreign Office in London." One of the attractions leading to the granting of the star was the Declaration of Independence, exhibited in the State Department Library until 1921. Another showstopper was the marvelous staircases; sadly two people tumbled to their deaths over the low marble banisters, so bronze railings were added to prevent further mishaps. The ostentatious building wasn't, however, universally popular; when told it was fireproof, General William Sherman cattily remarked, "What a pity."

As early as 1917 there was agitation to do away with what had by then become a relic. It was suggested that it be shrouded in a tidy classical style so as to match the formal (albeit lifeless) Treasury Building in the corresponding position on the eastern border of the White House grounds. The Depression came in time to save it, and the building managed to make it through that crisis intact. In July 1930, by act of Congress, it had been renamed the Department of State Building, reflecting the move of the other two departments to their own building. By 1949 the State Department, too, had moved out, and it was renamed the Executive Office Building when the White House took it over completely to house its overflow. In 1957 a new bureaucratic menace, the President's Advisory Commission on Presidential Office Space, recommended tearing it down and putting up a glass and steel box in its stead. That was probably the last serious threat to the building's existence; now it has "beloved" status.

According to the Reagan people, the economizing of the Carter crew is the reason the building has gone to seed. The grim and gray corridors, semilit by undersized light bulbs, strands of loose wiring tacked along the walls, chipped plaster, and the ugly security arrangements—railings and desks manned by guards blocking ground-floor junctions—make the place a prime candidate for a little Reagan beautification.

The glory of the Old EOB is the grand proportions of its offices, an almost extinct luxury today. Regardless of the status implications involved, the spacious and airy high-ceilinged corner suites in the building can assuage a considerable amount of bruised political sensitivities for not being in the West Wing. The Vice President maintains a large suite on the second floor (although his "primary" office is in the West Wing), following a tradition started by Lyndon Johnson as the first sitting Vice President to use it. The White House mail room is in the basement; every one of the 4,500,000 pieces of correspondence received by the White House each year is handled by the fifty-eight employees under the direction of the special assistant to the President for correspondence, Anne Higgins. (Only about 100 letters a week actually reach the Oval Office.) Higgins's staff is also responsible for the White House switchboard, located in a carefully guarded room in the basement; the phone center's twenty operators handle an average of 1,000 calls daily. The National Security Council and David Stockman's Office of Budget and Management are also housed in the building, as is the First Family's small two-lane bowling alley and a physical-fitness room open to a few dozen high-ranking (deputy assistant and above) presidential advisers.

Probably safe from urban planning tinkerers (unless it collapses of its own accord in the meantime), the Old EOB as architecture is still evocative of the country's flamboyant young adulthood and with care and restoration could as well be a proud part of the nation's wiser maturity. Would that some social elixir were found to permit its reopening to the ordinary citizens its occupants are attempting to govern.

V

Presidential Understudy

THE VICE PRESIDENCY

Th' prisidincy is th' highest office in th' gift iv th' people.
Th' vice-prisidincy is th' next highest and th' lowest.

FINLEY PETER DUNNE

CONTRARY TO POPULAR NOTION throughout much of the Republic's history, the honor of the office of the vice presidency is certainly not an empty one, although a few of its holders have seemingly been less than respectful of that honor. Even in recent decades vice presidential probity hasn't been something that could necessarily be taken for granted. For example, Henry Wallace, Franklin Roosevelt's second Vice President and a man who missed inheriting the highest office by only a few weeks, started his incumbency tolerably enough, but his performance later became such an embarrassment to the President that he was forced off the ticket in FDR's fourth run for the White House. His predecessor, John "Cactus Jack" Garner, is remembered for only one statement, the repulsive observation that the "vice presidency isn't worth a pitcher of warm spit." Richard Nixon, our last full two-term Vice President, filled his eight years relatively capably but later disgraced himself and whatever residual honor might have remained from those years. For undiluted venality, few officeholders at such high level in the country's history can top Spiro Agnew's staggering betrayal of the public trust.

This state of affairs has, fortunately, taken a brighter turn with the last four Vice Presidents. Gerald Ford wasn't in the office long enough to do anything especially memorable, and his own Vice President and successor, Nelson Rockefeller, isn't even generally remembered for *being* Vice President so closely is he identified with the New York governorship and with his even greater position as a result of his name and leadership in America's most affluent family. But the last two incumbents have brought to their office genuine stature—and even a limited measure of substantive power.

The relationships of Walter "Fritz" Mondale to Jimmy Carter and George Bush to Ronald Reagan have had many similarities. Both have been central figures in their respective administrations, enjoying an extraordinary degree (by historical standards) of presidential trust, and each has been brought forward to stand next to the President in terms of authority as well as the formalities of precedence. Jimmy Carter was the first President to give his Vice President an office in the West Wing as a symbol of that authority; now George Bush considers his large first-floor West Wing quarters—with Ed Meese and Jim Baker on either side—to be his principal office of the three assigned to him.

Though in the final analysis the duties of the vice presidency have to be seen as more formal and ceremonial than politically consequential, Bush performs one service for the President that can be measured in precise political terms: In his first year as Vice President, he was the principal speaker at dozens of Republican fund-raising luncheons and dinners, raising more than $3,000,000—all the while picking up valuable IOUs along the way for his own eventual expected run for the presidency. Bush not only meets with Reagan once a week to give and take advice over lunch but has one of the rarest privileges any President can bestow: unlimited access to the Oval Office, a liberty the Vice President doesn't hesitate to use.

Constitutionally the Vice President has two formal roles. The first is to serve as president of the United States Senate, a function only infrequently carried out in practice (and a job so minor that it is assigned to the most junior senators when the Vice President isn't acting as the Senate's presiding officer); the second, far more potentially important, of course, is to be the successor to the President in case of his death, resignation, or "disability"—the latter now controlled by the Twenty-fifth Amendment to the Constitution. Other than these functions, his role is precisely what the President wishes it to be; the Constitution provides no further job description.

Of all the Vice President's offices, his most splendid quarters are in the Capitol. The formal office, behind the Senate chamber, is a rococo confection with a Volkswagen-size seven-tiered crystal chandelier which once hung in the White House; in this room Chester Arthur took the presidential oath when James Garfield died and Vice President Henry Wilson died from a "congestive chill" after bathing in the Senate bathhouse. A few yards away, in the northeast corner of the building, is the Vice President's other, less formal Senate office. Both are, in a sense, ceremonial in that neither is used on a daily workaday basis, although the corner office serves as his *pied-à-terre* when he makes his intermittent visits to the Hill. (On rare occasions his presence in the Senate chamber may be crucial; the Vice President's vote, cast, it goes without saying, in the administration's favor, can be used to break a tie.) His most important job in the legislature is to serve as a lobbyist for the President, one former Congressman George Bush has performed with distinction for Reagan.

The primary constitutional reason for the existence of the vice presidency—serving as the President's successor or substitute if he can't fulfill his term for whatever cause—has been further defined in the Twenty-fifth Amendment, ratified in 1967. The proviso was designed to avoid a repeat of the kind of situation in which Woodrow Wilson lay paralyzed with a stroke for the final eighteen months of his second term and in which there were no legal means to resolve the impasse short of the President's resigning, which Wilson refused to do.

As far as the succession is concerned, there is no question when the President dies or resigns. The Vice President succeeds to the presidency, and that's that; he can then name his own Vice President, subject only to confirmation by a majority of the House and Senate. If both the presidency and vice presidency are vacant at the same time, there would go into effect the 1947 law which puts the speaker of the house (today Massachusetts Democrat Thomas "Tip" O'Neill) next in succession, followed by the Senate president pro tempore (currently South Carolina Republican Strom Thurmond), and members of the Cabinet in the order their departments were created—State, Treasury, Defense, Justice, Interior, Agriculture, Commerce, Labor, Health and Human Services, Housing and Urban Development, Transportation, Energy, Education.

The Twenty-fifth Amendment comes into force if the President should become "unable" to carry out his duties. In the event that it's the President himself who declares—in writing—his disability, the Vice President becomes Acting President without further ado. When the declaration is rescinded, the two return to their former positions. But if the President should be too sick (or, God forbid, too loony) to make such a declaration, matters could get sticky. In such an event, when the Vice President together with "a majority of either the principal officers of the executive departments [the Cabinet] or of such other body as Congress may by law provide" transmits to Congress in writing that the President is out of it, the Vice President then immediately becomes Acting President. Potential for real conflict lies in the final provision of the amendment, which deals with the President's getting his office back. He resumes the presidency upon written notice to Congress *unless* the Vice President (now Acting President) and the same group that declared him unfit decide to fight him. Congress then decides the issue, and must do so within twenty-one days; if two-thirds of each house still think he's unfit, the Vice President continues as Acting President. It would require evil men to thwart the honorable intent of the amendment, but the scenario is nevertheless one with the potential to keep the federal government in thrall for a dangerous period.

The office of the vice presidency has developed a sizable bureaucracy of its own. George Bush's staff now stands at fifty-seven employees (10 percent less than Mondale's, as the administration enjoys pointing out) on both the Senate and executive payrolls (the Vice President is the only federal officer with duties in more than one branch of government). Officially headquartered in the Old Executive Office Building, it is headed by retired Admiral Daniel Murphy as chief of staff and Richard Bond as deputy chief of staff, names which would loom large if George Bush were ever to become President. His other top aides have titles which pretty much match those on the President's staff—Assistant to the Vice President (press, appointments and scheduling, domestic policy, and so on) and Deputy Assistant (national security affairs, legal, administration, etc.). Among the aides there is even a personal photographer to the Vice President.

The staff member most concerned with the vice presidential social agenda is Susan Porter Rose, officially titled Chief of Staff to Mrs. Bush. Her large beige and white Victorian office on the second floor of the Old EOB looks across West Executive Avenue to the roof of the West Wing and to the Palladian windows at the end of the mansion's West Sitting Hall. The day of our visit was a somber one—Anwar Sadat had been murdered that morning, and we could see President and Mrs. Reagan publicly offering the nation's condolences from the north portico. Ed Meese and Caspar Weinberger were hurrying down the corridor outside Rose's office, obviously preoccupied with the day's portentous tragedy in Cairo. It seemed an inauspicious time to discuss the Vice President's social life, but Mrs. Bush's chief spokeswoman was very open and warm in talking about a couple she obviously regards as extraordinary.

The tall, elegant Rose, a Washingtonian for ten years, had worked for both Mrs. Nixon and Mrs. Ford in the White House's East Wing as an appointments secretary. These qualifications and a well-bred poise that is the mark of many of the Reagan administration's ranking aides led to her job on the vice presidential staff. She is the head of the four full-time employees working for the Second Lady, including a personal assistant, a social assistant, and a press secretary. There are also two part-time employees on the staff as well as some intermittent secretarial assistance.

If this seems an overabundant bureaucracy for the wife of the Vice President, consideration should be given to the life the Bushes lead. A primary role filled by any modern Vice President and his wife is serving as the country's second host and hostess. Not only do the Bushes attend most White House state functions, but they carry on their own substantial and hectic social schedule. Some is at the bidding of the White House to relieve the Reagans of a portion of the demands on their entertaining capabilities, but most is generated by the Bushes' own position. The formal vice presidential dinners and receptions follow the same general outline as their presidential counterparts. An example are the reciprocal dinners given in honor of visiting vice presidents. Not officially counted as state visits, most such affairs are "issue-oriented," as Susan Porter Rose describes them, the sort where, for instance, the vice president of Mexico might visit to discuss a "subpresidential" matter.

The Vice President receives $60,000 a year in "representational funds," a euphemism for an entertainment allowance. But when entertaining foreign officials—a very large chunk of the schedule —he can send the bills to the State Department. Even so, the $60,000 can be eaten up fairly rapidly, considering that Bush had all 100 senators to dinner in his first few months in office and that numerous societies, charity organizations, and the like are continually asking to be entertained by the Vice President and/or Second Lady. But like Fritz Mondale, the current Vice President is perfectly happy to let such organizations pay for their own canapés, cookies, and punch. Ms. Rose notes, however, that it's "not a criterion for being invited."

After more than a century and a half of the American Second Family's living catch-as-catch-can in Washington—some in surprisingly Spartan apartments (the Trumans), some in fancy hotel rooms (the Agnews), some in sumptuous mansions (the Rockefellers, naturally)—the Vice President of the United States finally has an official residence. It might have come a great deal earlier if it weren't for Warren Harding's wife's small-minded spite. In 1922 Mrs. John B. Henderson offered to sell cheaply her Sixteenth Street mansion (today the Spanish Embassy) to the government to serve as the official vice presidential residence, but Florence Harding wasn't about to have whom she considered the "upstart" Coolidges living in anything rivaling the White House. So that golden opportunity came and went.

Because until comparatively recent years the vice presidency was considered something in the nature of an honorary office, little more thought was given to finding an official residence. Even though of late the Vice President has become far more involved in the administration of government, what really got the ball rolling on a serious search for such a residence was the need for security. The choice of the widely scattered—and relatively indefensible—past vice presidential homes around Washington was dictated largely by personal income. All they had in common was the difficulty in protecting the inhabitants. In 1974 Congress finally found and designated a permanent official home for incumbent Vice Presidents and their families.

About two miles northwest of the White House—across Lafayette Park to Connecticut Avenue, out to Dupont Circle, left on Massachusetts Avenue to Observatory Circle—stands one of the *most* defensible houses in the capital. In 1881 President Hayes wanted the Naval Observatory moved from Foggy Bottom (even then the capital's smog made heavenly observing an on-again, off-again matter) to higher ground. The new location was then an isolated area, "away from the objectionable vibration of traffic." In 1892, for the sum of $20,000, a large white house—solid and sensible—was built in the middle of the twelve-acre observatory grounds. It served for its first thirty-five years as the residence of the observatory superintendents (whose job it was to "maintain continuous observation of the sun, moon, planets and fundamental stars for the determination of absolute positions"), becoming in 1926 the official home of the

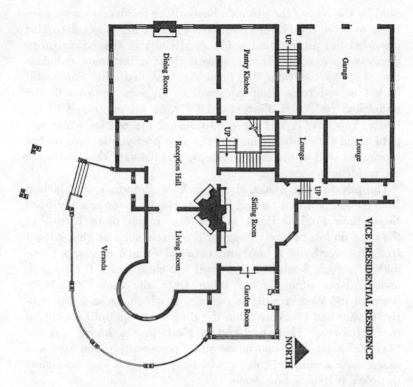

Chief of Naval Operations, the naval representative on the Joint
Chiefs of Staff and the nation's ranking sailor. Admiral's House
would be home to a succession of famous American admirals
and their families, including Chester Nimitz (whose daughter
remembers pitching horseshoes out in the backyard with Harry
and Bess Truman), down to its last naval occupant, Elmo Zum-
walt. (CNOs now live at Tingley House just inside the main
gate of southeast Washington's Old Navy Yard.)

When Admiral's House became the Vice Presidential Residence in 1974, the Gerald Fords were the first family eligible to
occupy it in its new capacity. Congress appropriated $315,000 to
redecorate it, and Betty Ford inherited the task of supervising
the upgrading. Since the house would still be financed and oper-

ated by the Navy (the grounds beyond the residence's lawn continue to serve the Naval Observatory), a young Navy decorator provided the professional guidance. Events in the Nixon presidency were moving rapidly toward their unfortunate culmination, and by the time the President resigned, the Fords still hadn't moved from their Alexandria, Virginia, house into the unfinished residence. Betty Ford left one bit of herself in the house, however; it was she who selected the official white and gold china with cobalt trim and the vice presidential seal on the border, as well as the crystal, linens, and flatware that still serve the residence's occupants.

Happily for the house, the next Vice President was Nelson Rockefeller. Not that he and his wife, Happy, ever actually *lived* there—their Foxhall Road schloss was much more them—but they did do lots of nice things for the place, such as giving it art treasures worthy of a museum: classical French clocks, a Coromandel screen, beautiful rosewood armchairs, and the magnificent Adams dining room table from the New York City home of the Vice President's parents, at which, he said, his family "always had breakfast from the time I was six until I went off to Dartmouth." Their best-known piece in the house was the Max Ernst bed, an enormous affair representing the sun and moon, with a sculpted tree intertwining the brass and mahogany uprights. It is, alas, now gone.

The first vice presidential family to live in the house was the Walter Mondales and their children. Mrs. Mondale, known in Washington as Joan of Art for her untiring efforts to promote the arts—and who served as Jimmy Carter's semiofficial ambassador to the arts—filled the house with original, eclectic, and mostly modern sculpture and paintings. The trouble was that it looked more like a wing of the Whitney Museum than a family home.

The current occupants—George and Barbara Bush—live in the house with only Fred, their aging cocker spaniel. All four Bush sons are married, and their daughter is a college student. By the end of 1981, $200,000 had been privately raised to redecorate the residence. Contributed by eighteen Texas families, all friends of the Bushes, the fund was run by the wife of Midland oilman Earle Craig, Jr., and is being used to refurbish the four first-floor rooms used regularly for official entertaining with items such as new rugs, chairs, sofas, and draperies. The object of the redecoration—to make the house less of a museum and more of a home—has already been largely fulfilled by the Bushes.

The best—actually the only—way for any other than an invited guest to get a good idea of the layout of the sixteen-room Vice Presidential Residence compound is to look at the remarkably detailed aerial view of it in Robert Cameron's book *Robert Cameron's Above Washington*. A driveway off Massachusetts Avenue, marked only by a large white ship's anchor, leads into the Observatory Circle grounds and, passing glass greenhouses and the old carriage house now serving as the Secret Service outpost on the estate, ends at a white guardpost manned by officers of the Uniformed Secret Service. Once through the inner gates, the visitor passes a small island in the driveway in the center of which is displayed another Rockefeller gift to the residence: one of the stylized bronze eagles used to decorate the presidential reviewing stand at Eisenhower's first inaugural. Looming above on the slight rise of the grounds is the sparkling white but less than palatial house, enlivened by a Romanesque turret at one end and a broad porticoed veranda with doubled columns enclosing two sides of the structure.

The inside is more cheerful than grand, a fact which has so far legislated against any form of opening the house to tours for the general public. The main floor has only seven major rooms, including the Garden Room fashioned from enclosing one end of the portico. The reception hall is warmed by one of three faces of the large central fireplace; the other faces are in the corners of the living room and sitting room-den. Off the hall are the dining room, the largest room in the house, with its own fireplace behind the Rockefeller table, and the living room made more interesting by the turreted corner housing a charming seating area. A formally arched alcove off the entry hall was where the Mondales put their grand piano, on top of which rested one of their ubiquitous artistic statements, an earthenware sculpture titled "Couch and Chair with Landscape and Cows."

The second floor isn't exactly palatial either. (The third story is essentially an attic floor and is used primarily for servants' quarters.) Other than the Bushes' bedroom—the room with the turret above the living room—there are only two other bedrooms. Susan Rose commented that the Bushes love to have their children and grandchildren visit, but "if they are all there at one time, it's too many."

As extensively as the house itself is used by the Bushes for both official and private entertaining, the grounds are the Vice President's particular delight. George Bush is today more Tex-prep than the New England variety, and perhaps for this reason outdoor barbecues are the special Bush form of hospitality. Tents are put up on the extensive but informal grounds, shielded from Massachusetts Avenue and public view by a long row of white pines, and one of their Sunday cookouts gets under way, with the Vice President himself doing the cooking.

The immersion of modern Vice Presidents into the thick of the nation's affairs of state—both political and social—provides inordinately useful on-the-job training for the only higher office to which any American can aspire. George Bush, not unnaturally, covets that one higher office, an observation borne out by his early 1980 run for the White House. Continuing this trend of fitting the incumbent to the high and honorable nature of the office, rather than the potentially disastrous pure ticket balancing of so many past elections, should help ensure that future George Bushes remain not the exception but the rule in American politics.

VI

Presidential Transport

"WE HAVE MOVEMENT"

There is the special luxury of knowing your trip will be crash-free.

SHEILA RABB WEIDENFELD

ALTHOUGH THE BUILDING is today a shell-shocked mockery of its former glory, buried somewhere within the bureaucratically inspired debris of Washington's Union Station is what was once a lovely frescoed suite of rooms which were designed and reserved especially for the use of the President, his family, and his guests. To have the nation's preeminent citizen mucking about on a crowded concourse was unimaginable. The thinking is pretty much the same today—only on a far larger and more costly scale. One of the foremost perquisites of the presidency is the luxury and pomp in which its holder is tranported to any point on the globe, at a moment's notice and in a manner in which his safety is as assured as the combined resources of the federal government can make it.

It is logically argued, of course, that the transporting of a President can't be compared with the movement of lesser beings, most especially because of the considerations of security. When Ronald Reagan leaves the White House, for example, to attend the opera at the Kennedy Center, a distance of perhaps a dozen blocks, thirteen cars are used to get him there in the requisite style, safety, and drama his office demands. The caravan approximates a small troop movement: two presidential limousines, two security cars, a staff car, two press vans, two police cars, two cars for presidential guests, a car for the White House Communications Agency, and, bringing up the rear, a car for the President's military aide and the first physician. But if the style of the executive branch has become uncompromisingly imperial today, it didn't start out that way when the nation was still in stiff-necked rebellion against anything smacking of trappings of royalty.

During George Washington's term in office, the presidential carriage was very much like anyone else's—nothing especially grand, certainly not yet a traveling bunker. A cipher was designed to distinguish Washington's cream and gilt coach, but he evidently thought it might appear a little too regal, so he never had it painted on. But to keep up appearances when he went out for a drive, the horses' mouths were washed out, their teeth picked clean, and their hooves blackened.

It wouldn't be until William Taft's administration that Congress even consented to appropriate funds for a White House coach. Until that time Presidents provided their own equipage or else walked. Millard Fillmore's wife accepted a magnificent carriage, complete with horses and harness, the gift of a group of rich New York friends of her husband, a ruse to save her hard-up husband any political embarrassment. On leaving the presidency, he sold it and bought a silver tea service with the proceeds. On the other end of the ethics scale was Grover Cleveland, so virtuous he measured the hay in the White House stables after he had been inaugurated and sent the outgoing President Arthur a check for it.

Lincoln had the use of a really handsome carriage, complete with a curved windshield (anticipating Detroit by some decades), also a gift of New York merchants. When the President wasn't being conveyed in this carriage, he could be found in his rakish brewster, which was a sort of early roadster with horses. The only noteworthy fact about Ulysses S. Grant's personal transportation is that he was the first President to get a ticket for speeding. He manfully commended the arresting officer for "doing his duty."

Teddy Roosevelt was the last President to use horse-drawn vehicles regularly. His successor, William Taft—who got that initial transport appropriation—started employing horseless carriages. The first presidential automobile was a Baker electric, followed in rapid succession by two Pierce-Arrows and a White Steamer. Taft was reported to derive an enormous amount of pleasure from his then very expensive cars, especially enjoying jaunts around the capital. Later Woodrow Wilson, in his eternal quest to inspire the civic good, reverted to a horse carriage on World War I "gasless days." (He also carefully observed the war years' "wheatless days" and "meatless days.")

It was during Coolidge's term in the White House that presidential motoring started to resemble modern standards from the angle of security. Secret Service men examined his planned routes beforehand, and an agent rode in the front seat with the President at all times. The first Lincoln, the car that has been the main presidential limousine ever since, was bought for Coolidge.

The second Roosevelt's best-known car was the *Sunshine Special*, a 1939 Lincoln convertible, leased to the government by the Ford Motor Company and used by the President's successor until 1950. When World War II started, FDR had it sent back to Detroit to have armor plating and inch-thick glass installed. Its name derived from Roosevelt's penchant for riding in open convertibles in parades in sunny weather.

Harry Truman used a 1949 Lincoln for a year but finally got an unmistakably presidential automobile in 1950. It has been only in recent years that American presidential limousines have attained the status attached to cars of European royal families, and it can be said to have begun with Truman's enormous whale-shaped Lincoln Cosmopolitan convertible limousine—then the absolute last word in sumptuous modernity. (Nine other somewhat smaller Lincoln Cosmopolitans, designed for Secret Service and backup use, were delivered with it.) Used all through the Eisenhower years—most memorably with the plastic bubble top Ike had made for it—it wasn't retired until after the 1961 inaugural parade.

Presidential limousines took on a tragic face with John Kennedy's navy blue 1961 Lincoln Continental convertible. The car, delivered soon after he became President and to which he was said to be quite attached, was the subject of an indelible photograph made at Dallas's Parkland Hospital, empty but for the crumpled bouquet of bloodred roses in the backseat. Leased to the government for $500 a year, it had been specially built with a wide range of roof combinations, a rear seat which could automatically be raised ten and a half inches from the floor, retractable floor stands for the Secret Service (which Kennedy wouldn't allow to be used on that last day in Dallas, reasoning that the agents would block people's view of him and his wife), and a great panoply of luxury accoutrements. It was more than twenty-one feet long, allowing two jump seats to be fitted in. Neatly encased in special panels in the passenger compartment were two handsome lap robes, each embroidered with the presidential seal.

From Dallas the limousine was flown back to Washington; shortly thereafter Lyndon Johnson had it returned to Dearborn for a complete overhaul. There were 130 other cars (later reduced by Johnson to 20) available to the White House at the time, including the 1961 black Crown Imperial Ghia limousine, with huge shark-shaped fins, that had been used by Jackie Kennedy. But Johnson decided instead to borrow F.B.I. director J. Edgar Hoover's tanklike Cadillac. The newly modified Lincoln was returned to the White House in June 1964, now weighing five tons, with eight pane-thick windows designed to stop almost any kind of projectile up to and including a cannonball. It was freshly painted jet black.

Nixon ordered a new 1968 Lincoln "stretch" Continental, another specially designed presidential version of the company's standard luxury line. It served as the primary presidential transport for four years, when its current successor, a 1972 Lincoln Continental sedan, was delivered to the White House garage. A black limousine with gray leather interior trim, it has a roof section that opens to allow the President to stand in the passenger compartment during parades—an almost extinct form of display in our security-conscious age. Surprisingly the over-twenty-one-foot-long car uses regular gas and (Ford points out proudly) "meets emission control standards." Designed by the Special Vehicles Engineering Department at Ford from a standard production limousine which was taken apart and rebuilt from the ground up, it now has a fourteen-unit aerospacelike master control module in the driver's compartment, a twin two-way communications system, a public address system, a rear bumper which folds down to serve as a platform for Secret Service agents, and a mechanically operated handrail that disappears into the trunk lid for the said agents to grab onto. Two dimmable fluorescent lamps were fitted into the passenger section so the President can be seen from the street at night—also now a rare form of presidential display. The brakes are oversize, the gas tank is the foam-bladder type used by planes and racing cars, and the whole thing has two separate air-conditioning systems. In case there might be some question of whose car it is, the presidential standard is flown from the left fender, and the American flag from the right, both illuminated at night by three miniature spotlights mounted on each fender. The car was literally built like a tank; it is designed to absorb a bomb blast directly underneath.

The remainder of the twenty-nine-car White House fleet consists of Chryslers—rented rather than owned—and two special 1975 Cadillac Fleetwood convertibles used as security cars by the Secret Service at official functions and parades. The black four-door limousines, modified to Secret Service specifications as convertibles by a private company, are equipped with twelve-inch-wide running boards extending along each side from front to rear wheel openings and transparent vinyl panels built into the convertible tops to allow scanning of rooftops. Between the

two front bucket seats is an additional bucket seat facing to the
rear so an agent can observe crowds and buildings during motorcades.

If American Presidents are today moved around on the
ground in luxury as great as any monarch, the same is not true
of their waterborne transport. Presidential yachts are now a relic
of the past, Jimmy Carter having decided before he even laid
eyes on the executive yacht that it would be a useful symbolic
gesture to rid the presidency of another imperial icon.

Official presidential yachts began with Teddy Roosevelt's
Mayflower in 1902. By the 1930s and early '40s, the President had
two vessels at his disposal; neither was remotely as splendid as
the British sovereign's *Britannia,* but both were seagoing craft
possessed of great comfort and dignity. The first and the grander
of the two was the *Sequoia.* Built in 1925, it became the official
presidential yacht during the last days of Herbert Hoover's administration. Franklin Roosevelt could hardly wait to get on it
when he became President in March 1933, but the passionate
weekend sailor and former assistant secretary of the Navy took
an immediate and intense dislike to what he considered a
"dandified boat." His real problem with the *Sequoia* (which
made a top speed of ten knots and got one mile to a gallon of
fuel) was probably the fact that its ladders and narrow passage-
ways made his getting around in a wheelchair very difficult.
Being carried from deck to deck was too great an indignity for
Roosevelt, so he ordered a more accommodating ship be found
to serve as his seagoing retreat and official ship of state.

What the Navy came up with for the President was an almost
new (launched in 1934) but nonetheless dowdy Coast Guard
cutter called the USS *Electra.* Abruptly withdrawn from Coast
Guard service in November 1935, the 165-foot-long patrol boat
became, after a thorough sprucing up, the new presidential
yacht, USS *Potomac.* Besides general cosmetic surgery to her
main cabins, including the addition of lots of polished brass, fine
wood paneling, teak decks, and new leather furniture scattered
around, there was one feature specially installed for the President: hidden within a second dummy funnel was a small hand-

operated elevator. It was a secret known only to the crew and a few of Roosevelt's staff, and guests were invariably startled to see Roosevelt wheeling himself out of an otherwise normal-looking smokestack.

The President used the *Potomac* regularly as a floating office as well as a pleasure vessel, especially enjoying taking close advisers with him down the Potomac to work on solving problems relating to the tattered economy. In September 1939, when the European conflict started, a warship started to accompany the *Potomac* every time it went out. A degaussing girdle was put around the yacht to protect it from magnetic mines, and the President told his worried advisers that "any Nazi torpedo would go right under" the shallow-draft vessel. Whatever the case, the Navy declared it unseaworthy in the fall of 1941, a move designed to force the President to forgo his increasingly dangerous hobby. That was the end of Roosevelt's yachting.

Harry Truman, a midwesterner to whom yachting was a totally alien activity when he succeeded Roosevelt, had the ship decommissioned in November 1945. (Truman used the smaller *Williamsburg* for his Potomac cruises; it was decommissioned by Eisenhower soon after he took office.) The Navy sold it to the Maryland Tidewater Fisheries Commissioners, and for the next fourteen years it served as a seagoing environmental research laboratory and as the official yacht for Maryland's governors. Until it sank in San Francisco Bay in 1981, a ruined derelict, it had been owned in turn by the Hydro Capital Corporation, Elvis Presley, Memphis's St. Jude's Hospital, a Fresno real estate broker, and a Long Beach bail bondsman. At this writing the owner is the Port of Oakland, which intends to turn it into a tourist attraction near the city's Jack London Square. It paid $15,000 for the forlorn and rotten hulk, down from the one and a quarter million 1934 dollars it had cost the taxpayers to build forty-seven years earlier.

Meanwhile, back to the *Sequoia*. After Truman got rid of the *Potomac*, he occasionally used the *Sequoia*, as did Eisenhower, Kennedy, and Johnson after him. Nixon would take it out more than any of his predecessors—eighty-six times, usually in the evening on the Potomac. The ship Jimmy Carter sold for

$286,000 in 1977 is now back in Washington. A group called the Presidential Yacht Trust bought it for $1,065,000, with plans to make it available to President Reagan to use for summer sailings on the Potomac (as well as for "special forums and special events"). While these plans were being made, the President (who rejected a suggestion made by some members of Congress that he buy a new presidential yacht) was looking around for a boat elsewhere, including among those vessels seized by the government in drug-smuggling raids.

In October 1981 occurred one of the most historic presidential journeys since such trips began with George Washington's being driven about in his cipherless carriage. Three former Presidents, all with reasons to dislike each other intensely on the ground, were at 31,000 feet over the Atlantic, behaving toward one another as the best of old comrades. The trip had been Ronald Reagan's idea, a unique and historic gesture of national mourning on the part of the United States to the Egyptian people on the death of their president, Anwar Sadat. The rounding up of the three former Presidents was the work of the superefficient White House transportation staff, which also made sure that the trio landed in Washington at precisely the same time to board the presidential helicopter to fly to the White House for the short farewell ceremony with the Reagans (themselves advised not to go because of the difficulty in providing adequate security). After the brief amenities all three were back on the helicopter again, flying to Andrews Air Force Base, where they embarked on the older of the two presidential 707s, the plane that had flown John Kennedy's body back to the capital from Texas and had carried President Nixon to China on his precedent-breaking journey.

Protocol might have created a problem with accommodation arrangements if it hadn't been decided earlier that the choicest spot on the plane—the presidential suite—was to go to Alexander Haig, who as secretary of state was the official leader of the party as well as the highest-ranking sitting officer of government aboard. (Under normal circumstances a former President outranks a current secretary of state by one notch on the table of

precedence.) The three former Presidents shared the less prestigious VIP lounge, along with Rosalynn Carter, the only former
First Lady attending the funeral, included in the party because
she and her husband threatened to go as private citizens if she
couldn't accompany him on the plane.

Spread out over the rest of the plane were, among others,
Henry Kissinger, now assigned to a considerably lesser space
than Haig, his onetime aide in his glory days at the White
House; Leonore "Lee" Annenberg, then chief of protocol, who
passed the time having everybody on board sign her copy of the
passenger manifest; Senator Charles Percy, being praised by
Nixon because he always "stood by the president in foreign policy"; and Defense Secretary Caspar Weinberger, undoubtedly
worried about what Anwar Sadat's death would do to the balance of power in the Middle East.

Enjoying themselves immensely were Carter in his comfy
beige cardigan, Nixon puffing on a Don Diego, Ford happy with
his butter pecan ice cream—all again right in the middle of the
action. What memories they must have been sharing of the years
when each commanded the plane, when each had been up front
in the big cabin, a host of minions fetching, catering, agreeing.
Few would disagree that life on this most sumptuous of presidential transport is life as it should be lived. Gerald Ford put it
nicely: "When they fly you on *Air Force One*, you *know* you're
President."

For the first 117 years of the Republic's history no serving
President had ever left the United States. Teddy Roosevelt was
the first; he traveled on the battleship *Louisiana* to open the
Panama Canal. At that, he was out of U.S. waters for only a few
hours. Even when Woodrow Wilson went to the Peace Conference at Versailles at the end of the first World War, one congressman introduced a resolution to declare the office of the
President "temporarily vacant" during his absence. It wasn't
thought fitting—or even constitutional—that the chief executive
should be away from American shores.

All this changed with the coming of World War II and
Franklin Roosevelt's need to meet with Allied leaders to plan the

war effort. At first his air transportation requirements (the Secret Service ruled out transatlantic ship travel because of the danger from German submarines) were met by a Pan American clipper under Navy contract; these glamorous flying boats epitomized America's air dominance during those years. His first flight was from Miami to Casablanca in January 1943. Not only was this the first time a President had flown, but it was the first such presidential visit to a theater of war since Abraham Lincoln toured Civil War battlefields.

So important to Roosevelt was his new mobility that in the autumn of 1943 a personal plane was provided for him. Dubbed the *Sacred Cow*, a name never made official but which would nonetheless stick with it for many years, the converted C-54 four-engine cargo plane was by the standards of its day a flying luxury hotel for the President. The interior was specially laid out so as to enable Roosevelt to get around the craft easily in his wheelchair. Because his favorite seat was right between the two pilots, a set of rails was installed so he could roll the chair up the slight incline to the cockpit. The Commander in Chief's 7½-by-12-foot stateroom had a swivel chair, a bed, maps on rollers, an electric fan, and a large bulletproof window; ironically, the fuselage around the window wouldn't have stopped birdshot. The plane's most memorable feature was its battery-operated elevator, which scooped Roosevelt and his wheelchair up from the runway into the plane's main cabin. The elevator also eliminated the need for telltale ramps at airports where the President was expected, an important consideration to wartime security.

When Truman succeeded Roosevelt, he was ecstatic about the plane. The new President loved to fly. Bad weather, turbulence, Bess's ill-concealed dislike for it—nothing bothered him or ever made him cancel a flight. The *Sacred Cow* was retired in 1947, and Truman got a shiny new Douglas DC-6, which he promptly named after his hometown—the *Independence*. Truman had it painted to resemble an angry American eagle; it was undeniably gaudy, but then so was the President. Though the nose was originally brown, the symbolism quickly dictated a change to gray. The *Independence* was decommissioned just before Eisenhower's 1953 inauguration.

Ike, of course, had to have something new and smart for the modern era he was ushering in, so he chose a Lockheed Constellation, one of the whale-backed, triple-tailed airliners popular with many of the international airlines of the time. Truman had almost gotten a "Connie" in 1949—one was being built on Air Force orders with the expectation that Thomas Dewey would win the election. The planned name for it was the *Dewdrop*, calculated to please Dewey when it would be ready and waiting for him on his inauguration day. When Truman was offered the plane after the beginning of his own full term, he was quoted as rejecting it with a parody of the then popular song, "I don't want it, you can have it, it's too big for me!"

Ike named his new plane the *Columbine II* (*Columbine I* was the plane he had used as European theater commander during the war) after Mamie's home state flower from Colorado. The waist section contained a twenty-foot-long stateroom for the First Couple, with brown leather chairs, two long couches which converted into three-quarter-size beds, and a handy little bar. Flying was Eisenhower's favorite mode of transportation, even though Mamie was terrified of it; the presidential pilots were always extra-solicitous about the First Lady's fears. The plane was replaced by the *Columbine III*, a Super Constellation, in 1954. Eighteen feet longer than the *Columbine II* and with a far greater fuel capacity and range, it was to serve the remaining six years of the Eisenhower presidency. His wife christened it with a flask of Colorado water.

To get back and forth to the Eisenhowers' Gettysburg farm from the White House, a small twin-engine Aero Commander joined the Super Constellation in the presidential fleet. The Secret Service originally vetoed it, contending that any plane carrying the President had to have four engines, but its convenience and Eisenhower's insistence carried the day for the little blue and white plane.

Just as Ike had ushered in a new generation of presidential aircraft, so did John Kennedy inaugurate the jet age for the White House. Although he used a DC-6 for the first year and a half of his administration, in October 1962 Special Air Missions —the Air Force unit at Andrews Air Force Base which controlled all the aircraft used by the President—acquired its first Boeing 707, which cost the taxpayers $7,024,000 and was the first plane to be popularly called *Air Force One*.

Originally the term "Air Force One" wasn't supposed to be the name of the President's plane. It was simply the radio call sign of any Air Force craft transporting the President; in other words, the term (even today) attaches to the President, not to the plane. But because it was so distinctive and because Kennedy hadn't followed the usual course of personally naming the plane, the press started using *Air Force One* to identify the 707. There is today another nearly identical 707 in the Special Air Missions stable; whichever the President is flying becomes *Air Force One*.

Raymond Loewy was commissioned to design the plane's exterior. Not wanting to emulate Truman's gaudy eagle decorations or the dreary military markings on Ike's *Columbines*, Loewy came up with the beautiful and unique design still used on both 707s—"United States of America" classically lettered on each side of the fuselage, the American flag on both sides of the tail, and the presidential seal on both sides of the nose. The design met with immediate public favor and even today lends the planes great elegance and style.

Little more than a year after the first 707 was delivered to the young President, it was used for his last journey from Dallas to Washington. Kennedy's heavy bronze casket was placed in the presidential bedroom at the rear of the plane, where his widow sat vigil next to it during the 1,000-mile flight. Lyndon Johnson had taken the oath of office in the forward cabin while it still sat on the ground at Dallas's Love Field, the compartment jammed with spectators and, because the engines and ventilation systems were shut down, an airless bake oven.

When Special Air Missions came under Johnson's control, he luxuriated in it to the fullest. On the spur of the moment he would leave Washington for weekends in Texas. To assuage reporters who felt he might be using *Air Force One* merely to enjoy himself, he'd admonish, "Now, boys, y'all know I work as hard up here as I do in the White House." There was no question, though, that he was just as uncouth in the air as he was on the ground. His pilot, Ralph Albertazzie, wrote of the time he saw the President yank a piece of unchewable gristle from a steak sandwich out of his mouth and hurtle it across the cabin, where it landed in a bowl of potato chips next to Lady Bird.

When Nixon took over, *Air Force One* became as much a hotbed of petty vindictiveness as did all the other presidential venues. According to Albertazzie, who remained the presidential pilot in the new administration, most of the grief was caused by Nixon's gung ho staff. A representative incident occurred when a second 707 was ordered to serve as the new primary transport for the President. Chief Nixon aide H. R. Haldeman was allowed to lay out the interior spaces and, in doing so, placed his own big staff compartment directly between the President's office and Mrs. Nixon's tiny sitting room, different from the arrangements on the existing 707, in which the staff area and the First Lady's cabins were reversed. The new arrangement allowed Haldeman to keep much closer watch over who saw the President. Mrs. Nixon objected to the plan, but the President wouldn't override his Svengali-like chief of staff. The minute Haldeman was dumped in the spring of 1973 Mrs. Nixon had the plane rearranged to match the layout of the first 707. This little test of wills cost the taxpayers $750,000.

The reason for the second 707 in the first place was fairly logical. Backup aircraft, necessary for staff and additional Secret Service agents, were no match for *Air Force One*'s more powerful and longer-range capabilities; it was therefore handicapped to the lesser abilities of the other craft. At Christmas 1972 the new plane was delivered; the interior came with more modern fittings than its sister ship, but the exterior was identical. The newer jet is now the primary aircraft used by the President.

Today Special Air Missions provides the President with a magic carpet to anyplace in the world on an hour's notice. The heart of the unit is still the two 707 jetliners familiar on every continent to tens of millions of people. Presidential pilot Lieutenant Colonel Rob Ruddick is successor to nine men who have held the position since Roosevelt's *Sacred Cow* was commanded by Lieutenant Colonel Hank Myers. The Reagans have made no major changes to the planes since the Carters except for the addition of the same kinds of framed photographs of the presidential couple on the cabin walls as are found all over the White House. The couple enjoys probably the most secure and luxurious flying in the world.

No presidential flight takes off without the chief executive's personal physician aboard. *Air Force One,* which is always given a clear priority over all other aircraft, never has to bother with holding patterns and other similar annoyances which affect commercial flights. Security in the Andrews hangars is airtight; the pilots themselves can't even board without checking in with the Air Police detachment. Food is bought on a random basis, never from the same place twice in a row. *Air Force One's* galleys are capable of turning out meals far superior to the usual airline muck. If they wish, the Reagans can have practically the same thing that is available in the White House kitchens. A typical lunch was served to the Nixons on the flight carrying them back to California on the day the President resigned: shrimp cocktail, prime ribs, baked potatoes, green beans, tossed salad, rolls, coffee. A typical breakfast was served to the Carters on a trip to Africa: orange juice, melon balls, French toast, scrambled eggs, sausage, blueberry muffins, coffee. The craft even has its own presidential china—gold-etched beige plates embossed with the United States seal; they were selected by Jackie Kennedy.

Each plane has a large three-room suite forward to serve as the presidential bedroom, a sitting room (the President's seat is on the side away from the door for security reasons), and a conference room as well as a lavatory. Between the suite and the cockpit are a small Secret Service seating area, the First Family's private galley, and an elaborate communications post. Running along the port side of the plane is a narrow aisle enabling traffic to bypass the First Family's quarters, which has its own interconnecting doors.

To the rear of the presidential suite are a staff compartment the full width of the plane, then an eight-seat VIP suite, and, finally, the pool reporters' area. (Most reporters covering the President follow his flight in their own plane, chartered by their employers, for which they are billed on a pro rata basis 150 percent of the regular first-class fare; this press plane usually precedes the presidential flight so the reporters can cover *Air Force One's* landings.) A larger galley and the lavatories are in the tail section.

Flying on *Air Force One* isn't entirely free of charge to the President and his family. If the purpose of his or a family member's flight is wholly personal, the President is billed by the Air Force comptroller's office at a rate determined annually and based on fuel costs, maintenance, and other miscellaneous items. During the Carter presidency, the hourly rate was around $2,500; today it's estimated by the Defense Department to be $5,566. To fly the Reagans from the White House to their Santa Barbara ranch and return cost $51,339.83 in late 1981, not counting the several dozen Secret Service agents and scores of Air Force ground support personnel. Since such charges could be ruinous to even the richest President, he has only to give a press conference or open some civic works project and the flight is "prorated," with the government picking up a good chunk of the tab. The President's party is billed for political trips.

The total cost of flying the President and his entourage on official trips—state visits, summit meetings, and the like—has risen to astronomical figures. When President Reagan traveled to the Caribbean in the spring of 1982 for a hemispheric minisummit combined with a private vacation, the total bill was reported to be between $3,000,000 and $5,000,000, which, by the way, covered only the three hundred people in the official party, not the two hundred members of the press who paid their own way. Included in the airborne caravan that accompanied *Air Force One* were three armored limousines, four armored cars, four Marine helicopters, one hundred fifty military personnel to repair and guard the vehicles, and, according to *Time* magazine, enough telephone equipment to "basically (redo) the Barbados phone system." As is standard with the President's travels, a fully-equipped hospital ship stood offshore.

The trip to the European summit later that spring was considerably more expensive—possibly $10,000,000—a figure *U.S. News & World Report* called conservative. Included in the huge party were two hundred presidential aides, one hundred fifty Secret Service agents, and two hairdressers for Mrs. Reagan. Britain's queen, with whom the President and First Lady stayed for two nights at Windsor Castle, was said to be "astonished."

The two 707s are not the full extent of the President's private air force. A large number of other planes—jets as well as small piston engine aircraft—are available for his use. The massive helicopters that ferry the President and the First Lady back and forth to Andrews from the White House, as well as to Camp David for weekends, are operated by the Marine Corps; the unit is known as HMX-1. When the President is aboard, that chopper becomes *Marine One*, and the call signal Nighthawk One. (Likewise, when he flies on an Army craft, it becomes *Army One*; on a Navy plane, it's *Navy One*.) The helicopters, like *Air Force One*, are now equipped with missile defense systems for the President's security. Headquartered at the naval air station on the northern edge of Bolling Field in the Anacostia section of the District, the three helicopters in the detachment stand ever ready to meet the President's needs.

On the same airstrip at Andrews with *Air Force One* is the Boeing 747 officially known as E-4 A-B National Emergency Airborne Command Post and sometimes referred to as Kneecap, from its acronym NEACP. Unofficially it's called the *Doomsday Plane*, an ominous but accurate description implying its true function. The $117,000,000 jumbo jet, painted to resemble the presidential 707s, gives Ronald Reagan, in his own words, "a sense of confidence." Well it might. First flown by Jimmy Carter, who described the journey as "a sobering experience," it will hold as many as ninety-four people, including a crew of twenty-seven and a fifteen-member "battle staff." The President would theoretically direct a nuclear war from the command compartment in the front of the plane. Its multiple decks contain radar gear, an intricate communications system (a five-mile-long copper antenna can be floated out behind the craft to keep in close touch with U.S. submarines anywhere in the world), and jamming, detection, and "countermeasure" facilities.

It is highly dubious that the founders of our Republic ever envisioned the tremendous gulf which would separate our President from those over whom he presides. The enormous panoply of power at his instant command—exemplified by the stateliness of his limousine and its attendant cavalcades and the power and instant communications capabilities of his jets and helicopters— make pale the perquisites of mere monarchs. Very far removed indeed is our President from the simple chief magistracy envisioned two centuries ago.

VII

Presidential Security

THE SECRET SERVICE

*The less freedom of action the people have, the more
their leaders have.*

RUFUS YOUNGBLOOD

FOR ALL THEIR MASSIVE MANPOWER, up-to-the-minute
gadgetry, and unparalleled access to information about which
nuts and homicidally motivated President killers are lurking
around, the guardians of the chief executive's life still can't keep
their man totally out of harm's way. They *can* make it extraor-
dinarily difficult, but not impossible, for assassins to do their
deeds. As long as the American President retains any freedom of
public contact, he will remain the potential victim of those who
would, to paraphrase John F. Kennedy, trade their lives for his.

In a monstrously unsafe world the President's well-being is a
matter of professional concern to a host of different protective
agencies, from military and civil police organizations and the na-

tion's foremost investigative agency to a wide range of covert intelligence services. But the chief guardianship of the life and safety of the President lies in the well-trained hands of a century-old branch of the Treasury Department: the United States Secret Service.

If during the first century of the Republic's history our Presidents were protected at all, it can best be described as on an "informal" basis. The tragic consequences of this laxity in providing security for the President was the loss of three chief executives in a thirty-six year span; earlier a fourth survived more by miracle than by right.

The near tragedy occurred in January 1835. Richard Lawrence, a British-born house painter and a psychotic who imagined himself to be King Richard III of England, aimed two pistols at President Andrew Jackson on the east portico of the Capitol. Both of the single-shot brass weapons miraculously misfired: the first shot had been aimed from a distance of thirteen feet, the second was discharged at almost point-blank range. Lawrence was ruled insane and spent the rest of his life in an asylum. The attack failed to inspire any efforts to provide for presidential safety.

What protection there was remained a casual matter, and Jackson's successors continued occasionally to receive threatening letters and were often subjected to abusive behavior. But the threats were never taken very seriously and, until the Civil War, Presidents continued to go about their duties without any kind of protective escorts. Even during that conflict Abraham Lincoln's safety was left to the perfunctory care of a military escort and a personal bodyguard, the latter a Washington policeman. Ironically, on the day he was shot Lincoln had met with his treasury secretary, Hugh McCulloch, to discuss a more efficient way to suppress counterfeiters—talks that led to the founding of the Secret Service three months later. (At the time no thought was given to the proposed service's providing protection for the President.) A few hours after the meeting Lincoln was murdered in an unguarded box in a downtown Washington theater. Carelessness had exacted a calamitous price, but—and almost beyond comprehension—still no political efforts were made to provide permanent protection for the President.

Sixteen years later the national nightmare happened again. Charles J. Guiteau was convinced that his unsolicited efforts to "help elect" James A. Garfield in 1880 entitled him to a federal job—the one he considered himself most qualified for was the consulship in Paris. When he didn't get it, he shot the President, who was walking to a train in the old Baltimore and Potomac Railroad Station in the capital. The .44 caliber revolver slug didn't kill Garfield outright, but two months of medical mismanagement did. Guiteau, who testified at his own trial that he had passed up three opportunities to attack the unguarded President, was convicted and hanged. Two bills were introduced in Congress to make it a federal crime to kill the chief executive; both died in committee. It was the first time such legislation was even considered. Failure to pass it was probably responsible for the success of the next presidential assassin twenty years later.

On September 6, 1901, William McKinley was scheduled to make two appearances at the Pan American Exposition in Buffalo, New York. The first, to deliver an address, passed without incident; the second, a public reception line, became a deathtrap for the President. His assassin, Leon F. Czolgosz, an anarchist (the urban guerrilla of the day), freely approached the handshaking McKinley, a handkerchief wrapped around his right hand, the hand wrapped around a .32 caliber revolver. As the President courteously reached for Czolgosz's unbandaged left hand, the assassin fired twice, at point-blank range, into the President's chest and stomach. McKinley died eight days later. The murderer was electrocuted. In retrospect, and even with allowance for the relative lack of security intelligence methods of the time, the most basic precautions should have prevented the tragedy. In fact, eighteen uniformed officers, eleven Coast Guardsmen, twelve Buffalo policemen, and several civilian guards were posted in and around the hall. There were even three of the Secret Service anticounterfeit operators there—sent as a courtesy by the local chief to help keep the reception line moving. But nobody had bothered to check Czolgosz's bandaged right hand.

At last, Congress got stirred up, and it looked as though it would actually do something about the appalling situation. Seventeen bills concerning presidential protection, as well as a joint resolution providing for a constitutional amendment to make it treason to kill the President, were immediately introduced. Another bill proposed that an amendment be added to make assault on the President a federal crime. Both died in committee, as did all seventeen of the others. But the Secret Service, the counterfeit-fighting agency, was ordered by the secretary of the treasury to provide a five-man protective detail for the new chief executive, Teddy Roosevelt. Roosevelt would later refer to it as "a small, but very necessary, thorn in my flesh." The expenses were paid out of federally appropriated counterfeit-suppression funds. In 1906 the Sundry Civil Expenses Act legalized the use of government funds for the express purpose of providing "protection of the person of the President of the United States."

For the next several years the President's new Secret Service protectors kept their charge safe. (One operative, though, had been killed in 1902, when a trolley car hit the President's carriage.) Roosevelt did become an assassin's target in 1912, but he was by that time a former President campaigning against Woodrow Wilson. The assailant shot Roosevelt through the chest; he recovered, and the would-be killer died in a mental hospital three decades later.

In 1917 the protection of the President's immediate family was authorized, and the first protective details guarding Edith Wilson came into existence. At the same time Congress made it a federal crime to threaten the President. The Secret Service continued to maintain its vigilance against counterfeiters (as it does to this day), but increasingly the agency's emphasis was switched to the security of the chief executive.

In 1922 President Harding requested the formation of the White House Police Force, upgrading the mansion's protection from the Keystone Kop-like jovials who had acted more as doormen than guards. The original thirty-three men were mostly comprised of transferred District policemen. Even this new force operated remarkably casually until one evening in May 1930 when a well-turned-out stranger sauntered past the guards at the gate and right into the White House itself. Both guards thought he belonged there because "he was dressed so well." The interloper marched into the dining room where President Hoover was having dinner, as though he were planning to join in. Hoover, understandably enraged, ordered the man thrown out. As it happened, the stranger wasn't a murderous sort; he claimed to be "just sight-seeing."

At nine o'clock that evening, the still-angry President had the head of the Secret Service on the carpet. The agent's alibi was that since the policemen at the door were not under his control, he had never been able to work out "satisfactory procedures" in concert with them. Hoover demanded the White House police be put under Secret Service control; within six weeks the normally indolent Congress had voted the necessary authorization.

Newly elected President Franklin Roosevelt almost didn't make it to the White House. A month before his inauguration he was passing through Miami, returning from a vacation cruise. At a political rally in a city park unemployed bricklayer Giuseppe Zangara—who blamed capitalists for the stomach pains he suffered—fired five shots at Roosevelt. None hit the President-elect, but one killed Chicago Mayor Anton Cermak, who had just been hailed by FDR over to his car, thus placing himself between Zangara and his target. The killer was tried and executed within thirty-four days. A bill was introduced in Congress to make it a federal crime to assassinate a President-elect. It died in committee.

With the onset of the war the activities of the Secret Service in matters of presidential protection took an enormous leap. The White House was closed to tourists, and the area around the mansion was subjected to far greater surveillance: Soldiers were on guard at all the entrances, the gates were barred, the roof was manned by machine-gun crews, and blackout curtains covered all the windows. The President's Hyde Park home was turned into an armed camp whenever Roosevelt visited it. When he traveled on a train, every inch of track was inspected beforehand, all switches were locked, and up to 150,000 soldiers stood guard on a single trip.

Harry Truman was the target of one of the bloodiest attempts ever made on a President's life. Even though his morning "constitutionals" always gave his Secret Service protectors the most grief, the assassination attempt came when he was napping. On November 1, 1950, as the President slept in the front upstairs bedroom of Blair House, two Puerto Rican nationalists—Oscar Collazo and Griselio Torresola—tried to shoot their way past guards at the doorway, presumably to track Truman down somewhere inside. (It later turned out that the two dimwits hadn't really thought out any kind of workable plan for their attack.) Torresola shot and mortally wounded a White House policeman, Leslie Coffelt; Coffelt returned the fire, killing the Puerto Rican with a bullet in the brain. Collazo was injured by shots from Secret Service agents assigned to assist the Capitol police in guarding the building. In the meantime, the Secret Service agent inside had grabbed a Thompson submachine gun the moment he heard the first shots outside. He planted himself in the center of the hall, covering the front door as well as the stairs and elevator leading to the President's quarters on the second floor. Even if the assassins had made it past the front door, they would never have been able to get around the machine gun.

Coffelt and Torresola were the only persons killed in the exchange of twenty-seven shots lasting nearly three minutes. Collazo recovered to be sentenced to death, but Truman commuted his sentence to life imprisonment. The incident bestirred Congress to broaden the Secret Service's mandate to include the President-elect and the Vice President under its protection. Ten years later an additional statute made it a federal crime to threaten the President-elect, the Vice President, and the Vice President-elect.

November 22, 1963, was the blackest day in modern presidential history, and the day's events in Dallas started a series of changes in the Secret Service that brought it close to its modern duties and strengths. The shots that killed John Kennedy also prompted the introduction of thirty-six assassination-related bills in Congress. In 1965 one of them was passed to make it a federal crime to assassinate, kidnap, or assault the President, President-elect, Vice President, or any person acting as President under the Constitution. That year the Secret Service received authority to protect a former President during his lifetime (which now costs the Treasury around $12,000,000 each year), and in 1968 additional authority was granted to protect a former President's widow until her death or remarriage. The same law covers children of former Presidents until they become sixteen. In 1968 Congress also extended protection to major presidential and vice presidential candidates and nominees. In 1971 foreign heads of state and government, as well as (at the President's discretion) distinguished foreign visitors, came under Secret Service protection. In 1974 the Vice President's immediate family was put under the protective umbrella, and in 1976 spouses of major presidential and vice presidential candidates were added to the list of protectees.

Meanwhile, the White House Police Force was also growing more sophisticated. As a response to the rapidly increasing number of visitors to the executive mansion, the force's size and responsibilities were greatly expanded; in addition, it received a new name: the Executive Protective Service. Besides guarding the White House compound, it was given the duty to protect any building in which presidential offices are located, as well as the Vice Presidential Residence, and to provide security for diplomatic missions from more than 130 countries in more than 500 locations around Washington (the latter had been a State Department responsibility up to this time). Since 1930 a part of the Secret Service, it again had a name change in 1977: to the United States Secret Service Uniformed Division.

When still called the Executive Protective Service, the division had its one moment, although a ludicrous one, in the limelight. Early in the Nixon presidency a small contingent was outfitted in Sigmund Romberg-inspired uniforms to serve as an honor guard for receiving distinguished visitors. The President apparently reasoned that traditions that because of their antiquity were acceptable in other countries would be equally accepted in this country. He was wrong. Had he done a little research, he might have found that Teddy Roosevelt had tried the same thing seven decades earlier only to have it end up as a laughing failure, too. The high-collared white jackets with aiguillettes and black holsters and Sam Browne belts, striped trousers, and gold-edged helmets reminiscent of Revolutionary War Hessian mercenaries—all designed by Washington tailor Jimmie Muscatello —are now gracing the marching bands of Southern Utah State College, a public school in Claghorn, Iowa, and an Austin, Texas, high school.

Today the Secret Service has more than 3,000 employees, including 1,550 special agents. Although it still has responsibility for suppressing the counterfeiting of United States currency and securities and for investigating the forging of government checks, bonds, and securities, by far its most visible activity is the protection of the President. Newly appointed agents are first assigned to the investigative side of the service; only those of obviously superior talent are eventually picked for the protective duties. New agents, who must be less than thirty-five when they start with the service, receive their initial training at the Federal Law Enforcement Training Center in Brunswick, Georgia. Those selected to protect the President and others covered by the agency undergo rigorous and extended instruction at the Secret Service Training Center in Beltsville, Maryland, just outside the District boundary. There, sometimes while being fired on, they practice moving a make-believe "President" through a variety of crowds, returning fire without hitting any of the pretend innocent bystanders. A replica of the White House and Blair House and their surrounding area, including Lafayette Park, has been built at the center at a cost of $1,600,000. Agents use the giant Hollywood-style set to practice protecting the President, his guests, and his staff.

Agents are required to take a marksmanship test every thirty days; if they fall below standards, they're transferred. They also return for formal supplemental training every six to eight months. A further form of training for agents assigned to chauffeur a presidential limousine is in the technique of evasive driving—the ability instinctively and instantly to get the President's car out of danger.

The service is divided into five "offices": Inspection, Protective Research, Administration, Investigations (the counterfeit and forgery people), and Protective Operations. The last includes ten divisions: Presidential Protective; Vice Presidential Protective; Dignitary Protective; Western Protective; Protective Vehicle; the Carter, Ford, Nixon, and Johnson Protective divisions (Jacqueline Kennedy Onassis gave up her agents when she married Aristotle Onassis in 1968; her two children lost theirs when they turned sixteen); and the Uniformed Division. (The requirements for the uniformed officers are considerably less rigorous than for the special agents; they can't fairly be described as simply the uniformed equivalent of the special agents.) The director of the service since early 1982, John R. Simpson, a career agent who before his promotion headed Protective Operations (and in 1968 served as head of candidate Ronald Reagan's security detail), is now conducting his organization's biggest expansion since it was founded in 1865, spending $10,000,000 to enlarge the Beltsville facility and hire additional agents.

The precautions taken to protect the President today are enormous in scope, with a few beginning to cross the fragile line which separates a free society from the trappings of a police state. Some view them, however, as a sort of weird American equivalent of the pageantry that surrounds foreign royalty.

The service keeps a computer list of about 25,000 people who in some way represent a danger to the President, by sending him hostile or threatening letters, being overheard to threaten him, having a tendency to insist on personally contacting the President or other ranking government officials to have imaginary grievances redressed, or posing some other overt danger. About 400 of them are considered particularly dangerous, and their whereabouts are constantly monitored. Sadly none of those involved in assassinations or assassination attempts since 1963—Sirhan Sirhan, Arthur Bremer, Lynette "Squeaky" Fromme, Sara Jane Moore, or John Hinckley—was on the list.

Whenever the President leaves the White House, agents go over every step of his intended route, checking for potential sniper hiding places and guarding corridors in buildings through which he will pass. Since the March 1981 attempt on Reagan's life, these visible security precautions have been significantly increased; the Libyan threat later in the year caused even more strengthening of his protective net. So many security people now surround him that they create their own crowd. One aide says, "The show is not an inconsiderable part of the protection. A certain number of people are going to be discouraged from attacking the President because the security *looks* impenetrable."

The President's motorcade now always includes a SWAT-team van, dubbed the War Wagon. The thirty or so agents (up to 150 agents travel with the President on his major foreign progresses) in the contingent—identifiable to each other by the small lapel button each wears—are armed with Israeli-made Uzi submachine guns, shotguns, first-aid supplies, and tools for prying the President out of a car crash. Maps of routes to the nearest hospitals are always carried. The President's car is parked in an underground garage whenever possible, and it is no longer always the lead car in motorcades. As the presidential limousine starts to move, agents may be seen murmuring into their shortwave microphones, "We have movement, we have movement." When Reagan is at an airport, there is almost always a car between him and the crowd. Appearances are usually unannounced these days, and all members of presidential audiences—even church congregations—must pass through airport types of metal detectors. Nancy Reagan considered canceling their Christmas Day 1981 church visit because she understood how offensive this last item is to the public; the couple has since nearly abandoned attendance at local church services for this reason. The Secret Service demands information on people who will be sitting near the President when he goes to a theater so they can be investigated beforehand. Elegantly dressed women at a Kennedy Center production of *La Bohème* attended by the First Couple set off the detectors with their metallic evening wear and had to be hand-frisked.

Security surrounding state visitors has been increased as well. When some foreign leaders enter and leave Blair House, Pennsylvania Avenue is closed to all traffic for thirty minutes beforehand. The south lawn welcoming ceremony audience is put through metal detectors, and its handbags and personal belongings are carefully checked, a procedure that can take the bloom off anyone's invitation to the White House. Paradoxically these metal detectors have developed a sort of perverse chic at Washington parties, where their presence often signals the attendance of very high administration officials.

The Uniformed Secret Service, normally on guard only around presidential and diplomatic buildings, is now being used to guard Reagan when he is traveling; small armies of the officers form an additional protective ring around the presidential party.

One of the most exotic categories of security apparatus, "a fabulous growth industry" according to one of its manufacturers, is bulletproof clothing. Made of fiber glass, bulletproof vests—the most usual "garment"—are both flexible and lightweight; they no longer look like water skiers' flotation jackets. Body Armor International, one of the biggest manufacturers, says they can be made in three "threat levels"—Level I ($325) stops a .22 caliber bullet and shotgun pellets; Level IIA ($415) will be dented only by a .44 caliber slug; and Level II—"really only for professionals"—will evidently stop a tank. (Absolutely nothing, however, will stop one of the new Teflon-coated bullets which will probably soon be a standard item in every homicidal lunatic's arsenal.) The obvious question is: Won't professional President killers and other like-minded miscreants simply aim for the head as a matter of course? The president of Body Armor says, "That's your smallest target. Also, you can move it. Your torso, that's the danger spot." Well, it must have convinced Nancy Reagan because she's now reported to have a bulletproof slip in her wardrobe.

If a democracy more than any other form of governance contains the seeds of its own self-destruction, then it's the assassin who most recklessly sows them. The removal by murder of a President is, of course, more than the loss of one replaceable man. It is the thwarting of a free system of government hard won and hung on to by the self-control and sacrifices of many generations. Still, Americans have taken it as a cultural right of our system that the President remains one of the people, occupying, temporarily, the most exalted position, but still one of us, one who is free to go to the people he governs in person and not merely as so many electronic lines on a glass screen. To have it any other way is to say, in effect, that the anarchists have won.

The area of decision the President's protectors will be facing ever more acutely in the coming years is how to let the chief executive remain free of a too protective cordon, yet to keep him from the dangers of those who know his death is one of the most onerous body blows the country can suffer. The most far-reaching danger posed to our society from its assassins is to the fragile line mentioned earlier between a free society and one that isn't. Whether the President's protectors make the right decisions will have a lot to do with keeping us on the right side of the line.

VIII

Presidential Envoys

DIPLOMACY
AND PROTOCOL

*"Let us agree not to step on each other's feet," said the
cock to the horse.*

English proverb

DIPLOMACY

THE PRESIDENT, though not a member of Washington's diplomatic community, is its head. Ambassadors are accredited not to countries, but to *leaders* of countries; an ambassador is the personal envoy from one country's head of state to that of another, a person theoretically charged with the authority to speak freely for the man or woman whom he represents. As such, it seems appropriate in a guide to the social institutions surrounding the presidency to include a chapter on how diplomacy and its handmaiden protocol function in official Washington.

First, it should be pointed out that diplomatic life in the nation's capital is not some sort of all-embracing mist clinging to every contour of the city's social layout. Only a tiny minority of Washingtonians—native or otherwise—ever attend a chic diplomatic cocktail party or a smart little soiree to honor the new first secretary at one or another of the embassies or even become part of the throng at a garden party held to mark this or that country's national holiday. For most Washingtonians, that world is represented by cars with diplomatic license plates taking up "their" valuable parking spots or items in the society columns about the latest social-climbing maneuvers of some minor ambassador. But for the select little slice of capital society that runs in these rarefied circles, and it is said that there are *no* strangers on the diplomatic social circuit, Washington is very much the place to be.

Simply put, the capital of the United States is the diplomatic center of the world. Even New York and its United Nations crowd are looked upon as an outpost of Washington, that group's own importance immeasurably enhanced by its proximity to the diplomatic Fort Knox on the Potomac. Money and power are what give the American capital its attractiveness—"aid" money that has for decades flowed in a one-way gusher, power that still makes America the hedge of last resort against the economic and social vicissitudes so much a part of so much of the world.

Washington has the largest diplomatic community on earth, with not only the usual national embassies but also some two dozen missions accredited to the Organization of American States and the European Communities Commission, all with full diplomatic status. (Occasionally the ambassadors overlap, some accredited to the United States as well as to the OAS and even the United Nations.) Four times a year the State Department publishes a blue-covered booklet called the *Diplomatic List,* which can be had by anyone interested in spending $2 for it. It contains the names and (most of the) addresses of every foreigner with diplomatic status in Washington, a group which currently numbers around 1,600 plus families. (It should be pointed out that not all foreign nationals employed by their embassies have diplomatic status; the 6,000 or so clerical and domestic people are listed in another publication, also available at the government bookstore.)

The list is an invaluable source of small but telling bits of realpolitik minutiae concerning the countries listed. For example, the West German Embassy usually has a sprinkling of "vons," but one will look in vain for any name with the old aristocratic preposition in the *East* German mission. In years past there was generally a nobleman or two at the British Embassy; in 1950, Second Secretary the Earl of Jellicoe's personal rank far outstripped that of the ambassador, a mere knight. National paranoia affects a growing number of the embassies which now no longer list their diplomats' home addresses. This might be expected of the Soviets, a paranoid folk to start with. It's understandable with the Israelis, who had their people's addresses listed until one was murdered in his Bethesda driveway. The East Germans and Czechs have, of course, always responded to Moscow's lead, but now Uruguay and Turkey and Kuwait, among others, have opted to follow this course.

Another observation from the *Diplomatic List* is that diplomacy is still very much a man's world. The overwhelming majority of accredited diplomats are men; most countries don't have a single female on the list—this including some countries which produce the most rhetoric about the equality of their citizens. (Much the same is true even with the United Nations. There are only four female chiefs of mission among the 156 United Nations delegations; the American ambassador is one of them.) There is one woman ambassador listed—Her Excellency M'alineo N. Tau from Lesotho, who lives in Bethesda with her husband, Maama. In reference to women, the instances in which the titles Miss, Mrs., and Ms. are used provide a small insight into the listers' sociopolitical complexion: Miss and Mrs. by the few Latin American countries with women diplomats; Ms. preferred by the "people's democracies" with such envoys.

There are a few diplomatic missions in Washington which don't represent the de facto government back home. Because this country has never recognized the Baltic states' 1939 takeover by the Soviet Union; Latvia, Lithuania, and Estonia—now all

Soviet "republics"—still have their own make-believe independent legations (a step down from a full-fledged embassy) in
Washington.

The nearly 150 nations with diplomatic recognition in the
United States—a number growing at a pretty good clip as more
oceanic atolls join the community of independent countries—
don't include every state in the world. The United States government doesn't recognize Albania, Vietnam, Cuba, Iran, or Iraq.
(The last three have "protective powers" watching out for their
interests, though; Cuba's interests are "protected" by Czechoslo-
vakia, Iraq's by India, and Iran's by Algeria.)

Most of the embassy mission heads in Washington now have
full status as ambassadors extraordinary and plenipotentiary, a
term describing a diplomatic agent who is accredited as the personal representative from one head of state to another. The ambassador is the head of mission, or highest-ranking officer in the
embassy. When for some reason an ambassador hasn't been sent
from another country which is recognized by the United States
government, the mission will most likely be headed by a chargé
d'affaires, usually the second-ranking person at the embassy,
who takes temporary charge until a new ambassador arrives—or
until bad relations between the countries have been settled
enough to permit the return of a recalled (one formally brought
home by his government, usually in pique) ambassador.

Just about the worst thing that can happen to a member of
the diplomatic community is to be declared *persona non grata*—
Latin for "person not wanted." This can come about in two
ways. Before an ambassador is sent to his new post, the sending
government inquires of the receiving government whether the
new ambassador will be acceptable. Usually it's a foregone conclusion that he will be, but now and again there's a flap.
Recently John Gavin's appointment as the U.S. ambassador to
Mexico was in question because it was perceived by the Mexican government that the former actor didn't have the proper
background credentials for the post; the contretemps was eventually cleared up, and Gavin went to his new post. But sometimes a receiving government isn't amenable to persuasion. In
1885 the American minister-designate to the Austro-Hungarian

Empire wasn't acceptable to Vienna ostensibly because he had made some unpopular political statements in his prior post, but really because his wife was a Jew (the note from the Austrian government put it rather less blatantly: "upon the certainty that his domestic relations preclude that reception of him by Vienna society which we judge desirable for the representative of the United States . . ."). The minister-designate withdrew rather than force a showdown. In 1913 the Mexican government refused an ambassador from Washington because of his alleged mistreatment of laborers at his Mexican mining property, and a few years later the American government rejected a German envoy on the ground that he was under indictment for fraud at home.

The second instance in which an envoy can be "*png'd*" is when a diplomat serving in a country does something so reprehensible that his host country has no choice other than to kick him out. This was recently the case with several Libyan "diplomats" who were engaged in overtly anti-American political activities. A note from our State Department to the offending country stating that the "presence of so-and-so is no longer acceptable to the United States" is the way in which a government is formally notified, and it can be the result of political, civil, or criminal offenses. Since diplomats are immune from prosecution, a declaration of *persona non grata* is the only course a government can take to rid itself of a patently offensive member of the diplomatic community. It might be noted that one reason it actually has to be invoked so rarely is that the offending country will usually recall an offender before the host country is forced to *png* him.

Within each diplomatic mission there naturally exists a pecking order, usually identifiable by title. The ambassador is at the top and is followed by an officer usually titled minister or minister-counselor (this is the person who generally becomes chargé d'affaires in the circumstances described above). In the larger embassies (an embassy is technically the ambassador's residence, and the chancery is the working office, but following common usage, we'll use "embassy" here to refer to the mission as a whole), such as Great Britain's or France's, there might be several counselors following the minister. (Think of ministers as vice presidents and counselors as assistant vice presidents, and you've got the idea.) First, second, and sometimes third secretaries come next, all heading departments (in the larger missions) or doing individual tasks (in the smaller ones) in diminishing degrees of importance. At the bottom of the career diplomat scale are the attachés, the strictly task-oriented junior officers. Almost all embassies have a contingent of military, naval, and air attachés. Some missions have exotically titled attachés—Nuclear Attaché for France, for instance. Others have attachés whose real duties involve spying ("intelligence gathering"), but whose titles are considerably more prosaic. The attaché is the lowest category ranked as a diplomat.

If a newly designated ambassador to the United States is acceptable, which is to say, there's nothing overtly unacceptable about him to the State Department, one of the first things he'll do when he arrives in this country is to present to the secretary of state letters formally recalling his predecessor together with his own new letters of credence. Once that's done, he's classified as an appointed ambassador and can deal officially with the State Department. But to become a full-fledged envoy and to be allowed to deal with all other American officials, he first has to repeat this ceremony with the President.

There are simply too many ambassadors today for the President to receive each new envoy in a separate ceremony (and most countries change their ambassadors every two or three years), so as soon as six or seven new ones have collected in Washington, a mass ceremony is scheduled for them all on the same day. This is not to say, however, that they all see the President at exactly the same time. Protocol officers have spaced their individual arrivals at the White House Diplomatic Reception Room entrance at fifteen-minute intervals. The day the curator, Clem Conger, was showing me around the mansion was one of these presentation days. Marine buglers and drummers form a semicircle on the Blue Room balcony overlooking the arrival area, and as each limousine—supplied by the State Department and bearing the flag of the new ambassador's country—swoops up to the entrance, ruffles and flourishes are played while the party is getting out of the car. Each time the marines started up anew, Conger and I would go to the window to see if we could identify which country was coming in. It was easy to tell Korea because the ambassador's wife was wearing the unique dress of Korean women, but none of the others was so distinctive. The inclusion of spouses in the ceremony was a Carter innovation and has been maintained by President Reagan.

The party is escorted into the Library for light refreshments—tea and cookies—and awaits the signal to start down the Ground Floor Corridor for the Oval Office. All this has to be done quite carefully to keep the groups from running into each other and to preserve at least the illusion of exclusivity. Once in the Oval Office, the ambassador presents his staff and family to the President, who accepts the proffered letters of recall and credence—the latter is a formally written request from the ambassador's head of state asking our head of state to "give credence and place all trust" in what his representative will do and say in the name of his government—and then hands them off to an aide, unread. (The letters of credence for the head of the first Japanese mission to the United States in 1860 was seventy-eight inches by eighteen inches, a great long golden pleated thing on exquisitely printed heavy card stock, bearing the shogun's cipher, which rather archly translated as "He who determines the coordinates.") He is now a recognized ambassador, and everybody settles down for a brief chat. ("Are you and your family enjoying Washington, Mr. Ambassador?" "Yes, Mr. President." "What do you think of the weather?" "So *hot*, Mr. President.") The new ambassador, now fully accredited and ready to get down to some serious partying, is then driven home.

Home for the ambassador is generally a wonderful place to be driven to. Indeed, if it weren't for all the ambassadorial housing requirements, Washington would have long ago lost many of its mansions to the wrecker's ball. There are two major diplomatic quarters in the city, the Sixteenth Street corridor and the far more fashionable Massachusetts Avenue area. (Many other missions are sprinkled over the far northwestern reaches of the city.) Before World War II Sixteenth Street was the classiest residential street in the District, and many of the biggest embassies were ensconced in the great mansions lining it from the White House northward. After the war it deteriorated until it now is on the edge of some of the city's worst slums; in 1968 Fourteenth Street two blocks to the east was nearly destroyed in the riots following Martin Luther King's murder. But several of the embassies have remained on Sixteenth Street, and as more young professionals are returning to its solidly built old apartment houses, it is showing strong signs of urban gentrification.

The best-known and largest diplomatic establishment is that of the Soviet Union on the lower part of Sixteenth, nearest the White House. Quartered in what was once the family mansion of railroad sleeping car builder George Pullman, the building now looks like a Victorian hedgehog, the roof bristling with a forest of sophisticated communications antennas. The interior is decorated with huge posters of Lenin, an ironic touch in the former home of a dedicated world-class capitalist. The local offices of Aeroflot—the Soviet national airline—are on the corner, which is handy. The Russians also have a large complex on Connecticut Avenue above Georgetown, as well as other bits and pieces of Washington real estate, in which they conduct their prodigious diplomatic activities. Their local version of a dacha is a forty-five-acre retreat on Maryland's Eastern Shore, a locale in which they're not likely to mingle with much of America's proletariat.

Soviet Ambassador Anatoly Dobrynin has served the longest continuous period as an ambassador to the United States, the (sole) qualification which permits him to be called dean of the Diplomatic Corps. His predecessor in this honorific, Guillermo Sevilla-Sacasa of Nicaragua, had been accredited to Washington since 1943 and lasted until his country abruptly and radically changed its political complexion, a circumstance which in all probability won't rob Dobrynin of the title. The Russian envoy has served since 1962; his nearest runner-up, the Ivory Coast's Timothee Ahoua, arrived four years later.

Many of the other missions are in the new Embassy Row— Massachusetts Avenue between Scott Circle and Observatory Circle, with a large concentration at midpoint around Sheridan

Circle. A few can fairly be called palaces, the French Embassy being a good example. Set on four acres at the edge of Rock Creek Park, the beige château is presided over by Ambassador and Mme. François de Laboulaye. His father having filled the same post in the thirties, Laboulaye has lived a third of his life in Washington (he was born in the city when his father was secretary to the ambassador before being appointed the top envoy). The ambassador's wife, Antoinette, has the pleasant privilege of calling on the Mobilier National in Paris, the French national storehouse of furnishings, to fill the mansion. The dining service was made exclusively for French embassies around the world and for the French presidential palace, with the plates costing $200 each. Naturally such splendid dishes are complemented by mountains of sterling and Baccarat, all shimmering with reflected light when laid out for luxurious dinner parties under the mansion's huge crystal chandeliers. In an elegant Gallic touch, place cards are sometimes fresh camellia leaves with names written on them in white ink.

The Belgian embassy residence, further out on Foxhall Road, looks very much like a small European palace; it is actually an exact copy of the Hôtel de Charolais, an eighteenth-century town house on Paris's own Embassy Row. Its Louis XVI salon has been called one of the most beautiful rooms in America.

An erstwhile "fun" embassy was that of Iran. Ardeshir Zahedi, the shah's ambassador to the United States (and his one-time brother-in-law), entertained thousands of guests when the Massachusetts Avenue embassy was the most popular in the capital. The envoy averaged two parties a week during his tenure. For a while after the ayatollah took over back home, "revolutionary guards" occupied the building, creating a diversionary spectacle to the passing motorists on the avenue. Since Jimmy Carter kicked the whole crew out, the building has sat forlorn, as though it might be waiting for the worm to turn again. The Algerians—now Iran's proxy in the United States—are responsible for taking care of it.

The Japanese Embassy is a case of diplomatic prodigality. Until recently the embassy residence was a perfectly lovely

Georgian-style house, not very Japanese, but identifiable for what it was by the elegant gold stylized chrysanthemum—the imperial coat of arms—on the front. Built in 1931, the Massachusetts Avenue mansion now serves as chancery offices. The new ultramodern residence on Nebraska Avenue, farther out in the northwest part of the District, boasts two acres of floor space on the first floor alone. It also has a second floor and two floors belowground. The building cost $12,000,000 and is supposed to represent the best of Japanese culture and technology. The capacious Great Hall—nearly as large as the White House's East Room—is eighty-one feet long, thirty-three feet wide, and twenty-one feet high. Two thousand people can be fed from the ambassadorial residence's kitchens, and fifty bedded at one time in the various suites; the rooms used to have numbers on the doors, but Mrs. Yoshio Okawara, the present ambassador's wife, has painted different flowers on each to give the rooms individual names. The stylized chandeliers drip crystal icicles. There's the traditional teahouse out back, its nearby lake stocked with golden carp. As for the ambassador and his wife, their private apartments are a cozy retreat furnished in high Chippendale.

The grandest embassy in Washington, and one of the most princely houses in America, is that of Great Britain, set in its own ambassadorial compound just below the Vice Presidential Residence on Observatory Circle. Only in this country would such a home have an ordinary street address—3100 Massachusetts Avenue—instead of a palatial title. The British Embassy is unusual in that it was built specifically to serve as such, as opposed to the converted mansions which house many of the missions in the city.

The property, twenty-one and a half acres (slightly larger than the White House grounds) in a subdivision originally called Pretty Prospect, was acquired by His Majesty's Government in the early 1920s. Foreign governments weren't required to take out building permits for their diplomatic buildings, but the British very courteously did so anyway, at the same time informing the President of their plans and discussing the new complex with Washington's Fine Arts Commission. Sir Edwin

Lutyens, one of the most prominent British architects and famous for the viceregal palace he designed in New Delhi, was chosen to design the complex. What he devised was a splendid pair of nobly proportioned buildings—a U-shaped chancery facing the avenue and, connected to it at a right angle by the ambassador's study, a typically English manor house of the Queen Anne period to serve as the residence. It was designed to house a 70-man diplomatic staff, 300 secretaries, janitors, chauffeurs, and even its own full-time house painter. The wings are red brick trimmed with white stone and capped by steeply pitched roofs and towering chimneys. Both the chancery and residence are fronted with columned porticoes, the chancery's in the style of the late seventeenth century, the ambassadorial home in that of the early eighteenth century. The embassy is decorated in a sort of ducal style—lots of portraits of various monarchs, marble pilasters, intricately carved woodwork, crystal chandeliers, and many cut-stone cartouches bearing the cipher of George V, sovereign when the embassy was built. Several years ago a new glass and steel chancery was constructed, an unfortunate (architecturally speaking) appendage to the otherwise-regal setting. At the edge of the grounds—facing Massachusetts Avenue—is a statue of Winston Churchill straddling the embassy's border, thus one foot on British soil (all diplomatic property is considered extraterritorial), the other on American—a fitting symbol of his importance to both countries.

The grounds are the site of Washington's hoariest but most coveted annual bash: the sovereign's birthday garden party. Nothing very exciting happens except that mobs of people eat mountains of strawberries covered with cream. Inflationary pressures have long since done away with the legendary Devonshire cream that was once flown in from England to grace the berries.

As one might expect, entertaining is the primary reason for the generally opulent proportions of Washington's embassies. The lowest form of diplomatic party making on the social scale is the cocktail reception, of which there might be four or five in a single evening spread all over town. Ambassadors, or at least one of their chief underlings, are expected to make an appearance, which is all the brief visitation really is. When so many appearances are expected before an ambassador goes to the evening's much more important dinner party, he can only say hello and run; doing so does fulfill one of his diplomatic obligations, however. It is the dinner party—really only an extension of the ambassador's working day—where any substantive business is gotten down to. Usually about twenty important people are invited, all to have delicious but most likely catered food (which helps to explain why Washington can support an inordinately large number of catering firms).

For something on a really stellar magnitude, an embassy will pull out all the stops. At the British mission, a royal visit grants such license, and the entertaining is carried out on a lavish and regal scale. When the queen visited in 1976, arrangements for which took nine months, Washington had an *event*. Lady Ramsbotham, wife of then Ambassador Sir Peter Ramsbotham, avoided a potentially nasty early-evening protocol gaffe by her quick thinking—President and Mrs. Ford's limousine arrived before the queen's (the head of state is always last to arrive in his own country), so Lady Ramsbotham very sensibly suggested to the First Couple that they drive around nearby Washington Cathedral for a few minutes, thus allowing the queen time to arrive from Blair House. It's these sorts of things that can prematurely age diplomats—and their spouses.

The embassy was decorated with 5,000 roses in the queen's honor, a gift from the American Rose Growers Association. The entertainment which the Ramsbothams laid on for the queen featured performers from the Yehudi Menuhin School in England, a marked cultural improvement over the Captain and Tennille, who had serenaded Her Majesty at the White House state dinner the previous evening. The party ended on a lovely note: a piper leaning against a magnolia tree, playing "A Lament to George III." For their successes in Washington, the Ramsbothams were posted to the governorship of Bermuda, where they could recover from such intensive merrymaking.

The agency of government most closely related to the diplomatic community is the State Department, the senior department of the executive branch of the American government. It is headquartered in one of the world's ugliest buildings in a part of Washington called Foggy Bottom, so named for the swampy miasma it once was. The building, covering four square blocks and composed of seven floors of office space, houses most of the 8,500 domestic State Department employees (out of a total of about 14,000 worldwide). In 1980 the department ate up a budget of $2,354,139,256.69, five times more than that of ten years earlier.

The State Department is primarily responsible for the conduct of America's business with other governments, but it also has two domestic duties: first, the storage and use of the Great Seal of the United States, the steel die on permanent display in the building's Exhibit Hall which annually impresses the American coat of arms on 2,000 to 3,000 treaties, international agreements, ambassadorial, Foreign Service, and Cabinet officer appointments, letters of accreditation and recall, and ceremonial communications from the President to foreign governments; and, secondly, the performance of protocol functions for the federal government. A lesser-known facet of the State Department is its headquarters building's magic eighth floor.

One of the great surprises in Washington is the magnificent Diplomatic Reception Rooms, sitting like a château atop a barracks. Surpassed in the capital by only the state floor of the White House in their richness and beauty, these rooms—seen by relatively few tourists each year—are far off the usual capital sight-seeing track. A reservation through the department, or arranged by a senator or congressman, is needed to see them. So little known are they, so interesting, and so much a part of official diplomatic Washington that a short detour here to tell their story shouldn't come amiss.

In January 1957 President Eisenhower and his secretary of state, John Foster Dulles, laid the cornerstone for the immense building which would house Dulles's department; by 1961 it was finished. Its style, if it has one, might be called Dullesian—an amalgam of early modern notions of what a really grand federal office building should look like. An eighth-floor penthouse for official entertaining was added to the block-and-a-half-long structure; its decor matched that of the rest of the building, a bit plusher perhaps, in deference to its function, with some pseudo eighteenth-century doodads, but low-ceilinged with wall-to-wall carpets over cement floors, floor-to-ceiling window walls, exposed steel beams, and lots of utilitarian Scandinavian-style furniture in "electric" colors. Its transformation into an accurate period setting for one of the greatest collections of early Americana in the United States is due almost single-handedly to the White House wizard we've already met, Clement Conger, who serves equally competently as curator of the State Department's Diplomatic Reception Rooms and chairman of its Fine Arts Committee.

The process got started soon after the building opened. Mrs. Christian Herter, wife of the secretary of state who had recently succeeded Dulles, asked Conger's help in "doing something" to improve the rooms' appearance for the first official dinner to be held in them, one to honor Greece's Queen Frederika. Sharing Mrs. Herter's distaste for what the anonymous GSA decorators had wrought, he volunteered to start a program to furnish the rooms in a manner he thought would be fitting to their purpose. With little appreciation at the time for the task he was taking on, but with the self-confidence that came from six years as deputy chief of protocol, Conger went to work. How he succeeded was very much due to a remarkable ability to convince people that they should give their treasures (or their money for him to buy treasures) to their country—the same tactic he would later use with equal success at the White House. "Most collectors," says Conger, "overcollect, and I offered to solve their storage problems."

Prodded by patriotism, pride, and the joy of tax deductions, the owners of many millions of dollars' worth of the country's finest historical furniture and furnishings took Conger up on his offer of a niche in the department's Valhalla, doing so in the shortest time such a rich collection had ever been assembled. Conger rates it as the fourth or fifth greatest in the country— after the Du Pont collection at Winterthur, the American Wing of New York's Metropolitan Museum of Art, and the Boston Museum and about equal to the Dearborn collection. It is the *only* time it was done without the backing of a great fortune.

The curator has used his charms and skills in a variety of ways to assemble the department's windfall. When he isn't outright asking an owner for a specific piece of furniture or a painting or whatever it is he wants, he'll solicit—in the nicest possible way, of course—money to replace what he's already paid out for earlier pieces. That way the funds are continually renewed, and the donor's name will go on a piece just as if he had given it from his own home. Occasionally some unfortunate in need of a quick tax deduction will race in to see what can be found. A few years back one such woman picked out $75,000 worth of not-yet-assigned furnishings, wrote out a check to cover them, and has been coming back to do the same thing every year since. Between the finding and the funding, Conger stays busy; since about 30 percent of the collection is only on loan and may be recalled at any time by its owners, the curator is constantly haunting auction houses for replacement pieces.

The results are breathtaking. The suite of rooms is used mainly by high State Department officials—but also by the President, Vice President, and Cabinet officers—for between 500 and 1,000 functions every year. The rooms are witness to more nationally and internationally prominent visitors than any others in America. Unhappily only about 60,000 tourists go through the suite each year, a small fraction of the 1,500,000 who visit the White House. Foreign governments have taken relatively greater notice than have Americans visiting their own capital. Eleven countries have sent representatives to study the rooms in hopes of doing something similar at home; Australia has already started its own version, also financed solely with private funds.

Coming out of the elevator at the eighth-floor lobby (the button for this floor can be operated only with a special key), the curator and I entered the exact match of a foyer of a rich planter's mansion in tidewater Virginia around the turn of the eighteenth century. Everything has been altered to disguise what had been merely a utilitarian elevator lobby before Conger's transformation. The white ceiling, raised five feet (as have those in all the completed rooms in the suite), now shines with splendid and authentic antique crystal chandeliers. The tan wood walls are topped with faux marble moldings, the same treatment as in the pilasters. The floor is covered with veined diamond-shaped marble tiles.

Around the corner, the Entrance Hall continues the tidewater pattern, but the ceilings are further enriched with a delicate plasterwork frieze. Rare Oriental carpets cover the floor. As with the rest of the rooms, the enormously valuable pieces of furniture are arranged to suggest what might have been a private home. Conger pointed out a shell desk on loan and valued at a half million dollars. "Possession is nine-tenths of the law," he joked, obviously hoping that the piece will remain in the collection.

Turning another corner leads into the fifty-four-foot-long Gallery, the mid-eighteenth-century woodwork of which was designed after Mount Pleasant in Philadelphia's Fairmount Park. At the north and south ends of the spacious corridor are elegant Palladian windowpanes cleverly disguising the original steel window casements, the outside walls still conforming to the modern exterior of the building. The Gallery is lined with superb pieces of furniture and art, cabinets filled with china once belonging to America's founding families, and Oriental carpets, some nearly 300 years old. The profusion of riches led Conger to comment about these rooms (as he did about the White House) that "we could never start over here again—it's too expensive now and we couldn't find the money." The fact that the total value of the State Department's furnishings is now conservatively estimated at $24,000,000 would tend to bear him out.

An example of the sobering expense is the recently completed women's lounge (officially the Martha Washington Ladies' Lounge and the Dolley Madison Powder Room) off the Gallery, what Conger calls "the most elegant ladies' room in the Western Hemisphere." It took $475,000 to create the authentically designed Queen Anne suite. The lavatory has four reproduction mirrors—copies of one owned by John Quincy Adams—over the sinks; they cost $3,000 each. Antique fire buckets serve as wastebaskets. Each toilet stall has a marble arch overhead and dainty painted louvered wooden doors. The exceedingly handsome faucets are gold-plated. This luxury ladies' loo is not, alas, open to female tourists, being reserved solely for invited guests.

The next room, one of three principal chambers of the suite, is the John Quincy Adams Drawing Room (the rooms were named by Secretary Dean Rusk for his predecessors who later became Presidents), called by critics "the most beautiful eighteenth-century style American drawing room in the United States"; it was constructed in 1972 in the manner of a great Philadelphia salon. The predominately Chippendale-style furniture, arranged in a series of conversation groupings, consists of virtuoso examples of the finest early Federal crafts. John Hancock's mahogany secretary desk is probably the most valuable artifact in the entire collection. Nearby is the Treaty of Paris desk, on which John Adams, John Jay, and Benjamin Franklin signed the final version of the treaty which ended the Revolutionary War. Across from it is a table desk designed and used by Thomas Jefferson, possibly even for drafting portions of the Declaration of Independence; President Nixon used it for the signing of the certification of the Twenty-sixth Amendment, establishing the eighteen-year-old vote. The Benjamin West painting over the mantel, "The American Commissioners," an unfinished work showing the American signers of the preliminary Treaty of Paris (unfinished because the British signers never showed up at West's London studio to be painted in) and once owned by publisher Cass Canfield, was cajoled away from Canfield in one of Conger's less subtle examples of arm twisting. Canfield had lent the portrait to the State Department but refused to sell it outright. Since Conger wanted it badly for the room where it was "meant to belong," he had an expensive and exact copy made. He hung the original over the mantel and invited Canfield to a reception in the room, which included Secretary Rusk and the French prime minister. At Conger's connivance, Rusk appealed to Canfield's patriotic impulses, suggesting that he take the copy home and leave the original to the State Department, a plea the distinguished head of Harper & Row agreed to. The painting thus became the permanent possession of the American people and the special pride of the curator.

The Thomas Jefferson State Reception Room—a transition between the two largest rooms on the floor, the Adams Room and
the Benjamin Franklin Dining Room—is a splendidly proportioned space, surrounded with brilliant Wedgwood blue walls,
white marble niches holding busts of George Washington and
John Paul Jones, a cut-glass Adams chandelier, and the focal
point, a nearly life-size statue of Thomas Jefferson in a pedi-
mented half rotunda recessed into the end wall. A Palladian
marble pillared screen topped with a segmented fanlight window leads into the Franklin Dining Room, which, at nearly 100
feet long by 45 feet wide, will hold 250 people for a formal
seated dinner, up to 1,000 for receptions. It is the least successful
of the rooms, partly because of the immense and jarring Great
Seal of the United States, the marble walls, and the lack of
warmth found in the other spaces. Its greatest attraction is allowing visitors to wander out the glass doors onto the terrace
where the trees on the Mall seem like a green carpet and the
Lincoln Memorial like a magnificent marble doll's house.

There are two additional rooms to the rear of the Franklin
Room, neither open to the public tours. These smaller chambers
—the James Monroe Reception Room and the James Madison
Dining Room—are the private entertaining preserve of the secretary of state. Both are as finely furnished as the rest of the
floor, but neither has yet been architecturally renovated. Consequently they still have the wall-to-wall carpets over the concrete
floor, plate glass windows, and walls of modern wood paneling,
as well as the original low acoustical ceilings. One factor delay-
ing their completion is that they're located directly over the secretary's seventh-floor office; when work on them begins, the
hammering and banging are going to make life unpleasant for
the incumbent secretary for a while. Another factor is that the
window pilasters are weight-bearing and can't therefore just casually be ripped out. The planned solution—an expensive one—
is to set a fireplace in the window wall with cabinets on each
side hiding the offending beams.

State Department waiters reportedly love to work the functions held in the Madison Dining Room, usually very high-level working breakfasts and luncheons and thus the scene of some very interesting table talk. Lest any state secrets be compromised, all the help are required to have security clearances. Very often the secretary's guests are ranking foreign leaders, and interpreters are required at table. The Carter administration people let the interpreters join right in at the meal, a practice Conger found "totally inappropriate—they were supposed to be interpreting, not eating."

Before we left the State Department, the curator took me one floor down to the secretary's suite. Past blue-blazered guards stationed at each end of the secretary's Reception Hall is a gallery illuminated by nine crystal and gilt chandeliers and lined with museum-quality paintings, the most magnificent being Ferdinand Richardt's enormous "Niagara Falls," a gift from Gulf Oil. It's assumed that foreign visitors are especially interested in the American West, so there are a number of paintings of Yosemite and other western scenes. The secretary's Reception Room is furnished with the leftovers from upstairs; unhappily it still has the "Hot Shoppe" light fixtures that were installed when the building was new. On the day of my visit the secretary was in New York discussing the world's fate with Andrei Gromyko, so Conger and I had a look around Haig's office. Less awe-inspiring than the Oval Office, it is nevertheless far more expensively furnished with American antiques—Hepplewhite chairs, a number of valuable oil paintings, a Chippendale walnut tall case clock, Sheraton sofas, an antique Kerman rug. The Exercycle in the corner looked like overalls at a ball.

Before we leave this extraordinary display of American masterpieces of decorative arts, it bears repeating that the *entire* collection was paid for by individual contributors—"the generosity of the American people," as Assistant Chief of Protocol Patrick Daly put it. Not a single item was bought, nor a single beam moved, with tax dollars. It's unusual to see such a mass of treasures outside a museum's cold formality, but here they're the setting for daily entertainment and hospitality and enjoyment.

The collection inspires not a small amount of pride for the taste and skills so fortunately abundant in the nation's youth.

PROTOCOL

Protocol may be thought of as the grease in Washington's official gears. Without it, the capital's diplomatic community would come to a virtual halt, ambassadors and attachés banging pell-mell into jealously guarded prerogatives, hostesses at a loss as to where to seat the guests, the big boys free to use their size always to take home the marbles. The modern meaning of the word itself comes in a circuitous fashion from the Greek *prōto-kollen*, meaning "first glue" and referring to the sheet of paper pasted to the front of official notarized documents, thus giving them a seal of authenticity. It evolved to signify more broadly the proper framework for drafting diplomatic documents and has now commonly come to stand for the recognized form for international courtesy and etiquette—the establishment of precedence and rank according to strictly adhered-to guidelines. In short, the planet's social *Robert's Rules of Order*.

Today protocol is a minor cottage industry in Washington. "An Executive Course in Protocol" has been offered each week in *The Washington Post* for nineteen years by Mrs. Gladstone Williams. For those whose social education is incomplete, Mrs. Williams will teach (for $165) European and American table manners, foreign and American titles, faux pas (if you commit one, she recommends that you "just smile"), toasts, and, most especially helpful, her own "original method for seated dinners without a servant, without the hostess leaving the table."

In the nation's early days President Jefferson didn't have a handy adviser like Mrs. Williams to answer the questions of social etiquette that the president of any new country can be expected to encounter. Take the problem of seating at his formal dinners in the new executive mansion. Since Jefferson didn't want to parrot the stylized and highly prescribed usages then current in Europe, he devised what he called the "pele mele" system, whereby a circular table was set up in the Elliptical Saloon so that anyone could take any seat at state dinners without regard to rank or title. This innovation didn't survive his presidency; his successors replaced "pele mele" with established old-world protocol regarding seating. One of the social forms he originated stuck, however. Whereas Washington and Adams had bowed to their guests, Jefferson initiated the custom of shaking hands instead. Innovations have been slow to come in the years since.

Books on official protocol and etiquette were very popular in this country in the mid-nineteenth century to help untutored visitors know the right thing to do. An 1857 guide called *Etiquette at Washington* gave the following advice for visiting the chief executive:

> The mode of obtaining access to the president is ordinarily exceedingly simple. An individual who desires to have an interview with him is shown into an anteroom, where he awaits his turn for admission. When it arrives, the messenger announces his name to the president, accompanied by his card, and he is forthwith ushered into his presence. A visit of this nature should not be extended beyond five or six minutes, because it must be remembered that, however agreeable it may be to the person visiting, yet so important a personage as the president of the United States never has any time to spare. After conversing for a few moments, he retires, delighted with the suavity of the president, and elevated in his own estimation.

The President customarily held a public levee once a week during the middle years of the last century; from noon until 2:00 P.M. the general public would gather and the chief executive would grace the assembly with his presence, rather like modern papal audiences. The guidebook went on to warn attendees that it was "considered an unthinkable breach of etiquette to approach him on business on these occasions." Former chief executives were advised in turn that they would be "breaching etiquette" if they returned to the seat of government "unless called again to the presidential chair."

New congressmen were given advice on the best way to conduct themselves while in the capital. "It is in bad taste for a husband and wife to be much together in company, as they can enjoy each other's society at home." In the sad event of a death in the family, "notes and letters should be sealed with black sealing wax during the entire period of mourning." Since many of the greenhorn congressmen were just in from the wilds of the western frontier, table etiquette was a subject of some gravity, and the newcomer was warned that "the business of a knife is to divide the food, not to eat with. The fork should invariably be used for this purpose. The fork may be assisted in its office by a piece of bread held between the thumb and the first finger of the left hand. It is *not* proper to collect a large mass of refuse around your plate."

Slowly Washington took its place with the old-world capitals in refinement of its matters of protocol and etiquette. But it would be many years before the American government had its own official protocol office, a function filled in most foreign countries by the court chamberlain's office. Washington had continued to follow Europe, which since 1815 had codified rules on protocol according to guidelines laid down by the Congress of Vienna. But in 1919 a "ceremonial unit" was established at the State Department to handle the visit of Belgium's King Albert to President Wilson. Although it was the origin of a protocol department, it wouldn't become permanent until 1925, when Coolidge's secretary of state, Frank Kellogg, established a formal Division of Protocol.

The new bureaucracy continued to grow (like everything else in government) to meet the needs of Washington's rapidly expanding diplomatic community. Today the office of the chief of protocol is staffed by fifty-three persons, including ten at the State Department-run Blair House and two in the New York headquarters of the American ambassador to the United Nations. Its annual budget stands at $1,500,000.

The office is divided into three sections, each headed by an assistant chief: Visits, Ceremonial-Administrative, and Diplomatic and Congressional Liaison, the latter split between Embassy Services and Accreditation. For the first year of the Reagan administration, the chief was Leonore Annenberg—called Lee by her friends—the wife of former ambassador to Great Britain and head of the *TV Guide* publishing empire, Walter Annenberg. In March 1982 Annenberg was replaced by a former Washington journalist, Selwa "Lucky" Roosevelt, wife of a grandchild of Teddy Roosevelt and a longtime capital social fixture. Like all her predecessors since 1957, the fifty-three-year-old Roosevelt was given the rank of ambassador along with her appointment.

The chief's official job description is also a good summary of her department's duties. Besides advising the President, Vice President, and secretary of state on matters of national and international protocol, she is responsible for the planning of all state and official visits to this country, as well as the same visits our President makes abroad; planning and carrying out all public events in which the diplomatic community is involved; coordinating the presentation of credentials ceremonies; acting as the official American adviser to all diplomats in the country on all matters affecting their status, accreditation, immunity, and credentials; clearing foreign military aircraft overflying the United States or foreign naval vessels visiting United States ports; and, finally, directing the management of Blair House. The most time-consuming tasks for the chief personally involve the coordination of ceremonials and visits at the White House; her staff's most pressing concerns are with the care and pampering of the diplomatic community, especially finding housing space both for embassy personnel and for the ever-growing needs of the chanceries themselves.

An issue of paramount importance to diplomats is rank and its adjunct, precedence (which is, incidentally, correctly pronounced pre-ceé-dence, not préss-i-dence). To avoid the obvious difficulties that would ensue if diplomats' precedence weren't strictly codified, internationally accepted protocol defines the relative standing between diplomats of otherwise equal rank in any capital on the sole basis of the dates on which their credentials were presented. Since official dining occupies a disproportionately large percentage of ambassadorial duties, the seating of ambassadors—the reflection of their official precedence—is always decided in this manner.

By the rules of international protocol, the diplomatic chiefs of mission have their own relative ranks. Papal nuncios—ambassadors from the Vatican, usually bishops—come first in Roman Catholic countries. (The United States does not exchange ambassadors with the Vatican; Great Britain started again in 1982 after a four-century interruption.) Next are ambassadors extraordinary and plenipotentiary, today the garden-variety heads of mission. Ministers plenipotentiary—diplomatic agents accredited to governments rather than to heads of state—are next, followed by the chargés d'affaires. When serving abroad, the head of a mission ranks over any other representative from his home government.

Now and again problems come up when an extremely distinguished person, but one without official rank, attends a diplomatic function. (It's safest to assume that *any* function involving diplomats is to be considered a diplomatic function.) For example, Alice Roosevelt Longworth held no official rank in her widowhood, but it certainly wouldn't do to seat the former President's daughter and speaker's widow at dinners below every third secretary and his spouse. So the special category of "dehors protocol"—outside protocol—was established, giving the host a little leeway in treating such persons with appropriate respect.

Occasionally there'll be some fuss caused by an unresolved conflict of precedence or a seemingly unfair protocol ruling. Until the early fifties hosts knew better than to invite the Chief Justice to any sit-down dinner at which a foreign ambassador would be in attendance; the relative precedence between the highest American judicial officer and a foreign ambassador was never decided, each firmly believing he outranked the other and thus merited the higher-ranking place at the table. Harry Truman finally put an end to the bickering when he ruled that the Chief Justice takes precedence over ambassadors. (The President's word on such matters is law.)

American ambassadors carry the extremely high precedence which goes with their office only when they are actually in the countries to which they're appointed; at home, either under orders or on leave, they rank far down in the official order of precedence, just below the comptroller general and just above the mayor of Washington, D.C.

A universal feature of protocol is that women take their husbands' rank, but not vice versa—men derive no rank from their wives. This makes for the preposterous sort of situation in which a woman senator will be outranked by any senator's wife whose husband is senior to (has served longer than) the woman senator. In the State Department every effort is made to provide regal hospitality for wives of distinguished foreign visitors, but husbands of such visitors are left pretty much to their own devices. A visiting first lady is treated almost as a head of state in her own right as far as honors are concerned and usually has her own full schedule of visits, the theory being that she has the same rank as her husband. A first husband—Denis Thatcher, to name a prominent example—isn't accorded any such frolicking.

This lack of sensitivity to the changing role of women relative to men is still firmly entrenched in most of the world's countries. Even though American customs are becoming less conscious of sex, the majority of embassies still reflect their social customs at home and persist in usages that appear sexist to more liberated eyes.

Another matter over which the rules of protocol hold sway is that of courtesy titles. Since everyone who has one exercises an inordinate amount of concern for its proper usage, it would be expected that the rules governing their use would be very tidily nailed down. Although there is no court chamberlain in this country to smite offenders, the misuse of titles brands the culprit an untutored oaf.

The Honorable is the one courtesy title used by Americans in this country (other than ecclesiastical purposes). There's a long list of officials entitled to have their names preceded by it; included within the executive branch are the President and the Vice President, if addressed by name; Cabinet members and their deputy, under, and assistant secretaries; all levels of assistants to the President; and American ambassadors and ministers. A few of the officials from the other branches of government allowed its use are former Supreme Court justices (sitting justices are referred to only by their judicial title), judges, senators, congressmen and congresswomen, and mayors. The honorific is always used alone, never with other titles such as Mr. or Mrs.

(e.g., the Honorable John Smith, not the Honorable Mr. John Smith). The spouse of an Honorable does not share the title.

"Excellency"—either "His" or "Her"—is not used by Americans when they are in this country. The title is given to ambassadors in Washington, as well as to presidents of foreign republics, heads of government (i.e., prime ministers), and other high foreign officials. Most foreign countries do, however, refer to the American ambassador in their capitals as Excellency.

There are one or two other little points regarding the use of titles in the United States. Contrary to popular usage, former Presidents and Vice Presidents are not officially accorded those titles for life (but they do rate the use of Honorable). Retired governors, generals, admirals, and so on are so entitled, but not Presidents and Vice Presidents. The reasoning is that there can be only one President or Vice President at a time, whereas the other offices have multiple holders. That said, everybody *knows* that former Presidents continue to be called Mr. President forever. Some rules of protocol are not observed as closely as they might be.

A note about the misunderstood term "First Lady." It was first used to refer to the President's wife in 1877 in a magazine article describing Rutherford B. Hayes's inauguration, but it didn't become generally popular until 1911, when the ever-lovely Elsie Ferguson starred in a play about Dolley Madison called *The First Lady in the Land.* Even today the title has no *official* status, though it is universally used.

When speaking to the President, the Vice President, Cabinet officers, or ambassadors and ministers, the title "mister" is used for men, "madame" for women, preceding the office title. The surname is never used for any of these officers.

The distinction in Supreme Court titles should be noted: It's Chief Justice *of the United States,* but associate justice *of the Supreme Court.* The title "mister" before the associate justices' names was quietly dropped a few years ago in anticipation of the eventual naming of a woman justice; consequently all are addressed today simply as Justice Whatever. Chief Justice Warren Burger is addressed as Chief Justice.

If you're planning to invite both the Soviet head of state (that is to say, the chairman of the Presidium of the Supreme Soviet) and the first secretary of the Communist party of the Soviet Union to a social gathering, the latter takes precedence over the former, the only instance of a country in which the head of state is outranked.

A final tiny point of protocol to keep in mind: The sofa is the seat of honor in a living room. Especially its right side.

IX

Presidential Valhallas

LIBRARIES AND HOMES

Presidents earn their libraries the way pharaohs earned their pyramids—simply by reigning.

RICHARD COHEN

IMMORTALITY, the greatest prize of all those which may accrue to the presidency, was in the past also the least assured. Before Herbert Hoover's time each President had to accept that his posthumous fame would be left to the vagaries of history books, with occasionally a great monument raised to his memory by a grateful nation. Such hit-or-miss prospects are now a thing of the past. Modern Presidents have been blessed with twentieth-century sorts of pantheons in which their deeds and memorabilia will be enshrined for all time in the national memory circuit. Dotted across the country in ever-increasing degrees of architectural splendor, library-museum complexes have been built to house the evidence—great and trivial—of their lives and administrations. To have served in the Oval Office is the sole requirement for one of these shrines to be raised to one's memory, with greatness or mediocracy, success or failure having no bearing on it. The libraries have become, barring outright disgrace, automatic.

Although all have been built through private funding, the cost of staffing and operating the libraries is, as a result of the Presidential Libraries Act of 1955, the responsibility of the American taxpayer; the National Archives and Records Service, a part of the General Services Administration, is the agency of the federal government given the overall accountability for them. The stated justification for the government's spending $14,000,000 annually (the estimated 1983 figure) on them is that because they serve as the repositories for each President's official papers, their importance to history is beyond price. It would seem that serving presidential vanity is becoming as important a rationalization.

All but the last two of the last nine Presidents had their own library-museum complexes completed by 1982, starting with Herbert Hoover and ending with Gerald Ford. (Ford actually has a library *and* a museum, quite separate from each other.) The future of a repository for Richard Nixon's papers and memorabilia has just been decided, and Jimmy Carter's library is in the planning stages. (The federal government has since Carter left office paid $700,000 to store his papers until a library can be built; nineteen tractor-trailers were required to move the documents from Washington to a storage warehouse in Atlanta.) The libraries reveal much about the style and times of the men they were built to memorialize just as their steadily increasing magnificence marks the growing imperial nature of the office each has held.

Re-created on a 187-acre site in West Branch, Iowa—a small town nearly lost on the flat east-central Iowa farmlands—is the America of the thirty-first President's youth. Herbert Hoover's memorial is, by the standards of most of the other libraries, a modest repository, one housing memories of a man who even though remarkably dedicated to a life of public service is one of the most maligned of twentieth-century Presidents.

What is now the Herbert Hoover National Historic Site and Presidential Library had its origins in a visit made by candidate Hoover to his hometown in 1928, one that sparked his interest in restoring the house in which he had been born in 1874. Seven years after the visit, his son Allan bought the three-room frame cottage and several adjoining lots, and in 1939 a group of historically minded West Branch citizens bought it in turn from Allan and that year founded the Herbert Hoover Birthplace Society, completing the work of restoration which the former President's family had started. Eventually the structure became the nucleus for an entire West Branch neighborhood reflecting the late-nineteenth-century appearance of the boyhood years Hoover spent there. A blacksmith's shop was built near the Hoover house in honor of the trade practiced by Hoover's father, Jesse, and a Quaker meetinghouse was also later restored by the society. By 1962 the association had through private funding built the Presidential Library, and two years later, on Hoover's ninetieth birthday, it was deeded to the federal government. (The National Historic Site surrounding the library is under the administration of the National Park Service.) When the Depression era President died two months later, he was buried on a hillside overlooking the house in which he had been born and the library which recorded his life; his wife Lou's body was moved from where it had been interred in California twenty years earlier to join that of her husband.

The library itself is very different from the grandiose architectural statements the more recent ones have become. A relatively small Colonial-style fieldstone building combining the functions of library and museum, it is the least visited of these presidential institutions owing in part to its remoteness from any large population centers; only 61,000 people visited it in 1982. The library holds 3,100,000 pages of meticulously catalogued papers recording Hoover's extremely long public career, all available for scholarly research. The museum houses a partial replica of the Oval Office as it was during Hoover's presidency, as well as many artifacts he and his wife collected during their prepresidential years in China and Europe. One of the more eloquent displays is a map highlighting all sixty-one schools named after him in seventeen states; in Hoover's own estimation, "no greater honor may come to an American than to have a school named after him."

As might be expected, it was Franklin Roosevelt who first pointed out the need for a permanent central storage site for presidential papers, and it was his library that was the first to come into existence—approved by Congress, built, and opened to the public all within his lifetime. The library together with the manorial family homestead forming the Franklin D. Roosevelt National Historic Site in Hyde Park, New York, has just celebrated the Roosevelt centenary, the hundredth anniversary of his birth. Part of the library-museum has been set aside as the Eleanor Roosevelt Gallery, the only such separate annex honoring a President's wife.

Franklin Roosevelt was a man acutely aware of history and the importance of the Roosevelt family to it. In 1938 he and his mother, Sara Delano Roosevelt, offered their home (the President didn't assume full jurisdiction of the estate until Sara's death in 1941) to the United States government, with the proviso that Eleanor and her children would retain the right to live in it for the rest of their lives. The following year Congress acted on the President's suggestion that a presidential library be established and maintained by the government. Built by a private foundation on sixteen acres of the Hyde Park estate, the buildings and grounds were turned over to the government on July 4, 1940; the museum section opened a year later (although the archives were not made available to scholars and researchers until 1946). In 1944 the secretary of the interior declared the whole estate a national historic site, and a year after the President's death his widow waived the family's residence rights. Today the mansion—named after the city of 20,000 people two miles to the north, which, ironically, was never carried by its most famous son in any of his electoral races—and Val-kill, the cottage which Eleanor had built to escape the big house and her mother-in-law, form with the library-museum a complex which is visited by a quarter of a million tourists each year.

The core of the library is the 16,000,000 pages of Roosevelt's papers, including an immense and rich store of World War II documents, nearly all of which have been declassified and opened to the public. The President's 15,000-volume personal library is also stored here. The comparatively modest fieldstone building houses an FDR museum containing presidential memorabilia as diverse as his model ship collection, his message to Congress calling for a declaration of war on Japan, some thirty honorary degrees, a gold tiara that was a gift from the sultan of Morocco, and the 1936 Ford phaeton which Roosevelt had built with special manual controls to enable him to drive it along the back roads near his Hudson Valley home.

The central attraction for the majority of the visitors to Hyde Park is the mansion itself. As the Summer White House for twelve of the country's most eventful years, the house had an enormously significant place in the national consciousness, as closely associated with the person of Franklin Roosevelt as were his upthrust cigarette holder and his dog, Fala. The original house, located on a bend in the Hudson River called Crum Elbow, was a typical Victorian mansion, built in increments (the earlier parts dating to the beginning of the nineteenth century) and surrounded with a veranda, the whole topped with a widow's walk overlooking the river. The Roosevelts had lived in the vicinity for generations, and with the patrician assurance that springs naturally from very old family money, they saw no need to compete with the palaces being put up by their very rich but far less socially secure neighbors. The house in which the future President was born in 1882 was not given its familiar gray stucco, neo-Georgian façade until 1916, at which time it was also enlarged so that it contained thirty-five rooms and nine baths. After that little more was done to the comfortable but slightly tatty interior, although when the British king and queen visited in 1939, Sara used the occasion as an excuse to fix up the sitting room with some new chintz curtains and upholstery. After the President's death Eleanor moved permanently into her cottage, Val-kill, leaving the mansion she had quietly disliked to the tourists. Shortly before she died in 1962, she made a twenty-four-minute tape recording describing the house, which is now used by visitors as they walk through the rooms.

Today, for $1.50, tourists can inspect the home that was for so many years an outbuilding of the White House. During the last year of his life Roosevelt would take short but needed breaks every two or three weeks from the oppressive atmosphere of wartime Washington to visit the mansion on the Hudson. Although in his mature years he was never to enjoy its beauty and tranquillity as a private citizen, he is today buried with Eleanor in the rose garden in the lee of the home he loved so well.

In January 1982, a few days before the centennial of Roosevelt's birth, a fire heavily damaged the house. Much of the roof, attic, and third floor were destroyed, and the ceiling of the room in which King George VI had slept in 1939 collapsed. Damage to the main floor was mainly caused by water from the firemen's hoses. Repairs were started immediately, and by the spring of 1983 the mansion's restoration was nearing completion.

With the Harry S Truman Library and Museum in Independence, Missouri, the art of the presidential library-museum moved into the age of the imperial presidency. Perhaps it is a fitting reward for the becoming modesty the thirty-third President displayed in life that his memorial should be a white marble colonnaded palace in the heart of America. In a larger sense, though, the whole city of Independence is a memorial to Harry Truman. Intimately associated with the town in which he lived from his early youth until his death in 1972, Truman was universally known as the Man from Independence, its number one citizen.

The library-museum was built with the contributions of 10,000 individual and institutional donors on land given by the city of Independence; the complex was opened to the public in July 1957 with the proud former President presiding at the ceremonies. During its first years Truman loved to escort groups of visitors through the museum and lecture schoolchildren in its auditorium. The building itself is a large curved structure, two wings flanking a glass-fronted and colonnaded portico. A courtyard to the rear is the setting for the President's simple white marble tombstone; the plot was designed so that Bess's resting place balances that of her husband alongside. What was Truman's private office is in a wing that was set aside for his personal use; it is still closed to the public.

The foyer contains a huge florid mural painted by Thomas Hart Benton called "Independence and the Opening of the West"; the painter and the former President spent many hours together when it was being painted, eventually becoming close friends. Through the doorway in the center of the mural a corridor leads to a replica of Truman's Oval Office, accurate down to the photos of Bess and Margaret, a portrait of FDR, and the sign on his desk he alluded to in his White House farewell in 1953: "The papers may circulate around the government for a while, but they finally reach this desk, and then there's no place else for them to go. The President, whoever he is, has to decide he can't pass the buck to anyone."

The library is the setting for 13,000,000 manuscript pages chronicling his career, especially the turmoil-filled eight years he served as President. Now that fewer than 1 percent of the documents remains classified, there has been a surge in researchers and writers anxious to study the now much-admired President, as well as the 350 of his official and personal associates who gave their own papers to the library. "The Truman period is in high gear as far as research is concerned," says library director Benedict Zobrist.

The library is far from being the only monument to the thirty-third President in Independence. The entire neighborhood around his home on North Delaware Street is now the Truman Historic District, forming a corridor leading north from his home to the library grounds. The upper portion of the historic district has been marred by urban development, but the part nearer the Truman house remains largely unchanged from when he was President and even earlier; most of the houses date from the mid-nineteenth century to the early twentieth century.

The Truman house, which was officially designated as the Summer White House from 1945 to 1953, was built by Mrs. Truman's grandfather on the lot he bought in 1867. In 1893 Mrs. Truman's mother moved into her parents' house after the death of her husband; Harry and Bess inherited it from her mother in 1952. The two-and-a-half-story clapboard house, a modest home for a modest couple, became famous with the presidential vacations spent there during the Truman White House years. The President would start out on his constitutional every morning down the quiet streets, often turning into what is today Truman Road, a major artery leading into Kansas City a few miles to the west. The neighbors wouldn't have dreamed of bothering him; only the reporters found his behavior noteworthy. Bess Truman continued to live in the house in which she was reared until her death in 1982. The tidy lawn encircling the home is filled with oak trees and flower beds and looks out on a simple neighborhood of a kind now only familiar to many Americans in memory. The wrought-iron fence around the house, installed at the Secret Service's insistence, was the only part of it paid for by the federal government.

One hundred and fifty miles west of Independence is Abilene, Kansas, the center of America's wheat-growing heartland and the boyhood home of Dwight Eisenhower. The pride of Abilene and the focus of the town's exit on Interstate 70 is the monumental Eisenhower Center, the five-building memorial to the President who presided over the end of America's age of innocence.

The nucleus of the center—the first element to be opened to the public—is the family home, the small Victorian frame building the Eisenhower family bought in 1898, when the future President was eight years old. When the widowed Ida Elizabeth Eisenhower died in 1946, her six sons deeded it to the Eisenhower Foundation on the conditions that it would be preserved forever without change and would always be open to the public free of charge. Today it is maintained exactly as it was at the time of Mrs. Eisenhower's death; to describe it as simple is nearly an overstatement—virtually the only element that might distinguish it from any other plain midwestern house of the period is the brightly patterned Oriental rug in the front parlor.

What was a typical middle American neighborhood when the

family lived in the house is now a thirteen-and-one-half-acre cleared track forming the Eisenhower Center. Most of the land is grassy lawns, planted with shade trees and crossed by a grid pattern of pathways. The other four buildings are roughly at the four corners of the site, with the homestead in the center. First of them to be built was the museum, opened by the then President on Veterans Day in 1954. Its 30,000 square feet of galleries hold 18,000 pieces of Eisenhower memorabilia, ranging from his Croix de Guerre and the ungainly Buick limousine staff car he used as Allied commander in Europe to a mannequin displaying Mamie's pink brocaded gown worn for a 1957 state dinner given for England's queen; the official gifts include a gold and silver model of a mosque from the Pakistani government, a crowned and robed doll model of the Infant of Prague, and a mélange of swords and firearms given by admiring governments all over the world. Curiously the museum doesn't contain a replica of the Oval Office, full-scale or any other scale.

The library is housed in a windowless limestone building, opened in 1962, and more lavish than the museum. Sixteen million pages of manuscript not only record the President's official life but also include the papers of Eisenhower's senior aides, most prominent being his two secretaries of state, John Foster Dulles and Christian Herter. Papers of twenty-three of the ranking officers serving under the SHAEF commander, from Mark Clark to Walter Bedell Smith, are also on file.

As with the rest of the center's buildings, the funds to build the library were raised through public subscription. The complex was turned over by the Eisenhower Foundation to the federal government in 1966; it is, like the others, administered by the GSA through the National Archives.

Two other smaller structures complete the grouping. The Place of Meditation, a chapel built in a style which epitomizes modern architecture in the years Eisenhower was President, contains his tomb alongside those of Mamie and their firstborn son, "little Icky," who was four years old when he died of scarlet fever in 1921. A recently constructed visitors' center consists of an auditorium and the sales desk where tourists can buy a wide range of books, tapes, and postcards featuring Ike and Mamie as the central figures.

The opening of the John F. Kennedy Library in October 1979 brought these institutions into their third generation—the space age, if you will, of the presidential library-museum. The first to be plagued by the increasing contentiousness of American society, the I. M. Pei-designed Kennedy Library is a fitting architectural symbol of the era John Kennedy rang in with his call for "an American on the moon in the 1960's."

The origins of the library go back to November 1961, when the President announced that he would ask his friends to build a library to house his presidential papers, following the tradition established by his four predecessors. On his last trip to Boston, in October 1963, he decided that the most appropriate site would be a twelve-acre piece of land overlooking the Charles River and adjacent to his alma mater, Harvard University; it was at that time the site of the repair and storage yards of the Boston Transit Authority. After the President's death the Commonwealth of Massachusetts bought the land from the transit authority and donated it to the federal government to serve as the setting for the proposed library. A committee headed by Robert Kennedy started a campaign which collected $18,000,000 to build the facility, and the brilliant and controversial architect I. M. Pei was commissioned to design it. Everything seemed to be going along smoothly.

Then the "neighbors" started to realize what such an institution, drawing an anticipated 1,000,000 tourists a year, would do to the neighborhood, possibly even imparting a carnival-like air to the country's foremost grove of academe. The opposition to the building was through legal means able to have construction stopped for several years, the litigation costs meanwhile seriously eating into the building fund. Finally, in 1974, the opponents settled for a plan which would permit the archives (library) to remain in Cambridge if the directors agreed to build the museum—the function which would draw the overwhelming percentage of visitors—somewhere else. The library directors were reluctant to separate the two functions, believing it would jeopardize the facility's integrity. But when in 1975 the board announced it would be amenable to the split, the University of Massachusetts immediately offered a site for the museum function at its Columbia Point campus on the southern edge of Boston. Obviously dispirited at having to abandon the Cambridge plan and all the associations President Kennedy had with that location, the board nevertheless accepted the offer, deciding to locate the entire complex on the site. In late 1975 Massachusetts took back the Cambridge land and gave a twelve-acre site adjoining the university campus overlooking Dorchester Bay. On June 12, 1977, Jacqueline Kennedy Onassis, her two children, Senator Edward Kennedy, and Rose Kennedy presided at the ground-breaking ceremony, all overturning a few mounds of earth with shiny new shovels; twenty-eight months later the memorial was finally opened. Sixteen years had passed since the death of the man it was built to honor.

Describing the library's appearance is difficult. Pei designed his usual highly unusual combination of geometric forms, including a nine-story wedge-shaped concrete wing attached to a slightly lower glass pavilion; two theaters in a round podlike structure protrude off one corner. It isn't exactly pretty, but it does have a space age aura about it. The exhibits in the museum are the standard presidential library-museum fare: 750 display photos, some mural-size, recording JFK's life; a thirty-minute introductory film; a representation of the Oval Office. Part of the museum has been given over to a display of Robert Kennedy's life, a thoughtful and generous tribute to the President's younger brother. The archives house 8,500,000 pages of Kennedy papers. David Powers, the close personal friend of the late President and Camelot's official "greeter," is the museum curator.

The major problem facing the library is the dearth of visitors. Even though it is still the second most popular of any of the presidential libraries, the expected 1,000,000 annual visitors have turned out in reality to average fewer than 400,000. The director, Dan Fenn, Jr., blames it on two factors: its location and its title. Built near a low-income housing area with a reputation for violent crime is one drawback; the other is that many people think that because it's called a library, it really is just a library. Tourists aren't especially interested in reading.

What served as the Summer White House during Kennedy's thirty-four months as President is near Boston, on the Cape Cod peninsula jutting into the Atlantic, about sixty miles south of the library. For those short years a generation ago, because of a group of three white frame houses directly on the shore of Nantucket Sound, the well-to-do summer colony of Hyannisport was one of the most important places in the world. In 1926 Joseph Kennedy, Sr., first rented a clapboard summer cottage on Hyannisport's Marchant Avenue; three years later he bought the property and expanded it into a rambling, trigabled house, surrounded by manicured lawns and gardens. His children grew up there, and his second son celebrated his election to the presidency in the house. Jack Kennedy had bought an eleven-room house around the corner in 1956, three years after his marriage, and Bobby later bought the third, all forming the famous compound. Because of the way the family drifted in and out of any of the houses, it's more accurate to call the three together, rather than just the late President's own house, the Summer White House. All are still owned by the widows of the men who lived there during the glory days.

From Herbert Hoover to Lyndon Johnson the number of pages of presidential papers increased more than tenfold. In Austin, Texas, 36,000,000 pages of letters, memos, reports, dispatches, and doodles fill the Lyndon Baines Johnson Library. The most monumental in appearance of any of the libraries-*cum*-shrines, the Johnson memorial accurately mirrors the outsize nature of the man it was built to immortalize and apotheosize.

Like other recent Presidents, Lyndon Johnson began to think about a library shortly after he succeeded to the presidency. As a site on which to build, sentiment initially favored either San Marcos, where he had attended Southwest Texas State University, or Johnson City, the family fief where he had grown up. But when the University of Texas offered to provide a building for his papers on its Austin campus, the President accepted the proposal. In conjunction with the new library, the university would establish the LBJ School of Public Affairs to honor the state's first President. Construction began in 1967, and it would be the first presidential library ever built on a college campus. In May 1971 the building was dedicated, with Richard Nixon the principal speaker.

Sitting on a high thirty-acre site overlooking Austin and the State Capitol dome, the eight-story travertine marble building, unrelieved by ornaments or windows, resembles a giant end table. The east and west walls are eight feet thick at the base and curve upward to the underside of the eighth floor, which overhangs the walls by fifteen feet on either side. The plaza is decorated with shooting fountains and quiet pools, and a broad greensward is decorated with Texas oaks. The whole complex cost nearly $20,000,000 to build and furnish.

In its functions as an archive and a museum, the Johnson Library is a stunning success. From the second-level exhibition hall the ceiling rises unimpeded to the seventh floor, with the glass walls displaying the nearly 40,000 neatly shelved red buckram boxes, each affixed with a gold presidential seal, holding the 36,000,000 pages of presidential history. Very few of the 700,000 annual visitors—the library is the biggest tourist attraction in Texas after the Alamo—ever get the chance to see any of this archival material. Only historians and researchers are granted access to the papers (only those papers dealing with foreign affairs still have significant classified portions). Permission to use any of the material is given only after a research application has been approved.

The most popular exhibit is the seven-eighths of life-size Oval Office replica on the top floor, but also on display are such items as the bridal gowns and bridesmaid dresses worn at the two Johnson daughters' weddings, the enormous feathered hat which topped Carol Channing in the mini *Hello, Dolly!* production staged at the White House, dozens of valuable state gifts given to the Johnsons, and more than 4,000 cartoons caricaturing the President, all emphasizing his Texas-sized ears and nose. Most poignant is the display of the Vietnam War years as seen through the President's eyes. It was the war that cost Johnson a full second term, and more than anything else he wanted the American people to have the chance to see the explosive nature of those years as he saw it. "We wanted it to end more than they [the antiwar demonstrators] wanted it to end," said the President's widow. "The President's real fear was more from people who wanted to get the war over by dropping a nuclear bomb."

The library is now the central involvement in seventy-year-old Lady Bird Johnson's vigorously active life. A major remodeling, after ten years and 6,000,000 visitors to the library-museum, is focusing on presenting some of Johnson's programs in a new perspective. Mrs. Johnson has supervised the $3,000,000 exhibit that interprets her husband's Great Society programs, which the former First Lady hopes won't be lost in the current paring of social spending. "Everything goes by peaks and slopes and valleys," Mrs. Johnson said philosophically.

Across the plaza from the library is the Lyndon Baines Johnson School of Public Affairs of the University of Texas. The former President gave lectures at the school, a graduate facility which issues a Master of Public Affairs degree, between its opening in September 1970 and his death in January 1973.

An hour's drive from the library is what is called the President's country—the Lyndon Johnson National Historic Site stretching across Blanco and Gillespie counties and centered on the famous LBJ Ranch, the Texas White House for five years. The various memorials include Johnson's birthplace, a typical Texas farmhouse of the late nineteenth century; the President's boyhood home in Johnson City, the town named for his forebears; and the LBJ ranch house itself, still the country home of Lady Bird Johnson. (Mrs. Johnson also maintains an apartment in Austin near that of her recently divorced daughter, Luci Baines Nugent.) Shortly before Johnson's death he donated part of the ranch, including 200 acres of land and the house, to the National Park Service. Visitors can tour the ranch and see the exteriors of the buildings.

Speaking of her husband's library, Lady Bird Johnson said, "Most of all, it is the future: a place where history will be made and lessons learned." It can only be sincerely wished that many lessons be learned from the raucous and tragic years recorded so minutely in the Johnson Library.

It might be thought that a thirty-month presidency would produce a relatively modest presidential library, one reflecting the essentially interim nature of Gerald Ford's administration. Instead, he has become the first former President to have two entirely separate repositories cataloguing and displaying the papers and memorabilia of his years of public service.

The Gerald R. Ford Library at Ann Arbor, Michigan, and what is nominally its branch, the Gerald R. Ford Museum at Grand Rapids, Michigan, were built to mark the two cities most closely associated with the Fords' early years—Ann Arbor is the site of the former President's alma mater, the University of Michigan, and Grand Rapids was the town in which the future President grew up and from which he was elected in 1948 to Congress.

There was never any question in Ford's mind that his presidential archive would be deposited with the University of Michigan. In December 1976 he gave his papers as a gift to be deposited at the institution, the first sitting President to make such an outright grant to the government. Planning for the library building started almost the day he left office. Ground was broken in January 1979, and the building was occupied eighteen months later. A committee of old Ford friends and associates raised the $16,000,000 from 14,000 individual donors, including $100,000 from the shah of Iran, $1,000,000 from the Japanese government, and $200,000 from Saudi Arabia; $3,400,000 of that was spent on the library, the remainder on the museum.

The primary holdings of the library are the 14,000,000 pages of documents spanning Ford's career from Congress to the White House. There are also 700,000 feet of motion-picture film, nearly 300,000 still photos, and about 4,000 audio and videotapes. As with all presidential libraries, the papers of many of the President's closest associates have also been given to the archive.

The building, on a site donated by the university, is a fairly uninteresting two-story glass-and-brick structure, the architectural focal point being the lobby opening onto an outdoor plaza. A glass-supported bronze railing staircase rises under the large skylight. An office for Gerald Ford's use has been furnished with the desk he used as House minority leader.

The museum is much more fun. The idea of splitting the archival from the tourist function which the Kennedy planners found so unattractive was no problem at all for Ford. After all, few people ever find themselves honored with their very own museum in the town in which they grew up. The Ford shrine overlooks Grand Rapids across the Grand River; the long angle of the triangular building (the idea came to the architect one night when he was "folding a cocktail napkin") mirrors the city's center, the windowless rear pointing to a busy interstate freeway.

The grand opening of the museum turned out to be a presidential summit of sorts. President Reagan was there, as were Mexico's President José López Portillo and Canada's Prime Minister Pierre Trudeau. Carter and Nixon weren't invited, though. Ford explained it was *his* occasion, and the presence of the two former chief executives "would tend to undercut that." But 2,500 other invited guests were, and the weeklong extravaganza was the biggest thing to happen to the town since furniture.

There is, of course, the obligatory reproduction of the Oval Office, the only full-scale replica in any of the libraries, a nice little fillip for the Ford reliquary; former aides of the President say it looks so realistic that "it's really spooky to stand in the place." There is also a full-scale mock-up of the Grand Rapids Quonset hut which housed the first Ford for Congress campaign headquarters in 1948. Framed on display is the letter pardoning Richard Nixon, the act which many believe cost Ford the presidency to Jimmy Carter. A photomural called "Five Days in the Presidency" presents a minute-by-minute outline of the White House crisis management during the 1975 *Mayaguez* incident, an affair which resulted in thirty-eight dead, three missing, and fifty wounded Americans in the costly military rescue of a privately owned American cargo ship captured by Cambodia. Near a fountain and reflecting pool alongside the front glass wall of the museum is an alcove, the eventual burial site of the thirty-eighth President and his wife.

Unless unforeseen circumstances arise to prevent it, the Carter presidential library will be built in a kudzu patch a couple of miles northeast of downtown Atlanta, a location that was, ironically, used by General William Tecumseh Sherman as a campsite for his army as it cut its famous swath of destruction through Georgia during the Civil War. At the end of 1982 a very real deterrent to the plan which could force Carter to look elsewhere is the highly indignant anger of the local neighborhood activists who vehemently object to the planned 2.3-mile parkway that would connect the Carter shrine to the city. Even though the developers have promised to make the road "as attractive as possible," with adjoining jogging trails and chic little "jogger johnnies," the preservationists nonetheless plan to throw their bodies across the path of the first bulldozer to break ground.

The library complex itself is expected to include not only the Carter library-museum, but an amphitheater, a research center under the aegis of Emory University and, to complete the 219-acre spread (to be officially called the Carter Center of Emory University), an international mediation facility where disputes between nations could—theoretically—be resolved in private, with the former President personally offering his good offices to guarantee a harmonious setting.

The projected cost for the Carter Center (not counting the parkway, which will, if it's built, be paid for by motor tax revenues) is a fairly immodest $45,000,000, donations toward the accumulation of which have been solicited by Carter at a reunion of his former White House staff. It was suggested that $5,000 might be an appropriate contribution, in light of the largess many were making on the lecture circuit as a result of their presidential associations.

Since presidential libraries are inherently celebrative, all so far have been essentially museums extolling the virtues and attempting to redeem the faults of the Presidents in whose names they were built. The archival function—serving as repositories of the administrations' recorded histories—is a subliminal one, there for the use of the scholar and history but ignored by the great majority of visitors. This duality was at the crux of the difficult negotiations conducted between Richard Nixon and Duke University in Durham, North Carolina.

Because Nixon was graduated from Duke University Law School in 1937, it was where he turned after his planned presidential library at the University of Southern California collapsed in the ashes of Watergate. The request to Duke to donate land for the library met with an immediate barrage of opposition from Duke's students, alumni, and, most important, faculty. The university's president, Terry Sanford, staked his own high prestige on advocating the library, stating "no collection of presidential papers is likely to be more studied over the next 100 years." Duke Professor Richard Watson summed up the opposition, saying, "We'd all love to have Benedict Arnold's papers, but we don't want a Benedict Arnold building on campus." A bare majority of the faculty sided with Watson, recommending rejection of the planned library by a 35–34 vote. The executive committee of the university's governing board by a 9–2 vote ignored the faculty recommendation, approving a library with the proviso that conditions for its construction must be worked out "in accordance with the purposes of the university." In addition, to avoid what one professor called the "normalizing of the Nero of our times," it was recommended by a nearly unanimous vote of the faculty that any presidential library-to-be must not include a museum. To do so, it concluded, "would tend to glorify the former President and also be a tourist attraction."

In any event, the intricately worked-out plans for the library on the Duke campus had fallen through by the end of 1982, and the several tons of Nixon's papers stored in the National Archives in Washington were as far as ever from a final home. But in April 1983, plans were announced for an 80,000-square-foot library facility to be built in San Clemente, California, the site of the former President's Western White House. Money for the new presidential library was to be raised by a Richard M. Nixon Archives Foundation. The sponsors announced that the library would include a public exhibit area "dealing with the major issues and events of the post-World War II period in which Richard Nixon played a role."

Whether or not the Duke site would have turned into a tourist attraction is something the Four Seasons Investment Company of San Clemente might speak to. Its venture into the world of Nixonia produced a local museum called A Bit of History. Filled with *Air Force One* ashtrays, White House Christmas cards, and other such bits of presidential flotsam from the Nixon White House years, the museum has reportedly been a resounding financial flop for the Four Seasons people. Expecting 1,000 visitors each day, the museum has ended up with an average of forty—and sometimes as few as six. The situation was blamed on the intransigence of tour bus companies serving the area.

It hasn't yet been decided where the eventual Reagan library will be located, but Southern California is the likeliest possibility. Other Presidents who have chosen their hometowns or home states have either been closely associated with them during their adult lives or else weren't strongly identified with any other single home. Neither Tampico nor Dixon, Illinois, Reagan's birthplace and boyhood hometown respectively, is likely to become the site of a presidential library; his alma mater, Eureka College in Eureka, Illinois, with 463 students, is an equally improbable location.

Ronald Reagan has lived in Southern California since he was a young man—nearly forty-five years—but the house in which he and his wife lived for a quarter of a century before moving to the White House is a dubious candidate ever to become a historic site, much less a presidential shrine. It is located in the ultra-swank Pacific Palisades district of the city of Los Angeles, a lush and prestigious residential community overlooking the Santa Monica mountains and beaches. When the Reagans went to Washington, they had to choose one of their two California residences—either the Pacific Palisades house or their Santa Barbara ranch—as the official Western White House, the property on which the government would then be authorized to spend whatever federal funds necessary to install a security network capable of protecting a vacationing chief executive. The ranch was chosen, probably because of its greater privacy and the fact that to secure the Palisades house would have caused a substantial hardship on the neighbors. The house was put up for sale shortly after the election at an asking price of $1,900,000; the joint listers were the internationally prestigious firms of Previews, Inc., and Coldwell Banker. By the end of 1981 no offers had been received, and brokers were quietly putting out the word that the owners would take a considerably lesser sum to get it sold. In February 1982 it finally was purchased—for $1,000,000.

The General Electric Company built the house in 1956–57 at a cost of $27,000 for its then chief public spokesman. The eleven-room house, on the higher of two adjoining lots nestled against a steep hillside, is reached by a winding drive up from Sunset Boulevard through concealing landscaping. Really a nonhouse, the California contemporary is a series of large, irregularly-shaped spaces that flow into one another, divided by display shelves. The view is the crowning jewel of the expensive charms of this all glass, redwood, and Palos Verdes fieldstone building. Called the Queen's Necklace, the long sweep of Santa Monica Bay is lined at night with countless lights from Malibu to the Palos Verdes Peninsula, a spectacular sight from the house's redwood deck. Many of the furnishings—sofas, chairs, lamps, and knickknacks to remind the First Family of what was once home —have been moved to the White House.

About 100 miles north of Pacific Palisades is the Reagans' escape hatch from the pressures of Washington: their ranch 2,400 feet up in the Santa Ynez Mountains overlooking the Pacific Ocean and five of the Channel Islands floating offshore. Named Rancho del Cielo—"Ranch in the Sky"—the 638-acre spread northwest of the wealthy retirement city of Santa Barbara contains little other than natural vegetation, a few head of cattle, seven dogs, four horses (including Mrs. Reagan's bay, No Strings, and, until its death in the summer of 1982, the President's Little Man), a few simple outbuildings, and a five-room 100-year-old adobe ranch house. Where the Reagans used to reach their vacation home by a seven-mile switchback road from the coastal highway at Refugio State Park below, now the President and First Lady are flown on *Air Force One* to nearby Vandenberg Air Force Base or Point Mugu Naval Air Station and helicoptered up to their mountaintop Western White House.

When Reagan first saw the ranch in 1974 during his last months as governor of California, he got what his former aide Nancy Reynolds calls one of his few "bad cases of the wants . . . he loved it the moment he saw it." Even though his financial advisers counseled him against buying it, Reagan put up the $527,000 price, a value that has since tripled.

The falling-down ranch house was restored with his own and his wife's hands and those of only a few close friends. It now contains two bedrooms, two bathrooms (no bathtubs), a living room and enclosed porch, the largest room in the house, and a kitchen with Reagan's "wine cellar"—a wine rack holding the President's small but impressive collection of fine French wines. The furnishings are rustic—lots of Mexican rugs and wicker, as well as collections of cowboy and Mexican hats and silver-and-turquoise belt buckles. As is inevitable wherever Nancy Reagan uses her considerable decorating talents and financial wherewithal, the tone is quietly luxurious.

When the ranch was chosen to be his official vacation home headquarters, Reagan declared, "I don't want to spend one penny more than necessary [on alterations], but I want to spend everything that I need so I can function there as President." The resulting bill came to about $750,000, a small fraction of the $3,500,000 spent on Nixon's two vacation houses at Key Biscayne and San Clemente. The Reagan alterations included the installation of a helicopter pad, a hangar, some house trailers, and a Secret Service command post. Supposedly the majority of the expenses are "recoverable." When Reagan leaves office, the GSA will pack most of it up and take it away.

Postscript

THE AMERICAN PRESIDENCY has become of late an office in which anything like resounding success is a virtual impossibility. Doubtless there will always be men and women willing, indeed anxious, to give it a go, but good intentions are no longer enough to carry the day. Americans are highly unlikely ever again to feel the sort of collective paternal warmth they had for Ike, the feeling that whatever danger they faced, the *President* could handle it. The sixties ushered in the age of contention, and Vietnam confirmed it. Today we take the President's temperature every five minutes, dissect every nuance, comment on and analyze and second-guess every syllable. Modern Presidents are conditioned to a Sam Donaldson's shouting questions at them every time they stick their heads outside their own front doors.

What we now elect to the presidency is our own illusions, turning even on inauguration day into delusions and cynicism. As society's complexity continues to dilute our unity, as the single-minded simplicities of interest groups and spoilers wear down the government's ability to govern, as the weakest of nations can with contempt control and diminish our role in international affairs, so do our attitudes toward the presidency reflect the influence of these new forces on the American people.

Up to now our Presidents have—in the aggregate sense—

served the country admirably. Not perfectly, but where in the world today do the rights of the governed act as more of a constraint on their governors? If the President has withdrawn into secure parameters, what rational person would wish on the nation, let alone on the man, another Dallas? If the President's concern for posterity and its judgment of him sometimes seems overly acute, who in the cockpit of history has ever been otherwise? If the First Family live and entertain in a degree of luxury unreachable to most of their countrymen, wouldn't it perforce be hypocrisy for them to be playing at false modesty? Not, in fact, since Harry and Bess Truman has the presidential life-style been anything but one of unabbreviated luxury. Even if a President doesn't bring inherited or self-earned wealth with him to the White House, today a deluxe way of life goes with the job. The chief executive's salary—$200,000 a year (since 1969) plus another $150,000 for expenses ($50,000 taxable and the remainder, for transportation, not taxable)—doesn't begin to convey the lavish life-style accorded any modern President as a consequence of the office he holds. The widely decried new White House china cost less than is spent each year on taking the President's official pictures. Where the big bucks go is into such items as Camp David, the private presidential air force, the maintenance of the White House as the most public private home in America, and the massive costs of keeping the First Family safe. It's difficult to imagine its being any other way now—the chief executiveship of the capitalist world can't very well go coach, and few people really expect it to. In the absence of authentic royalty, most Americans don't seem to begrudge at least a little regality in the life of their First Family.

Appendix I

Order of Succession to the Presidency

Vice President
Speaker of the House of Representatives
President Pro Tempore of the Senate
Secretary of State
Secretary of the Treasury
Secretary of Defense
Attorney General
Secretary of the Interior
Secretary of Agriculture
Secretary of Commerce
Secretary of Labor
Secretary of Health and Human Services
Secretary of Housing and Urban Development
Secretary of Transportation
Secretary of Energy
Secretary of Education

Appendix II

Partial Order of Precedence (Unofficial)

The President of the United States
The Vice President of the United States
The Speaker of the House of Representatives
The Chief Justice of the United States
Former Presidents of the United States
The Secretary of State
The Secretary General of the United Nations
Ambassadors of Foreign Nations
Widows of Former Presidents of the United States
Ministers of Foreign Nations
Associate Justices of the Supreme Court
The Secretary of the Treasury
The Secretary of Defense
The Attorney General
The Secretary of the Interior
The Secretary of Agriculture
The Secretary of Commerce
The Secretary of Labor
The Secretary of Health and Human Services
The Secretary of Housing and Urban Development
The Secretary of Transportation
The Secretary of Energy
The Secretary of Education
Director, Office of Management and Budget

The United States Representative to the United Nations
Members of the Senate
Governors of States
Former Vice Presidents of the United States
Members of the House of Representatives
Chargés d'Affaires of Foreign Nations
The Under Secretaries of the Executive Departments
The Deputy Secretaries of the Executive Departments
Administrator, Agency of International Development
Director, United States Arms Control and Disarmament Agency
Secretaries of the Army, the Navy, and the Air Force
Chairman, Council of Economic Advisers
Chairman, Council on Environmental Quality
Chairman, Joint Chiefs of Staff
Chiefs of Staff of the Army, the Navy, and the Air Force
Commandant of the Marine Corps
Generals of the Army and Fleet Admirals
The Secretary General, Organization of American States
Representative to the Organization of American States
Director of Central Intelligence Agency
Administrator, General Services Administration
Director, United States Information Agency
Administrator, National Aeronautics and Space Administration
Chairman, Civil Service Commission
Chairman, Atomic Energy Commission
Director, Defense Research and Engineering
Director, Office of Emergency Preparedness
Director of ACTION
Director, Office of Science and Technology
Director, Office of Economic Opportunity
Director, Office of Telecommunications Policy

Appendix III

Dinner at the White House
Thursday, November 4, 1954,
at 8:00 P.M.

The President and Mrs. Eisenhower
Her Majesty Queen Elizabeth, The Queen Mother

SECTOR I

His Excellency the British Ambassador and Lady Makins
Lady Jean Rankin, Lady in Waiting*
The Hon. Mrs. John Mulholland, Lady in Waiting*
Air Chief Marshal Sir William Elliot, Gentleman in Waiting*
Captain Oliver Dawnay, Gentleman in Waiting*
The Vice President and Mrs. Nixon
The Chief Justice and Mrs. Warren
The Speaker (Joseph W. Martin, Jr.)

SECTOR II

The Secretary of State and Mrs. Dulles
The Secretary of the Treasury and Mrs. Humphrey
The Secretary of Defense and Mrs. Wilson
The Attorney General and Mrs. Brownell
The Postmaster General and Mrs. Summerfield
The Secretary of the Interior and Mrs. McKay
The Secretary of Agriculture and Mrs. Benson
The Secretary of Commerce and Mrs. Weeks
The Secretary of Labor and Mrs. Mitchell

* Member of the Queen Mother's official party

The Secretary of Health, Education and Welfare
The Hon. William Pettus Hobby (husband of the Secretary of HEW)

SECTOR III

The Hon. and Mrs. Harold E. Stassen (Director for Mutual Security)
The Hon. and Mrs. Rowland R. Hughes (Director of the Budget)
Senator and Mrs. Alexander Wiley (Wisconsin; Chairman, Senate Foreign Relations Committee)
The Hon. and Mrs. Sherman Adams (White House Chief of Staff)
Representative and Mrs. James P. Richards (South Carolina; Chairman, House Foreign Affairs Committee)
The Hon. and Mrs. Herbert Hoover, Jr. (Undersecretary of State)
The Hon. and Mrs. Corrin L. Strong (United States Ambassador to Norway)
The Bishop of Washington and Mrs. Dun

SECTOR IV

The Hon. and Mrs. Joseph E. Davies (former United States Ambassador to the Soviet Union)
The Hon. and Mrs. Walter S. Gifford (former United States Ambassador to Great Britain)
The Hon. Pearl Mesta (former United States Ambassador to Luxembourg)
Mr. and Mrs. Paul Helms (corporate executive)
The Hon. Paul G. Hoffman (former Marshall Plan administrator and former Studebaker Corporation president)
Mrs. Nicholas Longworth (widow of the late Speaker and daughter of Theodore Roosevelt)
Colonel and Mrs. G. Gordon Moore (presidential friend)
Mr. and Mrs. John A. Roosevelt (Committee on Government Contracts)
Mr. Charles H. Tompkins (President, Charles H. Tompkins Company, construction engineers)

Appendix IV

Official Dinner at the White House for Israeli Prime Minister Menachem Begin Wednesday, September 9, 1981

The President and Mrs. Reagan

Prime Minister Menachem Begin

Yitzhak Shamir, Minister of Foreign Affairs, and Mrs. Shamir

Dr. Yosef Burg, Minister of Interior, Police and Religious Affairs

Ariel Sharon, Minister of Defence

Ephraim Evron, Ambassador of Israel, and Mrs. Evron

Yehiel Kadishal, Director, Prime Minister's Bureau

H. Kubersky, Director General, Ministry of Interior

Major General A. Tamir, Assistant to the Minister of Defence for National Security

Brig. Gen. Ephraim Poran, Military Secretary to the Prime Minister

Maj. Gen. Yehoshua Sagi

Hanan Bar-On, Deputy Director General, Ministry of Foreign Affairs

Dr. Reuven Hecht, Adviser to the Prime Minister

Mattl Milo, daughter of Prime Minister Begin

Yaacov Agam, Israeli artist, and Mrs. Agam

Richard V. Allen, Assistant to the President for National Security Affairs, and Mrs. Allen

Leonore Annenberg, Chief of Protocol, and Walter H. Annenberg

James A. Baker, Chief of Staff and Assistant to the President, and Mrs. Baker

Senator Rudy Boschwitz and Mrs. Boschwitz

Rep. William S. Broomfield and Mrs. Broomfield

Vice President George Bush and Mrs. Bush
Senator William S. Cohen and Mrs. Cohen
Senator Alfonse M. D'Amato
Anne D'Amato
Michael K. Deaver, Deputy Chief of Staff and Assistant to the President, and Mrs. Deaver
Bruce Drake, New York *Daily News*
Madeline Feher
Max M. Fisher and Mrs. Fisher
Rep. Benjamin A. Gilman
Rep. Bill Green and Mrs. Green
Philip C. Habib, Special Presidential Envoy
Secretary of State Alexander M. Haig and Mrs. Haig
Senator Paula Hawkins and Mr. Hawkins
Martin Hecht and Mrs. Hecht
Jacob K. Javits and Mrs. Javits
Rita Kelhoffer
Rep. Jack F. Kemp and Mrs. Kemp
Jeane Kirkpatrick, U.S. Representative to the United Nations, and Dr. Evron Kirkpatrick
Eppie Lederer (columnist Ann Landers)
Samuel W. Lewis, American Ambassador to Israel, and Mrs. Lewis
Arthur Marshall and Mrs. Marshall
Robert McFarlane, Counselor, State Department, and Mrs. McFarlane
Edwin Meese III, Counselor to the President, and Mrs. Meese
Senator Charles H. Percy
Secretary of the Treasury Donald T. Regan and Mrs. Regan
Arthur Rosenfeld, editor, *Dayton Journal-Herald,* and Mrs. Rosenfeld
Milton Rudin and Mrs. Rudin
William Safire, columnist, and Mrs. Safire
Mort Sahl, comedian, and Mrs. Sahl
Andre-Michel Schub, pianist
Maurice Schurr, International Vice President, Brotherhood of Teamsters, and Mrs. Schurr
Dinah Shore
Albert A. Spiegel and Mrs. Spiegel
Jack Stein, Special Adviser to the White House, and Mrs. Stein
David H. Susskind
Andrew Susskind

Jacques Torczyner, member World Zionist Organization, and Mrs. Torczyner

Nicholas A. Veliotes, Assistant Secretary of State for Near Eastern and South Asian Affairs, and Mrs. Veliotes

Barbara Walters, ABC

Secretary of Defense Caspar Weinberger and Mrs. Weinberger

David Werblin, Chairman, Madison Square Garden Corporation, and Mrs. Werblin

William A. Wilson, personal representative of the President to the Holy See, and Mrs. Wilson

Herman Wouk, author, and Mrs. Wouk

Gordon Zachs, President, R. G. Barry Corp., and Mrs. Zachs

Robert M. Zwelman, National Commander, Jewish War Veterans, and Mrs. Zwelman

Bibliography

Aikman, Lonnelle. *The Living White House.* 6th rev. ed. Washington, D.C.: White House Historical Association in cooperation with the National Geographic Society, 1978.

American Heritage magazine eds., *The Inaugural Story 1789–1969.* Washington, D.C.: 1969.

Art of Diplomacy—Official Gifts to President John F. Kennedy and His Family. Framingham, Mass.: Danforth Museum, 1976.

Babb, Laura L., ed. *The Washington Post Guide to Washington.* New York: McGraw-Hill, 1978.

Boyarsky, Bill. *Ronald Reagan—His Life and Rise to the Presidency.* New York: Random House, 1981.

Buchanan, Wiley T. *Red Carpet at the White House.* New York: E. P. Dutton, 1964.

The Capitol. Washington, D.C.: Government Printing Office, 1981.

Cochran, Bert. *Harry Truman and the Crisis Presidency.* New York: Funk & Wagnalls, 1973.

Collins, Herbert R. *Presidents on Wheels.* Washington, D.C.: Acropolis Books, Ltd., 1971.

Crane, Katherine Elizabeth. *Blair House—Past and Present.* Washington, D.C.: Department of State, 1945.

Curtis, Richard, and Maggie Wells. *Not Exactly a Crime—Our Vice Presidents from Adams to Agnew.* New York: Dial Press, 1972.

Drury, Allen, and Fred Maroon. *Courage and Hesitation.* Garden City, N.Y.: Doubleday, 1971.

Etiquette at Washington Together with the Customs Adopted by Polite Society by a Citizen of Washington. Baltimore: Murphy Company, 1857.

Ewing, Charles. *Yesterday's Washington, D.C.* Miami: E. A. Seeman, 1976.

Federal Writers' Project. *Washington—City and Capital.* Works Projects Administration. Washington, D.C.: Government Printing Office, 1937.

Ferris, Robert G., sen. ed. *The Presidents.* Washington, D.C.: United States Department of the Interior, 1977.

Ford, Betty. *The Times of My Life.* New York: Harper & Row, 1978.

Foreign Service Institute. *Social Usage in the Foreign Service.* Washington, D.C.: Government Printing Office, 1957.

Frank, Sid, and Arden Davis Melick. *The Presidents—Tidbits and Trivia.* Maplewood, N.J.: Hammond, 1980.

Freidel, Frank. *Our Country's Presidents.* Washington, D.C.: National Geographic Society, 1977.

Friddell, Guy. *Washington—The Open City.* Offenburg, W. Germany: Burda G.m.b.H., 1974.

Furman, Bess. *White House Profile.* Indianapolis: Bobbs-Merrill, 1951.

Gallagher, Mary. *My Life with Jacqueline Kennedy.* New York: David McKay Company, 1969.

General Services Administration. *Executive Office Building.* Washington, D.C.: Government Printing Office, 1964.

Gurney, Gene, and Harold Wise. *The Official Washington D.C. Directory.* New York: Crown, 1977.

Haas, Irwin. *Historic Homes of the American Presidents.* New York: David McKay Company, 1976.

Hagner, Helen Ray. *Social Precedence in Washington.* Washington, D.C.: self-published, 1929.

Hall, Laura Hope. *Social Usages at Washington.* New York: Harper & Bros., 1906.

House and Garden magazine eds. *House and Garden's Complete Guide to Interior Decoration.* New York: Simon & Schuster, 1970.

Hurd, Charles. *The White House Story.* New York: Hawthorne, 1966.

Hyatt, Richard. *The Carters of Plains.* Huntsville, Ala.: Strode Publishers, 1977.

Inaugural Committee, 1977. *Inauguration of President Jimmy Carter and Vice President Walter Mondale—A New Spirit.* Washington, D.C.: Duobooks, 1977.

Jensen, Amy LaFollette. *The White House and Its Thirty-four Families.* New York: McGraw-Hill, 1965.

Johnson, Haynes. *The Working White House.* New York: Praeger, 1975.

Johnson, Lady Bird. *A White House Diary.* New York: Holt, Rinehart & Winston, 1970.

Kane, Joseph Nathan. *Facts About the Presidents.* New York: Ace Books, 1975.

Keim, Randolph. *Official and Social Etiquette in Washington.* Washington, D.C.: Keim Publishing, 1889.

Kiplinger, Austin, with Knight A. Kiplinger. *Washington Now.* New York: Harper & Row, 1975.

Kiplinger, W. M. *Washington Is Like That.* New York: Harper & Bros., 1942.

Laird, Archibald. *Monuments Marking the Graves of the Presidents.* North Quincy, Mass.: Christopher Publishing House, 1971.

Leech, Margaret. *Reveille in Washington—1860–1865.* New York: Harper & Bros., 1941.

Leish, Kenneth W. *The White House—A History of the Presidents.* New York: Newsweek Book Division, 1977.

Lewis, David L. *The District of Columbia—A Bicentennial History.* New York: Norton, 1976.

Lincoln, Anne H. *The Kennedy White House Parties.* New York: Viking Press, 1967.

Love, Nancy, ed. *Washington: The Official Bicentennial Guidebook.* Washington, D.C.: Washingtonian Books, 1975.

Martin, Judith. *The Name on the White House Floor.* New York: Coward, McCann, & Geoghegan, 1972.

Maury, William M. *Washington, D.C.—Past & Present.* New York: CBS, Inc., in cooperation with the United States Capitol Historical Society, 1975.

McCaffree, Mary Jane, and Pauline Innis. *Protocol: The Complete Handbook of Diplomatic, Official and Social Usage.* Englewood Cliffs, N.J.: Prentice-Hall, 1977.

McConnell, Jane and Bart. *The White House—A History with Pictures.* New York: Studio Publications, 1954.

McLendon, Winzola, and Scottie Smith. *Don't Quote Me.* New York: E. P. Dutton, 1970.

Medved, Michael. *The Shadow Presidents.* New York: Times Books, 1979.

Miller, Hope Ridings. *Embassy Row.* New York: Holt, Rinehart & Winston, 1969.

National Archives and Records Service. *The Art of Diplomacy.* Washington, D.C.: National Archives Publications, GSA, 1971.

Neyland, James. *The Carter Family Scrapbook.* New York: Grosset & Dunlap, 1977.

Post, Robert C., ed. *Every Four Years.* Washington, D.C.: Smithsonian Exposition Books, 1980.

Radlovic, I. Monte. *Etiquette and Protocol.* New York: Harcourt, Brace and Co., 1957.

Reagan, Nancy, and Bill Libby. *Nancy.* New York: Berkley Books, 1980.

Reed, Robert. *Old Washington, D.C. in Early Photographs.* New York: Dover, 1980.

Report of the Commission on the Renovation of the Executive Mansion. Washington, D.C.: Government Printing Office, 1952.

Restoration of the White House—Message of the President of the United States Transmitting the Report of the Architect. Washington, D.C.: Government Printing Office, 1903.

Ryan, William, and Desmond Guinness. *The White House—An Architectural History.* New York: McGraw-Hill, 1980.

Safire, William. *Before the Fall.* New York: Doubleday, 1975.

Salinger, Pierre. *With Kennedy.* New York: Doubleday, 1966.

Shaw, Carolyn Hagner. *The Social List of Washington.* Washington, D.C.: Carolyn H. Shaw publisher, various editions.

Shuster, Alvin, ed. *The New York Times Guide to the Nation's Capital.* New York: Bantam, 1968.

Sibert, Jacqueline S., managing ed. *The Presidents.* Indianapolis: Curtis Publishing Company, 1980.

Sindler, Allan P. *Unchosen Presidents.* Berkeley: University of California Press/Quantum Books, 1976.

Smith, Timothy G., ed. *Merriman Smith's Book of the Presidents—A White House Memoir.* New York: W. W. Norton, 1972.

Sobel, Lester, ed. *Presidential Succession.* New York: Facts on File, 1975.

Squire, Anne. *Social Washington.* Washington, D.C.: self-published, 1929.

State Visit to Australia by the Honorable Lyndon B. Johnson 20/23

October 1966, Programme. Collection of the Library of Congress, Washington, D.C.

Symington, James W. *The Stately Game.* New York: Macmillan, 1971.

Templeman, Eleanor Lee. *The Blair House.* McLean, Va.: EPM Publications, 1980.

Ter Horst, J. F., and Colonel Ralph Albertazzie. *The Flying White House—The Story of Air Force One.* New York: Coward, McCann, & Geoghegan, 1979.

Truitt, Randle Bond. *The White House—Home of the Presidents.* New York: Hastings House, 1949.

United States Government Manual—1981/82. Washington, D.C.: Government Printing Office, 1981.

Washington Dossier magazine. Washington, D.C.: various issues.

Washington Standard Guide. New York: Foster & Reynolds, 1906.

Washingtonian magazine. Washington, D.C.: various issues.

Weidenfeld, Sheila Rabb. *First Lady's Lady.* New York: G. P. Putnam's Sons, 1979.

West, J. B. *Upstairs at the White House.* New York: Coward, McCann, & Geoghegan, 1973.

Whipple, Wayne. *The Story of the White House and Its Home Life.* Boston: Dwinnell Wright Company, 1937.

White House Historical Association. *The White House Guide—An Historic Guide.* Washington, D.C.: National Geographic Society, 1979.

White, Theodore H. *Breach of Faith.* New York: Atheneum, 1975.

Wood, John R., and Jean Serres. *Diplomatic Ceremonial and Protocol.* London: Macmillan, 1970.

Wright, William. *The Washington Game.* New York: Saturday Review Press/E. P. Dutton, 1974.

Youngblood, Rufus W. *20 Years in the Secret Service.* New York: Simon & Schuster, 1973.

Index

NOTE: Where a page number(s) is in **boldface**, it represents the primary reference or description.

124, 130, 137, 138, 148, 149, 150,
158, 194, 197–99
Resolute, HMS, 42
Reynolds, Nancy, 199
Reza Pahlevi, Shah of Iran, 78–79,
82, 160, 193
Richardt, Ferdinand, 170
Robb, Charles, 89
Rockefeller, Mrs. Nelson (Happy),
120
Rockefeller, Nelson, 113, 118, 120
Rogers, William, 92
Roosevelt, Alice (*see* Longworth,
Alice Roosevelt)
Roosevelt, Eleanor, 10, 19, 46, 89,
182–84
Roosevelt, Franklin Delano, x, 10,
11, 19, 21, 33, 38, 39, 40, 42, 52,
63, 65, 89, 94, 97, 105, 106, 107,
108, 112, 125, 128–29, 131–32,
144, 182–84, 185
Roosevelt, Sara Delano, 182
Roosevelt, Selwa "Lucky," 174
Roosevelt, Theodore, x, 9, 10, 26,
31, 39, 48, 60, 125, 128, 131,
143, 146, 174
Rose, Susan Porter, 116, 122
Rosebush, James, 47, 48
Ruddick, Rob, 135
Ruge, Daniel, 65
Rusk, Dean, 168
Ryan, William, 5

Sacred Cow, 132
Sadat, Anwar, 75, 81, 102, 106,
116, 130, 131
Sanford, Terry, 196
Scarfone, John, 77
Schmidt, Helmut, 77
Scouten, Rex, 50–51, 53
Secret Service, 15, 39, 102–103,
107, 125–27, 132, **140ff**
Sequoia, USS, 128ff
Sevilla-Sacasa, Guillermo, 159
Sharif, Omar, 75
Sherman, William, 110, 195

Shikler, Aaron, 19
Shore, Dinah, 83
Simpson, John R., 148
Sinatra, Barbara, 56, 75
Sinatra, Frank, 56, 75
Sirhan, Sirhan, 148
60 Minutes, 51
Smith, Walter Bedell, 187
Social Secretary to the White
House, 48
Sotheby Parke Bernet, 47
Speakes, Larry, 66–67
Special Air Missions, 133ff
State Department, 109–10, 146,
153ff
state dinners, 73ff
Stein, Mr. and Mrs. Jules, 32
Steuben (crystal), 92–93
Stockman, David, 111
Stone, Mrs. Edward, 100
Stringer, Karna Small, 60
Stuart, Gilbert, 25, 27
Sunshine Special, 125
Suzuki, Zenko, 79

Taft, William Howard, 10, 125
Tau, Maama, 154
Tau, M'alineo N., 154
Temple, Dottie, 76, 78
Thatcher, Denis, 176
Thurmond, Strom, 115
Tiber Creek, 8
Torresola, Griselio, 145
Treasury Building, 16
Trudeau, Pierre, 194
Truman, Bess, 13, 25, 38, 85, 92,
117, 119, 132, 184–86, 201
Truman, Harry, 11–12, 13, 20, 26,
33, 41, 42, 85, 89–90, 92, 97, 98,
101, 105, 117, 119, 125–26, 129,
132, 134, 144–45, 175, 184–86,
201
Truman, Margaret, 12, 36, 85, 105,
185
Twenty-fifth Amendment, 114–15